THE

....

HAPPY KID

....

HANDBOOK

....

THE

HAPPY KID

HANDBOOK

How to Raise Joyful Children
in a Stressful World

KATIE HURLEY, LCSW

JEREMY P. TARCHER/PENGUIN

An imprint of Penguin Random House
New York

JEREMY P. TARCHER/PENGUIN
An imprint of Penguin Random House LLC
375 Hudson Street
New York, New York 10014

Most Tarcher/Penguin books are available at special quantity discounts for bulk
purchase for sales promotions, premiums, fund-raising, and educational needs.
Special books or book excerpts also can be created to fit specific needs.
For details, write: SpecialMarkets@penguinrandomhouse.com.

Library of Congress Cataloging-in-Publication Data

Hurley, Katie.
The happy kid handbook : how to raise joyful children in a stressful world /
Katie Hurley.
pages cm
Includes bibliographical references and index.
ISBN 978-0-399-17181-9 (paperback)
1. Happiness in children.   2. Child rearing.   3. Parenting.   I. Title.
BF723.H37H87 2015
649'.1—dc23
2015022156

Printed in the United States of America
1   3   5   7   9   10   8   6   4   2

Book design by Ellen Cipriano

For Sean, Riley, and Liam—
you make the world a happier place just by being in it.

And for my mom—
the mastermind behind many happy memories.

When I was five years old, my mother always told me that happiness was the key to life. When I went to school, they asked me what I wanted to be when I grew up. I wrote down "happy." They told me I didn't understand the assignment, and I told them they didn't understand life.

—JOHN LENNON

CONTENTS

INTRODUCTION

The most important thing is to enjoy your life—
to be happy—it's all that matters.

—AUDREY HEPBURN

OPEN A MAGAZINE, turn on daytime TV, or check in with your good friend Google for a minute and you are likely to find (on any given day) an endless list of parenting theories, books that will make parenting easier, calmer, or quieter, and blogs and articles galore that promise to make you a better parent. Parenting experts crop up just about everywhere these days (guilty as charged) and there is no shortage of information out there when it comes to doing the job right or better or more efficiently.

Yes, somewhere along the way the word "parent" shifted from a noun, the role people fill when they have a child, to a verb, an action word that signifies the process of executing the most rewarding yet exhausting and frequently judged job in the world. Gone are the days of come-as-you-are parenting. Parents today must keep up with a never-ending list of parenting trends if they want to get the job done right. Or so those books, magazines, and blogs would have you believe.

What all of this information overload is missing, however, is the part about how the kids feel in all of this—what makes them thrive? Book after book will teach you how to correct the thousands of things that can (and will) go wrong along this parenting journey, but very few books focus on raising happy kids.

Did you know that happy kids enjoy better school performance, are more successful when it comes to making and keeping friends, and boast better health overall? It's true. Harvard University–based happiness and success expert Shawn Achor's research, chronicled in his popular book *The Happiness Advantage*, shows that a happy outlook and foundation leads to success.[1] In his second book, *Before Happiness*, Achor asserts that in order to attain happiness, you need the right perspective.[2] Achor believes that if parents work on their own happiness, they will raise happier and more successful children as a result.

There are a number of parenting books on the market that focus on putting an end to negative and frustrating behaviors. And for good reason. Parenting can be stressful. Sleepless nights make for very tired and cranky (and possibly prone-to-yelling) mommies. Lengthy tantrums are exhausting. And back-talking school-age children have the potential to send even the most Zen mama running for cover. There's no doubt about it, parenting is hard work and sometimes a quick fix seems like the best answer. But does the quick fix *really* hold up as children grow?

It's time to focus on raising happy kids instead. It's time to build our kids up, give them the tools to lead with happiness, and make sure that they know how to jump through the hoops along the way (should those hoops arise). And it's long past time to slow down, get back to the business of kids being kids, and put the small stuff into perspective. Life is short—you want your kids to live happy lives by learning to follow their passions, empathize with others, appreciate those around them, and manage and cope with their own stress.

PART I

RAISING HAPPY

One of the most difficult parts of processing the parenting information out there is that all these theories and ideas make you feel like if you just do this or that, parenting will be a breeze. Check in with any grandparent and I think you'll find that parenting has never ever been a breeze. It's a process. It involves trial and error. One-size-fits-all parenting simply doesn't exist in this world. And there is no retirement plan when it comes to parenting. Once a parent—always a parent.

Part I of *The Happy Kid Handbook* takes parents through a proactive approach to raising happy kids. Beginning with understanding the child's temperament and parenting each child as an individual and moving through various positive behaviors, Part I of the book is all about building the child's pro-social skills to raise happy kids. Areas addressed include: the power of play, understanding emotions, teaching forgiveness, building empathy and assertiveness skills, embracing differences, and cultivating passion.

1

Know Thy Child

Today you are You, that is truer than true.
There is no one alive who is Youer than You.

—DR. SEUSS

HAVING STUDIED CHILD DEVELOPMENT for years, helped count-less parents work through their parenting struggles, and stood in front of parenting classes as the expert on hand, I was pretty certain that I could handle any parenting dilemma. Stay calm, empathize often, and just keep swimming. I was ready. What I didn't count on was having kids with *entirely* different personalities.

I'm fairly introverted and my husband, Sean, is about the same (despite the fact that he is, indeed, a very successful bass player and often plays in front of crowds of twenty thousand). We can turn it on when we need to, but we don't mind hiding out and just spend-ing time together. At larger parties, you'll find us hand in hand, moving from one small group to the next. And then we head home for a glass of wine and some much-needed quiet time. All that small talk can be exhausting when what you really crave is some time on the couch and an episode or two of *30 Rock*.

We were both labeled "shy" as kids and we often spent time

playing alone. (Sean was known to climb into his crib as a toddler.) We both preferred hanging out with a close friend versus a large group of friends. We weren't lonely kids; we just didn't crave the interaction. Our rich internal worlds kept us company.

So it came as no surprise when our firstborn, Riley, seemed a little introverted around the edges. What *was* a surprise was the amount of talking she did from the minute she learned how to talk! Before she even celebrated her second birthday she was stringing together caveman-like sentences and once she started, she never stopped. At seven, she talks from 6:45 AM to 7:15 PM. No exaggeration. It's cute and funny and oh so sweet and we quickly adapted to having a nonstop talker who craves action. An introvert in the outside world, she is anything but at home.

But when she was just twenty-one months old, her little brother was born. And wow, was he a different child. High-intensity from the very first yelp, Liam had big feelings and he wasn't afraid to let the world know. And as his personality began to emerge, we realized how different the two kids would be. Also a talker, but only if he trusts you to listen, Liam doesn't go from dawn until dusk like his big sister. He needs downtime and alone time and "get out of my room and leave me alone" time. Where Riley tends to hang out somewhere in the middle of the introvert-extrovert scale, Liam pretty much defines introversion. He needs space to do puzzles, think about numbers, and play his drums. At five, he still naps. And when something is scary, frustrating, or confusing, his reaction is always the same: big, loud, and long. Riley tends to internalize her feelings until she can't hold them in any longer, but Liam lets them out with a fury. Every! Single! Time!

While Sean and I like to joke about our own level of introversion, Liam takes it to a new level. Big parties? No, thank you. Playgroups? I'm good; one friend is fine. Loud music, carnival rides, and screaming children running around? Pass the noise-canceling headphones and get me out of here! In fact, let's just go ahead and stay home in case I don't like it. He is the quintessential stay-at-home kid. He feels safe and secure in the comfort of his house, surrounded by his toys, and the people who love him anyway.

It didn't take long for us to realize that we couldn't simply set a list of rules and expectations and hope for the best. We have two children with very different emotional needs. While our daughter needs help slowing down and getting her feelings out, our son needs help coping with his very big feelings before they get even bigger. Time-out? Not a chance. That would leave her feeling lonely and him feeling lost. Reward charts? Only if they can be rewarded for very different behaviors and with a different set of standards. He needs constant input; she needs to learn to delay gratification. It's complicated, at best.

While some general rules work in our house (bedtime never changes and TV time is scheduled), we have found that we truly need to adapt our parenting style for each of them. Riley tends to worry at times, and needs a lot of one-on-one time to work through her worries to feel happy and confident. At times, I feel guilty that she gets more of me. But Liam craves space. He wants me nearby, but doesn't need constant input when he's calm. Where he does need extra attention is when something goes wrong. He can go from happy to utter frustration in seconds, and he needs piles of empathy and understanding to get through such an event. He also needs love and cuddles on the other end.

Whether you have one child or four, parenting is hard work. It's only natural for parents to create some sort of ideal in their minds—a blueprint of how they want their families to be. Some parents focus on academic success while others are more concerned with family unity. Whatever the parenting goal, it takes work and nonstop focus to get there. There are no vacations in the world of parenting, after all.

And it's easy to get caught up in the busywork of parenting. Between diapers, dishes, carpooling, and homework, there is always something that needs doing. The seemingly meaningless and yet very essential tasks that need attending to each day are exhausting. Parenting is full of to-do lists.

In all this running and doing and shuffling and accomplishing, parents often set a list of behavioral expectations for their children. These are the rules; it's up to you to follow them. It makes sense, when you stop to think about it. Rules and structure help kids thrive. When children know what to expect each day, they are better able to meet the expectations and they experience less anxiety overall. In theory, it makes for happy kids.

Here's the catch: No two kids are exactly the same. And while a general blueprint of rules and expectations takes the guesswork out of each day, children also need the opportunity to simply be themselves. While some kids seem to come out of the womb oozing empathy, others tend to be a bit more self-centered during childhood. While some children can cope with frustration without much drama, others scream and flail when something goes awry. In all likelihood, you can have three kids with three very different personalities. How can each kid shine when they are all bound by a general set of rules and standards with no room for change?

We have to parent the individual.

While a general list of rules about keeping your hands to yourself, using kind words, and not bossing others works for most kids, it helps to consider the temperament of each child before creating a master list of "house rules." A high-intensity child, for example, is likely to be prone to yelling in frustration when things aren't going his way. I would know. I have one of those. A "no yelling" rule is a setup for failure for a child who tends to experience big emotions. It takes time, practice, and a lot of patience to work through those big emotions and learn to react in a smaller way, and it wouldn't be fair to hand out consequences each time a high-intensity child raises his voice.

If you have a creative daydreamer on your hands, you might want to think twice about a "following directions the first time" kind of rule in your home. What might look like a child who simply isn't listening might actually be a child lost in thought, dreaming about her next great work of art. Kids who daydream tend to completely check out while lost in thought. They truly don't hear what you're saying. Instead of coming down on your little daydreamer for poor listening skills, it would be more effective to come up with verbal and nonverbal cues (tapping on the table twice, for instance, or simply saying, "When you're finished with your thought, I need your help") to help keep your child on track.

And anxious children can only handle so much criticism. Kids who struggle with anxious feelings are their own worst critics. They already come down on themselves for breaking rules or forgetting important tasks. Public reprimands can really crush their spirits. It's best to review expectations one-on-one in the case of an anxious child and help your child come up with solutions to avoid repeating the behavior in the future.

Teaching to individual strengths comes up a lot in academic settings. Parents often wish that teachers would focus on strengths-based teaching for each individual child instead of simply teaching to standards. It makes a lot of sense. Kids have different areas of strength. And while it's important to teach the basics to each child, it would also be great to help children hone their specific skills early on.

Parenting isn't much different.

Sure, you're not teaching literacy skills or something completely anxiety-producing like long division. (Do they still teach that? Please say no.) But parenting does involve a teaching component. With an end goal of independence, there are a lot of skills that require mastery along the way. And chances are that your children will master different skills at different levels.

How many times have you heard another parent describe an infant or toddler as an "old soul," a "free spirit," or a "worrywart"? As parents, we tend to create labels for kids and explain their behaviors or tendencies before another person has even spent a minute with the child. What we are really saying is, "This child is different. She has her own unique personality." As parents, we recognize that all children are not exactly the same.

So why on earth would we parent them in exactly the same manner?

Social convention often pressures us into having certain behavioral expectations for our kids. It can be hard to parent the quirky child who doesn't seem to fit any mold, but when we force our children to act a certain way, we are really asking them to act in ways that run counter to what feels natural to them. Some kids truly don't want to go on playdates. They might find them overwhelming. They might find them underwhelming. Or they might get all the social interaction they need in preschool or school each day. Liam has yet to ask for a playdate. He sees kids at the park and at preschool, and that's enough. I learned to stop scheduling them. He will tell me when he's ready, that much I know for certain.

When we meet children where they are and focus on their individual needs, we send the message that we understand them. Helping anxious children find ways to work through their worries instead of brushing them off, for instance, shows them that you take their worries seriously. When we stop overscheduling kids who need extra downtime, we show them that we get it—they need a break and we can work that into our busy lives. When we take the time to teach our high-intensity kids how to manage those big and scary emotions, we show them that we know that life is hard and sometimes you just need help. There's a lot to be said for understanding their strengths and accepting their limitations.

And before you start hearing the chorus of "That's not fair" in your head that you probably hear seven billion times a day, remember this: Fair isn't about everyone having exactly the same thing. Fair is about everyone having their needs met. Kids might rely on black-and-white thinking when it comes to fair and unfair, but fair is very much filled with shades of gray. And it's okay to teach your kids about those shades of gray. Explaining their differences and showing them that you are raising each of them in a way that best suits them teaches them a valuable lesson about embracing people for who they are.

Fair, as it turns out, is increasing your child's happiness by figuring out who your child really is.

While we all enter into this job with some preconceived notions about how it will go, the truth is that we can't be certain about the best way to parent our children until we actually get to know them. And if we want to raise happy kids? We have to parent the kids we have.

It would be foolish, of course, to pretend that this is easy. With multiple kids come multiple obstacles on any given day, and that is just plain hard. A structured day helps keep everyone on task and there are some rules that just aren't negotiable (no physical aggression comes to mind, and screen time should be limited). It takes time and practice to find what works for each child, and you just can't get it right every time. But you can work on finding a happy place for each child in the family.

So how do we parent the individual and find happiness for all in a house full of kids with busy schedules and nonstop action? We begin by understanding their personalities.

Introvert, Extrovert, or Some Other Vert?

A common mistake when it comes to discussion of personality is to rely on "either/or" thinking. I hear it in my office a lot, but I hear it on the playground just as much. When a child is outgoing and jumps right in, the parent is quick to label that child an extrovert. Which makes the quieter, less-likely-to-jump-into-the-new-situation little brother the family "introvert."

While the general labels might very well apply, it's useful to think of introversion and extroversion as a scale. Different kids have different personalities, and sometimes their personality traits shift based on environmental factors, social situations, and even time of day.

The truth is that everybody has a little bit of both. And some children truly change day to day. That child who clams up at the huge birthday party just might be the life of the party in the comfort of his own home, surrounded by close friends (like my little Riley). And the one who talks nonstop and wants to be surrounded by friends at all times might break down and sob uncontrollably when she's running on low energy, because even those who lean toward the extroverted end of the scale need a break sometimes.

Everyone needs both time alone and time spent with other people. The difference between introverts and extroverts is how much time they need of each to thrive. When you slow down long enough to truly observe each child and watch their patterns, you begin to recognize how much of each your children really need. (Dragging that introvert to three parties in one weekend is like taking him into battle, mamas; that one needs plenty of puzzles and independent play to recharge.) When the expectations placed upon kids are in sync with their specific personalities, kids experience self-confidence, a sense of accomplishment, and greater happiness.

Raising happy kids means striking the right balance for each child in the family, even if that means that you deal with the chorus of "It's not fair" from time to time.

So You Think You Have an Introvert?

Kids who hang out on the introverted side of the personality scale tend to exhibit a few of these behaviors:

- Take a "wait and watch" attitude
- Observe and process a new scenario before entering
- Need time to get acclimated, even among friends and close relatives
- Get involved in stages (watch first, talk about it, then join)
- Can appear anxious
- Can seem aloof, indifferent, or even rude because they often wait until they are comfortable before they interact with others
- Tend to concentrate on one person or one activity at a time
- Struggle with transitions (big and small)
- Think before they speak (most of the time, anyway)
- Need time to recover from loud or overwhelming events

No matter how strong their preference for introversion, whether they are extroverted some of the time or completely introverted all the time, these kids need downtime. Time spent around other kids is fun and engaging, but completely exhausting. They get their energy from time spent alone, when they can truly think their own thoughts.

Introverted children sometimes confuse their parents because they might actually appear fairly extroverted some of the time, but then clam up the minute they are thrown into a big party or a brand-new situation, even with friendly faces around. That's where the introversion/extroversion scale comes in handy. Most children have moments of both, but when we learn to determine their individual needs, we can lead them toward a happy medium. And that helps us to raise happy kids.

Tips for Raising an Introverted Child

Respect Their Privacy

Introverted children tend to have very rich internal worlds. Time spent alone with their thoughts and ideas energizes them. The single most important thing that you can do for your introverted child is to respect this.

They will ask you to play and they will play with other friends and siblings at times, but they might not include you in every little detail of their inner worlds. That's okay. They need that time to think, create, and just be alone. When you let them have that, you send the message that you understand.

Try to factor in at least forty-five minutes of downtime for your introverted child each day. When life is extra busy and sends your child running from activity to activity, increase the amount of downtime. They need this time to process what they've experienced and to reenergize. They will reemerge happier for it, that's for sure.

Respect Their Preferences

We live in a very social world these days. It used to be that you invited seven or eight kids to a birthday party; now the expectation seems to be that you invite the entire class . . . and their siblings. And playdates? They've taken on a whole new meaning. The traditional hang-out-with-a-neighborhood-bestie-for-a-little-while "playdate" of days past seems to have morphed into open-ended, long afternoons with "playgroups." While some kids do enjoy these larger (and longer) playdates, introverted children do not.

Introverted children tend to stick to one or two close friends, and do not need daily playdates. Take a deep breath, concerned parents. Playdate refusal and avoiding large groups are not behaviors indicative of a child who struggles to socialize. Introverted children just happen to thrive when they are one-on-one, and they don't crave extra playdates. To the introvert, a day at school is positively exhausting. Legos and dolls in the comfort of their own rooms can be a very welcome relief. They are perfectly happy just playing alone!

As for their birthday parties? Discuss before you plan. They are likely to ask for a small gathering or simply a family party. That's perfectly normal and should be respected. Happiness is feeling heard.

Understand Their Emotions

Introverted children tend to (big shock coming) process their feelings internally. Counter to their extroverted siblings, they might not blurt out their feelings every minute of every day. But they still experience the same shifting emotions as other kids.

Because they don't necessarily get their feelings out, introverts sometimes experience big meltdowns or tantrums. While a meltdown might appear to be related to a specific trigger, often it's just the final straw after a series of unspoken frustrations, worries, and overwhelming feelings. Once you understand this about your child, you can help your child learn to express his or her feelings throughout the day.

- **Create a feelings book:** Give your child a stack of paper with one feeling written on each page (e.g.: happy, sad, excited, frustrated, lonely, angry, etc.). Ask him to draw a picture of (or write a description about) a time when he felt each way. When the pages are complete, staple them into a book, read it out loud, and discuss each page.

- **Feelings Bingo:** This is a good one for kids who don't like to draw. Make Bingo boards (you can download these templates) using feelings faces in the boxes. Call out the feelings to mark off on the board. When the winner calls "Bingo!" discuss each feeling marked off on the board.

As important as it is to teach introverts to express their feelings, it's also important to normalize those big feelings. Given that introverted kids tend to keep their feelings hidden, they often fail to seek help from adults. They need to know that all feelings and emotions are okay and a part of growing up. Normalizing their experiences helps them feel a little less overwhelmed in what often feels like a very overwhelming world.

Understand How They Think

As we've already established, introverted children tend to get lost in thought. They also like to think things through before they speak. Especially before they commit to something that they might not actually want to do. The problem is that this quiet thought process is often misinterpreted as daydreaming or inattention. Particularly in the classroom setting.

Bottom line: Introverted kids need time to think. Demanding an immediate answer from an introvert is akin to telling your extroverted child to just sit still for once. Their brains need time to process the information and come up with an answer that makes sense to them.

With that in mind, there are a couple of things you can do to decrease the frustration, and increase the happiness, on both ends.

- Factor in extra time when you make schedule changes or need information (as in, what are you doing for that mandatory talent show?).
- Provide plenty of warnings for comings and goings and activity changes.
- Use timers to keep your child focused and on track. (That iPhone certainly comes in handy for parenting, doesn't it?)
- Expect big conversations (to sleep over or not to sleep over?) to take place over a few days. Give your child time to come back to you with thoughts and questions.
- Warn all teachers and caregivers—explain the best way to connect with your child.
- Don't push for immediate answers—even when it comes to poor choices. They need time to process before they are able to discuss and move forward.

Prepare Them for Events

Given the overwhelming nature of large and unpredictable events in the mind of your little introvert, you simply can't expect them to jump right into the bounce house with masses of giggling, screaming kids. And if they didn't even know that bounce house was happening? They just might fall apart before they even get out of the car.

Introverted children become physically overwhelmed by sight, sound, and touch. The party that seems to offer endless opportunity for fun for one child is likely to cause anxiety and panic for an introverted child. The real reason they hide behind you or cling desperately to your pants has less to do with fear of socializing and more to do with sensory overload.

While most parents seem to expect (or at least hope/want) their kids to simply join in and enjoy the fun, introverted children need much more preparation and close supervision in order to take part in the celebration.

How, exactly, do you prepare your child for these sorts of fun but mostly overwhelming events? With a few easy steps . . .

- Describe the event in as much detail as you can, at least one day in advance. Food, games, bounce houses, you name it. Let them know what's happening.
- Observe: Begin by simply letting them watch.
- Practice: The great thing about role-playing is that you can do it anywhere. Practice ways to enter a group.
- Help: Stay close and walk your child into the event or group play. Hang close until your child is settled.
- Go: Move back and talk to the other parents.

- Safety word: It can help to have your child choose a safety code word in advance. If it gets to be too much he can just utter the word and out you go.

Try to keep the big social outings short and sweet. All that overload is exhausting for an introverted child.

Understand How They Socialize

Introverts, in general, aren't big on small talk.

Salutations and idle chitchat feel like a huge waste of time to an introvert, who has likely been thinking about one particular topic for quite some time and would like to cut to the chase. Resist the urge to cut your child off and force him to go back to the social graces period of the conversation. Introverts are the happiest when they can finish their thoughts to completion. Let them speak. Then revisit the basic conversational skills by role-playing specific conversation starters ("Hi. How are you? Did you have a good day?" followed by "I learned something interesting today.").

It's very important to avoid public behavioral corrections with introverts. While they might sometimes make the wrong choice or forget their manners when they're on a roll, they do embarrass easily. They internalize these moments and shut down in response. Also, that amazing story that you interrupted because you worried about how someone else might judge his behavior took a lot of thought and effort. You want your child to gradually feel more comfortable with these interactions over time. It's best to support them in the moment, and then pull them aside to discuss any behavioral issues.

Teach Flexibility

Introverts tend to dig in their heels when they want what they want. In short, they can be stubborn. At home, it might not be such an issue. But at school? Yikes. Flexibility is required. Sometimes things change without much warning, and kids need to be able to accept those changes.

- **Use a calming phrase:** Repeating a calming phrase over and over when your child becomes upset about a change cues your child that you understand that it's hard, but you will help him through it. When the usual daily routine is interrupted due to travel, for instance, you might want to soothe your child by saying, "I know you miss your regular routine, but Mom is always here to help. Together, we can get through this." For an older child you can simply shorten this to, "Together we can handle anything."

- **Transition boards:** Create a felt board (or use a dry-erase board) with symbols that represent parts of your typical daily schedule. Make small changes each day and show your child that schedules and routines can change.

- **Friendship map:** When an introvert feels abandoned by a friend, it can be devastating. Because introverted children tend to stick to a close group, it can really hurt when a friend chooses a new friend for a day. Draw a friendship map that includes all the kids your child might enjoy. Talk about the fact that friends sometimes switch places on the map from day to day, but that doesn't mean that the friendship is over.

You can have fun and enjoy one friend one day, and another
friend the next.

When introverted children learn that they won't break every time
they bend, they experience higher self-confidence because they realize that they are capable of coping with change. This self-confidence
leads to greater happiness and less anxiety throughout the day.

Give up Some Control

The great thing about living in your own little introverted world . . .
is that you have complete control over it. That's not, however, how
the real world works. At all. In the real world, introverted children
are constantly trying to measure up to other people's standards and
follow what might feel like complicated lists of rules. Bottom line:
They have no control.

Giving introverted kids some control over their lives not only
builds their independence, it reduces their stress and increases their
happiness. It's not that they have to be in charge of every little thing,
it's that they need to feel like they can make some choices and have
some control. Allowing your child to assist with meal planning once
a week is a great place to start. Consider allowing your child to organize her room in a way that is meaningful to her, choose her own
clothing (as long as she dresses for the weather), and decide which
birthday parties and school events she would like to attend.

Giving introverted children the power of choice, and sometimes
even the power of veto, relieves them of the stress that can trigger
anxious and isolating behaviors. It tells them that we understand
them and we want to make choices that actually work for them, not
just for us. And that makes them feel happy.

Factor in One-on-One Time

The upside of parenting an introvert is that they do crave a lot of independent playtime. Suddenly things like showers and laundry feel doable on a daily basis. The downside is that, unless you really stay connected, you might accidentally experience a moment when you realize suddenly that you haven't spent much time with your introvert this week.

Unlike their louder, very vocal siblings, introverted children don't always cry out for one-on-one attention. But they need it just the same. When they don't have enough one-on-one parent time, they are likely to internalize feelings of sadness, anger, and even anxiety. They feel left out. Where's the happiness in that?

Carve out special time with your introverted child. A fixed special-time schedule tends to work well, as it takes the guesswork out of it for your child and decreases any anticipatory anxiety. Let your child choose the game, destination, or project and turn off all electronic devices. I guarantee that you will learn more about your introverted child during these special-time sessions than you will during the rest of the week.

Added bonus: Special time is guaranteed to increase the smiles and happiness. When children feel loved and understood, they also feel happy.

Promote Interests

Social convention tells us to focus on raising well-rounded kids. They have to be good at just about everything to really have a shot at a good future. Or so we are led to believe. . . .

Introverted children tend to have just a few interests, but they really thrive when they are able to showcase those interests. Take an interest in your child's interests. Get books on the subject. Take field trips that relate. Ask as many questions as you can and truly listen to the answers. Repeat the information back to your child so that he knows you are listening.

As parents, it's up to us to let go of the fear of others passing judgment. So what if your five-year-old thinks about NASA 24/7? Is he happy? Does he come to life when given the opportunity to share his knowledge and show you his latest Lego rocket creation? That's all that matters. When you let your introvert embrace his true passions, you send a very positive message. And that message is critical to your child's happiness.

While focusing on a few interests is important to introverted children, cultivating passion is actually important for all children. See Chapter 8 for more on increasing happiness by way of cultivating passion.

Or Maybe You're Raising an Extrovert . . .

Life with an extroverted child is action-packed. Doers by nature, these kids like to go, go, go! At times you might find yourself wondering if your extrovert might one day run out of things to say. Not a chance. Your little talking machine draws energy from those around her. She craves stimulation and interaction to recharge her batteries.

On the bright side, you will know every single thing that happens to your child at school every minute of every day. No creative questioning needed for this one. On the less bright side, the constant input can be exhausting. Don't fret, tired mamas, there are always ways to restore balance to the family while keeping a smile on each face.

Kids on the extroverted side of the personality scale tend to exhibit a few of these behaviors:

- Think out loud (Extroverts tend to think while they talk. It might sound like nonsense at times, but it's all part of the thought process.)
- Act first, then reflect on what they've experienced
- Jump into new social situations
- Crave playmates and conversation
- Direct their energy outward
- Crave variety and action
- Are expressive and enthusiastic
- Find energy in large groups

Extroverts can seem like they are constantly on the move and directing their energy so many places that they can't possibly have any kind of focus. You often hear them described as "spirited" or "high energy." While they do tend to be energetic little beings with a lot to say about everything, that doesn't mean that they lack focus. Their thought process is such that they need to talk their way through things and take a hands-on, action-based approach to find their focus. With a little help, they can learn to let their wonderful spirit guide them toward their goals and aspirations, while smiling all the way.

Tips for Raising Extroverted Children . . .

Embrace Their Social Nature

To shut down an extrovert is to completely crush her spirit. Being with other people and getting their ideas and thoughts out into the open is what recharges extroverts. They feel their best, and experience the most happiness, when they are encouraged to do what they do best—talk and get their energy out.

With that in mind, it's best to allow for plenty of social interaction for your extroverted child. They thrive in groups and love to move. Try to avoid highly structured social gatherings, as these can feel limiting to an extroverted child. Remember, sitting still and following a specific set of rules in school all day can drain an extrovert. Freedom to chat, express their thoughts and ideas, and move is crucial to feeling energized and happy.

And not all social gatherings require planning. Extroverted children tend to enjoy meeting new people. An impromptu trip to the local park is just as energizing and exciting as a playdate with ten close friends.

Emotional Overload

Given their tendency to wear their feelings on their sleeves, extroverted children can appear emotionally overloaded at times. It's important to remember that talking and sharing is how extroverted children process and work through their feelings and emotions. Try not to jump to conclusions about their emotional well-being; often they just need a good old-fashioned brain dump to get their feelings out. Life can be overwhelming for kids at times. That's perfectly normal under even the best conditions. Once they learn to release and make sense of their emotions, they are likely to experience more happiness. (Refer to Chapter 3 for more on understanding emotion.)

With that in mind, there are a couple of activities your child can use to get those feelings out in a meaningful way. (The visuals created by these activities can stay with your child long after the activity is complete if you hang them on the wall or paste them into a notebook.)

- **The color of feelings:** Have your child assign a color to each feeling they experienced during the day (red for angry, blue for sad, etc.). On a plain white piece of paper, ask your child to color as much of each feeling that she experienced during the day. If she was angry or frustrated a lot, the page might be covered in red, for example. After the coloring is complete, talk about what might have caused those feelings and what your child can do differently the next time.

- **Rain/sun/fog:** It's no big secret that the weather can affect mood, but weather also makes a great metaphor for feelings. Fold a paper into thirds and draw a sun on one panel, a rainstorm on a second, and a foggy day on the third. Ask your child to tell you what things made her feel sunny and happy, what made her feel sad or angry and rainy, and what left her feeling in between. Write them in the appropriate panel. Talk about ways to increase the sunny feelings the next day.

Help Channel the Energy

While some parents, particularly introverted ones, can find raising an extroverted chatterbox an exhausting task, it's important to remain patient and help them work through their extroverted energy.

Think out loud with them to help them find the solution to a problem. Or try chatting while engaged in building and crafting projects. They work best and feel happiest when actively sharing with others.

Extroverts need to direct their energy outward. It's what helps them find balance. Help your little extrovert find activities that both meet that need and make her happy. Plays, puppet shows, and comedy routines all provide both a creative outlet and an audience. Building projects and arts and crafts are other great places to direct that energy and provide the opportunity to connect and talk during the process. And, if you're up for it, consider allowing your child to create a series of "how to" videos. You are likely to get lessons in everything from throwing a perfect tea party to proper swinging form. Funny and engaging.

Be sure to allow for plenty of physical activity. Observe your child carefully to determine what kind of physical activity is the best fit. While some extroverted children crave the social aspect of team sports, others might feel restricted by rules and regulations. The best way to ensure the best fit is to simply talk it over with your child. Not to worry, she will happily oblige.

Teach Relaxation Skills

Although they don't like to admit it, extroverts need downtime, too. But some extroverted children simply don't know how to relax. Complete silence or flipping through books (also known as the introvert's paradise) threatens to deplete the extrovert of energy. An extrovert needs sensory input and stimulation.

But there are ways to teach children the art of relaxing in an extroverted manner. Quiet time is beneficial to an extroverted child in that it teaches her that she can be alone—she doesn't need an audience every minute of the day. While many extroverts find themselves wondering why anyone would ever want to be alone, the fact is that people are alone at times. Learning how to be alone is a valuable skill.

- Try guided relaxation: There are several programs and apps that will talk your child through a five- to ten-minute guided relaxation, complete with interesting nature sounds and pleasant imagery. (The Simply Being app is by far my favorite.)
- Try "Ready . . . Set . . . R.E.L.A.X."—a relaxation program for children that teaches progressive muscle relaxation and uses guided imagery in kid-friendly scripts.[3]
- Rely on audio books to keep reading interesting.
- Help your child find music that she likes and encourage her to just listen and dance on her own.
- Consider a child-friendly yoga DVD.
- Jump ropes and swings are both solo activities that can prove relaxing for extroverted children.
- Clay stimulates muscles and helps relieve pent-up stress and emotion.

Teach Active Listening Skills

Sometimes extroverted children have so much to say they simply forget to stop and listen. While they might be able to talk nonstop at home, this can become a problem at school, on teams, or in other classes. They do need to learn the art of give and take when it comes to conversational skills. And they really need to understand when it's best to just listen for a little bit (like, say, when the teacher is busy teaching).

The best way to teach listening skills is to model them. We tend to get frustrated when we feel like our kids aren't listening, but how often do we hit the autopilot and simply respond with "wow" or "uh-huh" at the appropriate intervals? When our children are talking, we have to stop what we're doing, maintain eye contact, and ask appropriate follow-up questions.

Here are a few more strategies you can work into family life to hone those active listening skills:

- Meet your child at eye level—if you're talking from across the room, chances are you're not really listening to one another.
- Repeat back: Ask your child to give you a recap of what you said. Do the same for your child when she speaks to convey your understanding.
- Play listening games: The continuous story is fun during family meals. One person starts the story with one sentence and then each person builds upon it along the way. It forces everyone to really listen and draw connections. Simon Says is always a winner when it comes to reinforcing listening skills because it requires both watching and listening. Multi-step obstacle courses are great for encouraging kids to listen and seek clarification.

Teaching listening skills requires time and patience. Extroverted children are full of thoughts and ideas that they need to get out. It can be hard for them to sit and listen. I often encourage children to count to four in their heads while taking four deep breaths before they respond to comments or questions. This allows them to relax their bodies and collect their thoughts instead of simply blurting out the first concept to cross their minds.

Focus on Taking Turns

When your mind is constantly full of good ideas that you need to get out into the open right this very second, it can be hard to stop and wait your turn. While we all tend to think of turn taking as a preschool skill that is generally mastered by the time kids move on to elementary school, very extroverted children can lag in this arena.

Turn taking is a critical social skill that takes you from the sandbox to the boardroom. While most adults take conversational turn taking for granted, it can be a frustrating skill to teach. Most of the time because the one who needs the skill fails to pause long enough to actually practice the skill. There are some great strategies parents can use to help kids internalize the process of taking turns.

- **Storyboards:** I have always loved storyboards when working on social skills with children because they combine creativity and real-life scenarios. Fold a piece of white paper (any old paper will do) in half three times to create eight boxes. Ask your child to come up with a story about two friends doing something fun together. Your child should draw the sequence of events, one action per box. When she completes the board, go back and point to boxes where one friend had to pause while the other did something or where one listened while the other spoke. Kids love to create their own action-packed stories, and this exercise teaches some valuable lessons while they tap into their creativity.

- **Nonverbal cue:** Learning to take turns can require frequent feedback. When a child is caught in a pattern of blurting out answers and thoughts as they arise, it can be hard to break that pattern. Have your child come up with a nonverbal cue to remind her to wait her turn. A simple thumbs-up or holding up three fingers (to signal "Take three breaths") can work wonders.

- **Play games:** Believe me, I know that the third round of Candyland is tedious at best. But board games provide excellent practice in both taking turns and following rules. Added bonus: Board games also sneak in lessons in coping with disappointment (we can't all get to the candy castle at the same time, you know). Take family game night seriously. And please stop letting your child win every time; that only creates real-world sadness when they play with other kids. Other good choices include: follow the leader, hide-and-seek, and farmer in the dell. Sometimes you just have to wait.

- **Sand timers:** Electronic timers are great, but good old sand timers are better for a child who is squirming with anticipation. You can buy little sand timers for two-minute, five-minute, and ten-minute periods of time. Start with the lowest amount of time and gradually work your way up. Being able to watch the sand and see time moving helps kids understand and see that their turns are coming soon.

Explain Other Personalities

While their introverted buddies are content and not particularly concerned with others when they enjoy solo time, extroverted children are often dumbfounded by the fact that anyone would ever want to take a break from talking and doing to just play alone. They just don't get it. As a result, they tend to follow other kids around and try to engage them.

It's important to teach your child to read nonverbal cues. Observe other children at play or even adults out in the world. Be sure to point out facial expressions and body postures. You can even do this with favorite books and television shows. Describe what cues people might be sending.

Explain to your child that some kids just need time alone to recharge their batteries. If you never stop driving the car, the car might break down. Everybody needs a rest, and some just need a little more than others. Everyone requires a unique balance to feel happy.

Increase the Hands-on Activities

In a world where academic success is highly valued, even in the youngest grades, learning has changed over time. Education appears to be on the fast track in many places these days (with the exception of Finland; I vote we all move there), which means that kids are learning at an accelerated pace. While some kids truly thrive in this kind of learning environment, others crave more creative outlets. Kids have different learning styles, and what works for some won't necessarily work for others. The fact is that not every parent has the opportunity, or finances, to handpick the perfect school for each child. Often, we get what we get. We can't tell the schools how to teach, but we can be supportive of the learning environment by volunteering in the classroom, heading up new programs for the school, joining the PTA or even starting a classroom garden. We can also help our children learn in a meaningful way at home.

Extroverted children tend to enjoy hands-on projects and learning through doing. Follow up their school learning with fun craft and cooking projects at home. Spend time at science museums or other hands-on learning museums in your area.

Yes, they need to complete the homework that is assigned. But they can also add their own ideas. A book report, for instance, can include a poster or a diorama. While it might seem like extra work for your child, chances are the hands-on projects will energize her and leave her feeling very happy (versus the worksheets or prompted writing assignments, which are likely to induce frowns and whining).

Or Maybe You Have Some Other Kind of "Vert"?

The truth is that most kids fall somewhere in the middle. Or their personalities shift based on environmental cues and the other personalities around them. While my daughter is always the life of the party at home (no matter the size of the crowd), she never jumps into a new situation with ease. We have to work our way up to it.

Kids caught in the gray area might thrive in certain environments (school, a favorite class, a family gathering) but completely shut down in others (a new class, a team sport, an overstimulating event). While it might seem like these mysterious kids keep us guessing, we can find their happy balance by watching closely and assessing often.

Common traits of those caught somewhere in between might include:

- Lively and energetic at home but quiet and reserved at school or in other large settings
- Enjoy time with playmates, but stick to a preferred small group of friends

- Crave social interaction for a period of time, followed by quiet time
- Comfortable and talkative in familiar social situations but quiet and clingy in new surroundings
- Shifting emotions and moods based on environmental factors
- Crave both variety and routine

Tips for Raising Some Other Kind of "Vert" . . .

Implement a Daily Feelings/Needs Assessment

When kids seem to change with the weather (or something else if you happen to be in Southern California, where there is no weather), it can be hard for kids to keep track of what they're feeling and what they need. They also might place internal pressure on themselves to live up to whatever personality they've carved out at the moment. That can result in stress and sadness. It's hard to feel lost and confused in the world.

Help them figure out where they stand each day with a simple assessment tool. Divide a paper into two columns. The first column should be labeled "Morning" and the second "Night." In the morning column, write a few questions (leaving space for answers). Start with something simple like "I am feeling . . ." and continue with things like "Something I am looking forward to . . . ," "Something I'm worried about . . . ," and "Something that might help me have a great day . . ." Again, begin the night column with "I am feeling . . ." and continue with things like "Something that went well today . . . ," "Something that was hard today . . . ," "Something that helped me problem-solve . . . ," and "Something that made me happy today . . ."

Knowing where they stand and talking through the ups and downs of the day helps kids learn to pay attention to their emotions and figure out what they need in order to feel happy.

Let Them Quit Sometimes

I know, I know, no one wants to raise a quitter! But sometimes quitting isn't about giving up; sometimes quitting is about self-preservation.

Kids are under a lot of pressure today, and these kids who hang out somewhere in the middle tend to be pleasers. They might sign up for a certain class (ballet, anyone?) because it seems like it would be a lot of fun (possibly because ten other kids from their school are enrolled), only to have regrets three months into the six-month class. Talk about it. Help your child work through it. Decide together what is the right choice, and talk about choices that might lead to happiness. Try to let go of the quitting part of quitting and focus instead on finding happiness for your child.

Pros-and-Cons Lists

When kids are caught in the middle, they can have trouble making decisions. Riley answers "I'm not sure" to half of the questions I ask her because she truly isn't sure. She knows that she loves big parties, for example, but she also knows that she doesn't love the feeling of exhaustion that follows big parties. So sometimes she just doesn't know which way to turn. Many kids struggle to make choices that suit them because they are caught between personality styles. They can use a little help sorting things out.

Grab a whiteboard and teach your child the power of a simple pros-and-cons list. Writing out everything you like and look forward to versus everything you dislike and might regret in a given situation can be very powerful. It can help kids decide what will bring the most happiness.

Family Meetings

A scheduled, weekly family meeting can do great things to increase overall happiness in the home, particularly for the kids who don't speak up often. Set aside a weekly time (not a meal—it should be free from distractions) to sit around the table and discuss what's working, what's not working, and what the family can do to change. Giving children a voice helps them feel heard. It also helps them learn to be part of the solution instead of simply waiting for things to improve.

Keep a weekly agenda handy and encourage your kids to add to it throughout the week as problems or questions arise. That way you can be sure to address all their needs throughout the week during the meeting. Working together to improve how the family communicates and functions leads to happier parents and happier kids.

Set Limits

While the ultimate goal tends to be to raise independent, HAPPY kids, this is a goal best accomplished in stages. Being a kid is confusing. Too many independent decisions can cause undue stress and pressure. Parents have to be the voice of reason, and often we have to just go ahead and make decisions for them.

You know your child best. If missing a birthday party will feel like the end of the world for your child, make it happen. But if running around all weekend will lead to stress, exhaustion, and potentially illness, make the hard choices. I've had countless kids sit on my couch and recite the same refrain: "I just want to be the kid."

Set reasonable limits and expectations (particularly for sleep schedules and pro-social behaviors). Talk about them with your child. Revise them as they grow. (Bedtimes can grow with kids, as can personal freedoms like walking to a friend's house.) But when things get confusing, be sure to be the parent your child needs you to be.

Understanding where kids lie on the introvert/extrovert scale is really only the tip of the personality iceberg, but it's a great place to start. When we slow down enough to truly understand each child as an individual, we can learn a lot about them. We can understand, for instance, that some kids seem to lead by intuition and see possibility around every corner, while others lead by their senses, and tend to take things at face value.

While it's certainly easier to attempt to treat each child in exactly the same manner, it's more effective to treat each child as an individual. The key to raising happy kids, despite the stress and ups and downs, is figuring out who your kids are first, and then working to meet their individual needs.

Once you've determined what makes your children tick, how each child responds to stress, and how to best help each child when the going gets tough, you can make decisions that best suit each of your children. As you read your way through this book on raising happy kids, try to pick and choose the strategies in each section that best suit each of your children. Some will work better for one child than another, and some might work for the whole family. Just remember to consider each personality as you help your children find their way toward happiness.

2

The Power of Play

It is a happy talent to know how to play.

—RALPH WALDO EMERSON

AVERY WAS NINE YEARS OLD when she first flopped down on my couch. I was working as a school-based therapist at the time, and Avery was assigned to me during her first week of school. Small in stature but large in personality, she sat across from me with her arms crossed and her mouth pinched into a straight line. Her scraggly chestnut hair looked like it hadn't been washed all week and the dirt collected under her fingernails meant that she was either a gardener or a master of fake hand washing. I suspected the latter. "I can tell that you're the least fun therapist at this school. You don't even have a dollhouse." I had my work cut out for me.

Her piercing, catlike green eyes seemed to see right through me as she sat upright on my couch, daring me to prove her wrong. For three weeks she stared me down for forty-five minutes at a time, refusing to talk *unless* she could talk about how boring my office was. Adopted at birth into a very conservative family, Avery was constantly at odds with who she wanted to be (outgoing, artsy, loud) versus who her parents expected her to be (quiet, appropriate, a rule follower). She was unhappy on a good day.

Sensing her need to work through her complicated feelings with more than just conversation, I bought and assembled the dollhouse that she claimed would change everything. It did. Her eyes lit up when she first caught a glimpse of it (although she did her best to conceal her excitement). Without a second thought, she sat down in front of it and began what would turn into a story line that took at least one year to resolve. Week after week she played through her feelings, giving me characters and words to fill in the gaps. Her directions were specific. I had strict orders to follow the script. The only changes allowed were her own. As the days turned into weeks, I began to notice a shift in her demeanor. She smiled when she saw me around campus. She waved to me as her bus rolled away. And sometimes she even stopped by for no reason at all.

Six months into her play sessions, her parents realized what was happening. Angry that she was "wasting" her time playing, they called and demanded that I work through a list of behavioral goals instead. These conversations can be difficult. Some kids tend to hold it together at school, only to explode at home. It's easy to understand why parents become focused on specific behaviors. But the underlying issues won't disappear unless kids work through them. Focusing on one behavior at a time is a short-term "solution," at best. As I described the changes I saw firsthand and how play can be used to improve behaviors, we discussed a new plan. Avery would talk for the first half and play for the second half of each session. Specific goals would be addressed, but she was free to work through her feelings in her own way after.

I worked with Avery for more than three years. The nature of her play changed along the way, but she never stopped playing. Even when she reached middle school. She looked older, she acted older, and she had adolescent thoughts and behaviors, but she loved to play just the same. Play stripped away the stress, anxiety, and anger for a little while. Play brought back her smile. Through our sessions she found her happy place. She learned to find peace with her conflicted feelings about her family. She transformed from a little girl filled with anger and hurt to an older girl filled with happiness and adventure. She learned to say exactly what she meant, even if she didn't get her preferred responses in return. She also learned to view the world through a different lens—that of her parents. After three years she finally learned to empathize with them, instead of lashing out at them every time something didn't make sense to her. She made peace with her family, her surroundings, and her dreams. She found her voice and, more importantly, she also found her place in the world.

The Benefits of Play

Play is the language of children. Through unstructured play, children learn to communicate, think creatively, work through their emotions, increase problem-solving skills and frustration tolerance, build social interaction skills (they learn to get along), and just have fun. Children who engage in regular free play experience increased verbal and cognitive skills, improved memory, improved oral language skills, and increased physical development (assuming some of that free play entails jumping, rolling, running, and other outdoor activities that might actually frighten parents at times). Unstructured play can be anything from dress-up and imaginary play to art projects to

Lego building to a fort that takes up half of the house (to name a few), as long as it's child-directed. The very essence of unstructured play is that the kids choose to play what makes them feel happy, calm, and inspired.

Unstructured play boasts many benefits, although these can be overlooked when academics take center stage. Play helps children develop the following skills:

- Turn taking
- Responsibility
- Problem-solving
- Empathy for others
- Assertiveness
- Coping with negative emotions
- Self-expression
- Feelings identification
- Social interactions
- Symbolic representation
- Higher-level thinking
- Physical strength, endurance, and balance
- Language development
- Creative thinking
- Exploring passions

And it doesn't stop there. . . .

All young children display creativity in one way or another. A common misconception about "creativity" is that it is restricted to the arts. If a child is more puzzle-oriented than painting-oriented, that child might be viewed as lacking creativity. Not to worry, though. That child will always be referred to as some sort of math whiz.

Creativity is not about painting a beautiful work of art or composing heart-stopping music. Creativity is about making new things and generating new ideas by tapping into the imagination. Creativity is about thinking outside the box (a phrase educators love to reference while piling on the worksheets and other exercises in memorization for, say, third-graders).

When we take the time to actually enter the world of the child, to sit down and play with them (not near them while scrolling through the Instagram feed), we see the creativity that children naturally possess. Through imaginative play, children create mini constructs of the world around them, as well as the world that exists in their fantasies. On any given day, they might play out their version of your life (complete with an exaggerated, or possibly accurate, version of just how much time you spend glued to technology), or they might tap into a magical world of fairies, dragons, and other stories that run through their action-packed brains throughout the day. Often, they merge both worlds in their play as they work their way through the various questions and points of wonder that occupy their minds.

Play Creates Connections

Beyond creativity, play helps children learn to relate to others. Stop by a school, a playground, or even just an empty field with a small group of kids and you'll find that children have a strong inclination to play with other children. Some have a difficult time entering play, so they wait and watch (inching closer and closer with each passing moment) until an invitation is offered. Others jump right in and command the action. Many hang out somewhere in between, joining the play but not necessarily running it. Regardless of how they enter the play, children learn to work together, solve problems, and consider the feelings of others when engrossed in group play. Empathy, after all, is a skill best practiced through play.

Arguments can and will arise during group play. It makes perfect sense. When you get a group of people together (no matter how small), ideas and perspectives clash. Everyone wants to play the role of the mommy or the baby. Three kids want to play some version of fire rescue while the other two dig in their heels and beg (make that yell) to play outer space. While well-meaning parents are often quick to jump in and do the negotiating for the kids ("Why don't you play fire rescue for the first ten minutes and outer space for the next ten minutes?"), it should really be the work of the kids to negotiate the play. When problems arise in the context of group play, children learn to think about the feelings of others, read facial cues and make the connections between facial expressions and emotions, identify the problem and come up with possible solutions, and cooperate effectively. Sure, they will need guidance (encouraging them to stop and look for facial cues, for example), but the nature of group play is that children *have* to learn to work things out if they want the play to continue. If they yell, argue, and hurt feelings without resolving the problem, the play is likely to come to an abrupt end (an important lesson for little ones).

Remember those quiet kids who wait for the invitation to join the group play? The more they engage in unstructured play with other children, the more they learn to assert their needs and feelings. Over time, they learn that they don't need an engraved invitation to join a group—they can join and leave at will. With practice, they also learn that their ideas have value and that they can speak up and share their thoughts on the nature of the play. Free play can help children find their voices and express their ideas.

Play Relieves Stress

As much as group play helps hone social interaction skills and improves problem-solving skills, unstructured individual and family play encourages mastery over fears, helps kids work through feelings of anger and other negative emotions, and restores balance when stress becomes overwhelming.

Sean travels a lot for his work, and night can be a particularly challenging time for Riley when Sean is on the road. When the lights go down, the worries creep in. An active brain during the day keeps anxiety in its place, but when the body starts to settle in preparation for sleep, the brain sometimes alerts the worry center in young minds. Translation? Why is it so dark in here and *what* are all those noises?

I've taken countless "camping" trips in darkened rooms with nothing but a flashlight (under the command of Riley, of course), some favorite books, and a few graham crackers to keep us nourished. In the controlled darkness we listen for owls, get to the bottom of unknown sounds and shadows, and tell stories (some spooky, some not) for entertainment. Following the command of our fearless leader, we wander through dark forests and save trapped animals. We soothe each other to drift off to sleep and rescue one another when we feel scared. Together, we take control of the darkness.

Play helps children master their fears. When they are allowed to play on their own terms, that is. Through various forms of unstructured play, children push themselves to the limit—they try to figure out what they can handle. They take control of the fears that lurk beneath the surface. Leading the play helps them assume the power position over the source of the fear, whether it's darkness, monsters, spiders, or any other common childhood fear. That power differential changes everything. Over time, children begin to internalize that feeling of power and gain control of their fears outside of the play.

Play helps children work through many emotions. Using the doll family to work through her internalized feelings of anger and frustration, Avery was able to practice ways to express her anger without hurting others and learn to communicate her needs to her family members. In the beginning, there was a lot of fighting, yelling, and running away. Avery wanted an escape from the life she didn't think was meant for her, and each time the anger began to trickle out in her play, she had the girl doll pack a bag and run away to New York.

Resolving issues through play can't be forced. Children need to work through their feelings and explore the possibilities on their own terms. For a while, it seemed like Avery was stuck. Until one day she dared to wonder aloud what the parents would feel like if the doll actually ran away for good. Would their lives be better off without her? It was at that moment that Avery shifted out of anger and into sadness. She longed for a different, less restrictive lifestyle and mourned the loss of the biological mother she never knew, but she also began to empathize with her adoptive parents. Staying in character, we practiced identifying feelings and staying calm in frustrating moments. It was not an overnight success. It took time and practice on Avery's part, and also on the part of her parents. But she was able to make peace with what she couldn't change and learn to assert her needs without resorting to negatively charged interactions when under pressure at home.

Play Is Everywhere!

The wonderful thing about play, of course, is that it doesn't need to occur in an office under the watchful eye of a trained play therapist for it to be therapeutic in nature. Children can access the power of play at any time in a way that is meaningful to them. Kids work through sadness, anxiety, frustration, and countless other uncomfortable feelings within the context of play.

Parents sometimes worry when kids make guns out of Legos, sticks, or even just their fingers. Why are they choosing violent play? Does a love of guns inherently signal deeper issues? The truth is that kids do these things to figure things out. They want to know what it all means, while worried parents overthink it and start placing restrictions on their play. This is a tricky area to navigate when it comes to play, particularly in light of recent school shootings. As parents, we want to protect our children from the horrors of the world, but we also want to be very certain that children understand that killing others is wrong. The problem is that kids are naturally curious about things. Chances are they saw something in an old cowboy-themed book or even in current children's films and books that sparked a curiosity about guns and shooting.

It's hard for kids to work through the differences between fantasy and reality, so they use play to try to make sense of these overwhelming concepts. Cutting off certain topics shuts your child down. It sends a very negative message. You might be trying to send a more global message (killing is wrong and guns are dangerous), but what your children hear is that they have made a big mistake (your play is bad). It's perfectly acceptable for a parent to feel uncomfortable with certain kinds of play, but it's important to talk about it with your children. Let them work through their curiosity and feelings and then follow it up with a discussion about that topic. In this case, a good compromise might be to allow Lego guns at home but not at the playground or school. Talking about your concerns with your children after play helps them process the information in a meaningful way.

When engaged in play, your child is embedded in a fantasy world that might include good versus evil and various weapons to help good (or evil) prevail. When they come out of play is the time to talk about the meaning behind the play. It's also important to remember that although kids work through thoughts and feelings in their play, it's also a lot of fun!

Slow Down—Children at Play!

Once upon a time oodles of playtime was the norm. These days, kids lack free time. In his article "Play as a Foundation for Hunter-Gatherer Social Existence" in the *American Journal of Play*, Boston College professor Peter Gray addresses the changes in free play over time.[4] Where children once spent after-school hours and summer days engaged in free play, children today are more engaged in competition and adult-directed activities. Gray maintains that noncompetitive forms of social play are essential for developing a sense of equality, connectedness, and concern for others. But many children are lacking in the opportunity to sit down and play.

I tend to agree. Kids are thrown into playgroups as infants, with an educator leading the charge. While I love the support and connectedness among moms that these groups inspire (being a new mom is no easy task, after all), the very directed manner of these groups can lead to learned helplessness. It also sets parents on a path of habitually enrolling kids in "age-appropriate" groups and classes. Babies and toddlers don't need daily structured classes. They might enjoy one or two, but what they really need is a few wooden blocks and a crayon when they can hold it.

Fast-tracking learning might seem like a problem within the educational system, but it's actually societal in nature. From the moment our infants enter the world we wait and watch for milestones. We hold toys just out of reach because someone somewhere along the line said that doing so will help babies learn to reach and crawl. We compare notes with other moms and pepper pediatricians with questions about every single thing that might go right or wrong along the way. Don't get me wrong; we do this from the bottom of our hearts. We want the very best for our little ones, and we want to set them off on the right foot. But in all this doing and thinking and "teaching," we forget to let our little ones develop at their own pace. We drag them around and enroll them in the best of the best, but we forget about the importance of sitting down on the floor and playing with a block. Often the fast-tracking begins before a child even enters a preschool classroom.

The great irony, of course, is that play actually *promotes* school success. Kids who learn through play test and develop ideas; are more motivated to learn; develop concepts; learn from other kids; work on oral language skills, storytelling, and sequencing; develop empathy for others; and work on emotional regulation. Learning through play sets kids up to be confident and competent learners.

When we take the time to slow down and let kids explore on their own, we actually set them up for better self-confidence and problem-solving skills (themes that often come up in the educational setting). If we control them from the very first moment and constantly direct their lives, we set them up for learned helplessness. If we let the child lead through play, we teach them that they are capable and that their ideas are important. It might not feel like sitting on the floor with a stack of blocks and a few barnyard animals is important work (particularly when the toddler music class that boasts a three-month waiting list promises to help develop important skills like language and communication), but it is. The simple act of playing at an age-appropriate level helps kids learn about and understand the world around them.

Colin was an excellent example of a child who thrived on play. At eight years old, Colin struggled to connect with other kids. He had a rich internal world that occupied most of his waking hours. Friends and school were simply the things he had to do in between his imaginary adventures. His parents traveled a lot for work, leaving Colin and his sister behind with a nanny. This imaginary play that kept him so busy was his escape hatch. It helped him feel safe and secure when his parents were away. Still, his struggle to relate to others was a concern for his parents. His singular focus on science fiction had them worried that he wouldn't be able to find many friends. They loved him exactly the way he was, but they wanted to help him expand his relational skills so that he had choices beyond his imaginary world.

Play was the key to getting him there. For many months his play centered on his favorite theme: science fiction. It didn't take long to discover that this type of play gave him the control that he so desperately craved. He missed his parents terribly. He couldn't find the words to beg them to stay, probably because he already knew the answer. Kids can be very perceptive, after all. And so I let him take the lead. For a while, the play seemed to go unresolved. He wasn't ready to complete the story—or so it seemed. Ever so gradually, I began to introduce different problem-solving strategies and new characters. He didn't resist. Over time, he began dividing up the characters evenly so that I could play a larger role. And then one day he looked me straight in the eyes (a rarity for this child) and conveyed his understanding of our "work": "I know what you're doing,

Kate, you're showing me how to be a better friend." Relief washed over his face as I met his statement with a smile and a nod. Finally, he knew how to connect outside of his imagination.

Between more intensive early education programs that no longer build much time for creativity into each day and extracurricular overload, kids are often too busy to get down to the business of play. And with all these expectations being placed upon children, it can be easy to forget that play plays a crucial role in social, emotional, and cognitive growth. In fact, in "The Crisis in Early Education: A Research-Based Case for More Play and Less Pressure," Joan Almon and Edward Miller break down the research on the benefits of play as well as recent causalities of the fast track to success. In this research, Almon and Miller found that both educators and physicians are finding a link between aggressive behavior in preschool and kindergarten and the stress that children experience at school.[5] Once a place for developmentally appropriate learning, preschool and kindergarten classrooms are now accelerating the learning process for young minds, and increasing stress levels as a result.

The reality, of course, is that accelerated learning is not the only obstacle when it comes to finding balance and providing sufficient unstructured playtime for children. Technology is a roadblock that seems to increase in size as it evolves. Discussions about technology can be polarizing among parents, as the love-its and hate-its always have a tendency to be the most vocal. Whether or not they join the discussions that tend to become inflamed in places like Facebook, many parents struggle to find balance when it comes to technology and kids.

Our children are growing up in a tech-savvy world, and we don't want them to be left behind. But we also don't want to raise kids who become so technology-obsessed that they forget how to play and interact without gadgets and games. Isolation can pave the way to a lifetime of loneliness. Where there's loneliness, depression usually isn't far behind. As such, educational games and apps are generally offered as a happy medium. If they're learning, what harm can come of it?

Unfortunately, it's not that simple. Time can tick away when kids are quiet and engaged, and many of these games and apps (yes, even the "educational" ones) are designed to keep kids coming back for more. With rewards and new stimuli appearing at well-timed intervals and what can feel like endless levels of play, these games and apps suck kids in and it's a struggle for them to get back out. "Everything in moderation" tends to be an excellent motto, but when it comes to use of technology we also need to tack on "with careful supervision." You decide what is "educational" in nature and you set and enforce the limits. And when time is up, you have to remove the source of temptation from sight. Out of sight, out of mind (or at least out of reach).

While many kids adapt to modified screen time, some become so fixated on what they're doing (and even addicted—yes, I said addicted) while engaged in video games and Internet use that they fall apart when access is denied. Too much screen time can negatively impact social interaction skills, problem-solving skills, and the ability to play without electronics and constant feedback. Too much technology is bad for the soul and detrimental to growing minds.

Play Comes to the Rescue

The hard truth is that lack of play decreases both curiosity and creativity and removes an essential coping strategy from the child's toolbox. You can talk at a child as much as you wish, but if you want that child to internalize adaptive coping strategies and improve communication skills, understand the concept of empathy, and work on social interaction skills, you have to let them play.

For many years I co-led social skills groups with a good friend and fellow psychotherapist. Ranging in age from five to eight, the children enrolled in the group struggled with various aspects of social interaction. They were the kids who struggled to engage with other kids, didn't make room for others to talk, failed to understand and implement the give-and-take policy when playing with friends, and generally felt left out and dejected as a result.

Parent after parent begged us for a step-by-step guide to teaching social skills to their kids. In their mind, a comprehensive list of problems and solutions would accelerate and ease the teaching process. In a lot of ways, that makes sense. A solution-based approach would allow parents and children to easily troubleshoot in the moment. The problem, of course, is that each group consisted of four to six kids with different personalities, different learning styles, and energy to burn. It wasn't as simple as teaching one specific social skill per session. We had to meet the kids where they were in the process and find exciting ways to engage them.

In the end, we merged the two concepts. We developed a curriculum (more of a skeleton, truth be told) for the parents so that they could reinforce the weekly topics and skills in between sessions. But within the group setting, play came to the rescue. Together, small groups of complete strangers created and developed the "perfect school," wrote and starred in plays about friendship, used art to express and share their fears and concerns about making and keeping friends, and used movement and play to practice being a good friend.

Through these weekly sessions, the kids found friendship, trust, and empathy. There were arguments, of course, and there was more than one tattler in the group, but they worked together toward common goals. They learned to observe before jumping in and think before reacting (or overreacting, as the case may be). And they walked away knowing that they were capable of making friends. We saw increased self-esteem, improved problem-solving skills, and better overall social interaction skills at the end of each session. But best of all, we saw anxious and defensive little kids evolve into happier kids who felt capable of finding friends in the world. For that, we can thank the power of play.

Play changes by age and stage, and not all play is created equal. While parallel play and imaginary play that mimics day-to-day life (that remote control makes a great phone, doesn't it?) is the norm for toddlers and preschoolers, older children (kindergarten and beyond) begin to engage in high-level play (think sustained play scenarios, multiple roles, symbolism, and planning). Dress-up fades away and imaginary nail salons become the new norm. Matchbox cars collect dust in the closet in favor of acting out *Star Wars* scenes. And some kids just want to get out and play a favorite sport. But although older kids can and do thrive within organized sports, they can still use some time for a good old-fashioned game of family (or neighborhood) whiffle ball. There is something to be said for playing your own way.

Kids need time to be kids—to play, write, draw, sing, dance, and be silly. It's how they find their place in the world. They discover who they really are by figuring out their likes and dislikes through the power of play. It also gives them time to bond with parents, siblings, caregivers, and other kids. Although kids might enjoy various team sports and art classes, it's essential to provide them with plenty of downtime to explore the world around them.

Tips for Promoting Unstructured Play

Let Go of Insecurities

Children don't have emotions about playing; they work through emotions *while* playing. Play, for children, is all in a day's work. They might have a specific story line in mind, or their play might be completely spontaneous, but, either way, they aren't afraid to sit down and play. And they tend to want to share their playtime with their favorite playmates: their parents.

Adults, on the other hand, do tend to have emotions about playing. They feel silly, insecure, or even anxious. They have long to-do lists running through their minds, and sitting down to play seems overindulgent—a waste of precious time. These intrusive thoughts can lead to an emotional block, making playtime with a child seem boring, trivial, and even frustrating. But we can't let our emotions and insecurities cloud our ability to help our children thrive.

Parental attitudes can affect the way kids play. If your child sees that imaginary play is a burden for you, she is less likely to engage in this crucial type of play. A child who doesn't engage in imaginary play lacks the same problem-solving skills, social interaction skills, and higher-level thinking skills that kids immersed in imaginary play develop over time.

Parents today struggle to cope with unpredictability. Scheduled activities keep the day rolling and provide a blueprint. Filling the downtime with more activities might make it easier for a stressed-out parent (no worries about how to pass the time when every waking second is accounted for), but it robs children of time to play, learn on their own terms, and create. It stunts their emotional growth. It's important for parents to learn to tolerate an unpredictable schedule.

It's also important for parents to take ownership of creating a playful environment. Instead of stressing about the potential mess, reframe your thoughts and consider the potential outcome (as in the smile on your child's face). Teach your kids to play. Get involved, get dirty, and leave your stress behind for a moment.

Our children don't need us to play with them every second of every day. In fact, many kids prefer solitary playtime at various points in the day to decompress and restore a feeling of calm. They do, however, need us to be present when we are engaged in play. It's not the quantity of the one-on-one playtime that matters the most, after all, it's the quality.

To that end, it's important to identify your own personal roadblocks to play and find some solutions. Playing the same Polly Pocket scenario over and over again for forty-five minutes at a clip can become monotonous for the adult, but chances are the child is working through something meaningful. Crawling around like a puppy at the command of a toddler can be exhausting and a little bit frustrating if you have an enormous list of errands to run or tasks to accomplish. It's more difficult for adults to get lost in a world of fantasy because we generally have other things on our minds.

Use parent-child playtime as an excuse to turn your back on the outside world (put AWAY the screens, my friends) for an hour. Instead of going through the motions with your child, take the opportunity to lose yourself in your own imagination. What would it feel like to live in a giant strawberry and run a successful café? What would be the rules of your castle should you suddenly find yourself wearing a crown? Children get lost in play because the thought of trying on new roles is exciting and awe-inspiring. Let go of your focus on the actual toy placed in your hand and allow symbolism to infiltrate your imagination.

Play without worry. Play without care. Play as if no one is watching. . . . Only then will you free your soul.

Make Time

Making time for play seems like a simple enough concept when you utter it out loud, but it doesn't always work out that way. Multiple children in a family translates to multiple schedules, appointments, and responsibilities. Children are enrolled in structured activities and team sports at very young ages these days, which cuts into what would be free playtime. And increased academic demands beginning as young as kindergarten in many areas means that homework is an issue. Bottom line: You have to make time for play.

It can take thirty to sixty minutes to plan, develop, and act out a high-level play scenario. You have to factor in time for brainstorming the theme, gathering props, choosing roles, setting the scene, and finally getting into the action. When unstructured play is continually disrupted to allow for more structured activities, children don't have the opportunity to work through the process that makes play meaningful on so many levels. They also learn to take shortcuts or avoid imaginary play altogether to avoid those frustrating interruptions.

In making time for play, kids have the opportunity to plan and develop their play scenarios without restrictions. They can get lost in the act of fantasy play because they don't have to watch the clock. That, alone, opens their minds and lets their imaginations thrive.

Schedule Weekly Parent-Child Playdates

I know what you're thinking—this is supposed to be unstructured. But that doesn't necessarily mean unscheduled. Parents are busy. Whether you work in some capacity or stay at home with your kids, there is always something that needs doing. The endless to-do list that fogs your brain (it's not just me, is it?) just might be the very thing that gets in the way of enjoying that unstructured playtime with your child.

Ensuring a weekly parent-child playdate where your child gets to set the stage and call the shots (within reason, anyway) for an hour gives your child a specific time to look forward to. Here's the thing: Resist the urge to plan something during this time. Play strengthens the parent-child bond because it's fun, free from rules and restrictions, and the child gets to lead the charge. Let go of your inhibitions, embrace your inner child, and eat the worm sandwiches being served at the restaurant. Or, if you have an older child, learn to knit, do some woodwork, or plant a garden together. Do whatever it takes to truly bond with your child because the better the relationship you have with your child, the happier your child will be.

Ditch the Fancy Toys

Let me be the first to admit that I love technology. Change can be a very good thing. But not necessarily when it comes to toys. And definitely not when it comes to play. Remember when wooden blocks were actually the only choice? Or when kids weren't struggling with video game addiction because, let's face it, you could only handle so much time playing Asteroids before you wanted to make a run for it?

Along with technology, education, and parenting styles, toys have changed over time. The Legos that once only existed in primary colors and required thought and imagination are now sold in overpriced buildable sets with step-by-step instructions to re-create your favorite movie and video game worlds. Following instructions? Check. Patience? Check. Creativity? Fail.

As much as loud, beeping trucks that resemble actual trucks at a construction site and Legos meant only to build Hogwarts are fun and exciting at first glance, they also have the potential to stunt the creativity of our children. A little bit of fancy is great, but we also have to get back to basics.

Try to balance the new fancy-talking, beeping, imitates-your-favorite-movie toys with building materials, dolls, and manipulatives that actually require thought and imagination. When given the opportunity, your child will reconnect with the power of free play and find happiness in the act of harnessing their creativity.

Support High-Level Play

If we want older kids to shift into high-level play, the kind that truly inspires creativity and symbolic play, we need to create a play-friendly environment. As a partially reformed control freak, I can understand when parents don't want creative and messy play to take over the home. What's calming for kids is not necessarily calming for adults. But for kids to truly benefit from play, we need to let go of "house perfect." Someday my home will mirror that of the latest Pottery Barn catalog and I won't find myself rebuilding the couch on a nightly basis (I will be sobbing from the lack of little voices in the house, though, you can count on that), but for right now, this house is meant for play.

The fact is that kids who grow up in play-rich homes experience stronger overall learning skills. They also learn to work through and cope with emotions along the way. Play-rich is not dependent upon a certain amount of toys or having the latest and greatest toys to hit the market. It means having a safe space to play without worrying about messing up the house, breaking something of great importance, or being made to feel like play is somehow detrimental to the state of the home. It means having the freedom to play, create, and imagine.

Creating a play-friendly environment does not, however, mean that your kids take over every room in the house without ever cleaning up. It also doesn't mean that you need to make peace with a giant cardboard pirate ship in the middle of your living room. It means that you offer an environment that encourages fantasy play.

Make props available in different spaces to inspire various play scenarios. The family room couch is the go-to airplane in our home, but if anyone needs to take a trip to outer space, they need to head to my office (that's what my children tell me, anyway). Riley's bedroom makes a great school around here, and Liam's room boasts the best safaris. Provide the canvas and a few tools to start the play, and let the kids take it from there. And then teach them how to clean up so that they can begin a brand-new adventure the next time!

Never Underestimate the Power of the Recycling Bin

Craft stores are great because they sell just about everything. It's one-stop shopping for your art-loving child. There are premade kits for every interest and enough art supplies to last a lifetime. They also tend to be expensive. I challenge you to get out of Michaels for under $80.

While all those kits and supplies are beautiful, inspiring, and fun to have on hand, they aren't entirely necessary. The key to tapping into a child's creativity through unstructured play (which includes art) is removing the need for instructions and perfection. When children are given the opportunity to create without expectations, they feel happy. Their work is truly their own.

Recycled art is one of the best ways to inspire true creativity in children. The great thing about being a kid is that they often see beyond the surface. A paper towel tube isn't just a cardboard tube in the mind of a kid; it's a spyglass. Or the mast of a ship. Or a tunnel slide at a park. You get the point.

Before you actually recycle that large bin of paper and bottles each week, give your child the opportunity to root through it in search of treasures. Resist the urge to label what you see and encourage your kids to think outside the box. Kids who create are happy kids.

The look of pure joy on my daughter's face when she discovered that she could finally make a zoo for her little animals with recycled strawberry baskets is burned in my memory. Happiness, it seems, is making something out of nothing.

Expand Play Themes

Young players can get stuck in a loop when it comes to play themes. Sometimes that's okay. Kids have a tendency to play out familiar themes (school, anyone?) or topics that trigger fear and other uncomfortable emotions (monsters, and ghosts, and bears . . . oh my!). It takes time to work through complicated emotions and sometimes playing out familiar positive themes is calming at the end of a long day.

But sometimes they're just not sure what else to do. As the play repertoire grows, so does vocabulary, oral language, problem-solving skills, and emotional regulation. As children try out new themes and work through different concepts and problems, they engage in higher-level thinking. It makes sense to help kids discover new areas of play.

Real-world experiences are a great way to inspire new themes and play concepts. Trips to museums, aquariums, zoos, and even local libraries can open the imagination to new possibilities. As can everyday errands. A large part of imaginative play is trying on new roles. Point out the various roles you encounter throughout the day. Everyone from the cashier and bagger at the grocery store to the divers and animal trainers at the aquarium are new and different roles to explore. Talk about how one librarian helps people find books, another checks the books out, and yet another reshelves the returned items. Lost in the moment and the scenery surrounding them, kids don't always see the details unfolding before them out in the real world. Help connect the dots so that they expand their worldviews and begin to try on new (and sometimes more complicated) roles.

Parents can also help develop new play themes by modeling use of props around the house and referencing experiences from the real world. Using loose change to buy a banana from the fruit bowl, for example, will remind your child about the grocery store trip. Making an old credit card into a "library card" might inspire a trip to the library. Subtle cues can inspire new themes for young children so that they don't get stuck in a loop.

Provide Theme-Appropriate Materials

Chances are that you have a ton of old stuff around your house that can and will inspire hours of unstructured play. Sometimes something as small as a loose Band-Aid can inspire an hour of emergency room fun. While I love to spring (and fall, winter, and summer) clean as much as the next person, I try to think about how my old things might be reused before I toss them. Used Target gift cards and reusable shopping bags provide endless grocery shopping fun around here, but there are hundreds of possibilities when you stop and think before you toss. These will get you started:

- Old concert tickets
- Used boarding passes from flights
- Old luggage (they have to pack!)
- Play money, real coins, and foreign currency (you know, for overseas trips on the couch)
- Postcards to keep in touch during those trips
- Extra photos
- First-aid supplies (empty Band-Aid boxes, unused medicine cups and droppers, gauze pads, etc.)
- Old textbooks
- Phone books (you don't use those anyway, right?)
- Plastic kitchen supplies
- Writing materials (for writing notes, making shopping lists, and taking messages)
- Old cell phones
- Scraps of fabric
- Old sheets (talk about a great roof for a fort!)

You get the point. A parent's trash is a child's treasure. Keep these little bits of inspiration in easy-to-reach bins and watch your kids create incredible, high-level play scenarios right before your very eyes.

Create a Reality-Based Dress-up Trunk

There is a good reason that your toddler insists on clomping around the house in your three-inch heels: She's trying to understand what it feels like to be you! Kids of all ages love to play dress-up in Mom and Dad's closets, but not all moms and dads want their closets raided day after day. That's okay; there is a simple solution for this one.

Create a reality-based dress-up trunk for your little ones. Before you donate all your unwanted clothing, sort through the pile to see what might be fun for your kids. This is also a good place to put the clothes that aren't actually appropriate for donating given the wear and tear. Choose items from both Mom and Dad to fill this trunk of possibilities, regardless of the gender of your kids. The point is to provide dress-up clothes that mimic the roles they encounter on a daily basis. When they run a library for the afternoon, for example, they might want to dress the part (or their version of the part, anyway).

Princess costumes and other dress-up items found at your local toy store are fun for a while, but nothing beats reality when it comes to creating your own fantasy world.

Provide Nonrealistic Props

A box of stuff that isn't really anything at all is just as important as the theme-appropriate props. When kids are given assorted items to create a play scenario but those items don't necessarily match the play theme they had in mind, they are forced to problem-solve. They might have to make a hairbrush into a microphone to start that concert on time or turn a plastic cube into a podium to make that important speech when running for president.

When kids are given nonrealistic props to incorporate into their fantasy play, they have to rely on higher-level thinking and imagination to make the props work. This helps them make the jump to symbolic play. Symbolic representation is the ability to separate the function of an object from the object itself. When a child uses athletic socks as bunny ears, for example, he understands that the socks represent the long ears. He no longer has to rely on exact representations in order to get lost in the fantasy play.

In the real world, that translates into better problem-solving skills and deeper engagement in the subject matter. But in the safety of the play-rich home, it really just makes for happier kids.

Take It Outside

A play-friendly home with all sorts of props is amazing, but the great outdoors opens up endless possibilities when it comes to imaginary play. Little kids are the masters of making something out of nothing, and props aren't always necessary. Liam and I are known to take long and winding safari walks to the park in search of lions, tigers, and giraffes. We hide behind trees and sneak up on the animals to avoid startling them. Then we capture them on film with imaginary cameras. And Riley loves a pirate adventure in the backyard. With sticks and leaves and a few fallen rose petals she can create a pirate meal to be served on the deck (the picnic table) before setting sail on her magic pirate ship (the swing set). It's nearly impossible to get her back inside for dinner once she leaves reality in favor of her pirate adventure, and sometimes dinner just has to be served on the ship.

You don't need fancy play equipment to inspire an outdoor adventure, and a walk through the big city can be just as inspiring as a walk through a small town or along the shore. Kids create their own fantasies with the tools at their disposal. When you are outside, the tools seem to be everywhere.

There are numerous benefits from daily outdoor play. When outside (even in the cold snow) kids are more actively engaged in physical play. Kids who play outside have better strength, endurance, and balance because they build their muscles and work on large motor skills. They also tend to sleep better and eat well. A growing trend among elementary schools is to turn recess into an extra physical education period to increase physical activity. This trend stems from recent spikes in childhood obesity. Kids don't have to run laps or do jumping jacks to improve their overall health, though. Running, jumping, scooting, and playing tag are all great sources of physical activity. Playing on the play structure, hula-hooping, and engaging in outdoor imaginary play are also sources of exercise for kids.

Recess is a time for kids to blow off steam and play at will after time spent sitting in the classroom. Turning it into exercise time takes the fun out of the one truly playful time kids have during an elementary school day. You can't control what happens during school recess, but you can bring back playtime in your own home.

Teach your kids the power of play. Make sure that they have enough time for imaginary play, messy play, outdoor play, and any other play that makes them happy. Prioritize this very essential part of childhood so that your kids can learn and grow at a pace that suits them. Your kids will be happier for it.

3

Understanding Emotion

Anyone who has a continuous smile on his face conceals
a toughness that is almost frightening.

—GRETA GARBO

JAKE WAS SEVEN WHEN he first started counseling. Despite his young age, he had already mastered the art of distraction and spent a good portion of each school day clowning around and making his classmates laugh. His smile was contagious and his eyes scrunched up into perfect little sparkling crescents each time he laughed. If you didn't know better, you would wonder what brought him to my office in the first place.

It was the stomachaches. And headaches. And sore throats. And muscle aches. In fact, it was a different complaint almost every single day. Week after week he sat on my couch and listed his various physical complaints. When I connected headaches to math, he laughed and said that math was no problem. When I commented that stomachaches seemed to crop up during PE, he told me to stop talking to his mom. Every time I asked him how he was feeling, the answer was always the same: He was happy. Everything was great. No problems.

But his teacher told a different story. He was struggling. He appeared anxious and felt sick each time the work was just a little out of reach. So I decided to do a little work with feelings identification. Either this kid was so guarded that he would do anything to avoid talking, or he simply didn't know how he was really feeling. For an entire session, we did nothing but play with a stack of feelings faces flash cards. This little game quickly revealed that he wasn't in touch with his feelings at all. Card after card, face after face, he guessed the exact same feeling: happy. For Jake, happiness was the only feeling that mattered. It was the only one that he could identify and process, and so he held it close to his heart. Even when anxiety sent him running to me with a host of psychosomatic complaints each week.

One thing I've learned over and over again in my practice is that countless kids coast through life without ever really understanding their emotions. They don't know what they're feeling. They don't know how to process their feelings. And very rarely do they draw the connections between emotional and physical health. It's a shame, really, this lack of emotional awareness. Because when you understand what causes your emotions and can truly identify what it means to feel happy, you can find your way to daily happiness.

When our babies first enter the world, we speak to and for them constantly. In an effort to understand their needs and figure out what each cry means, we watch carefully and run through the punch list to problem-solve the situation. Hungry? No, she just ate. Tired? Eh, she had a long morning nap. Wet? Please not again, I just changed her. Gas? Bingo! She needs to burp. As we frantically (while trying our best not to appear frantic) run through the possible causes, we soothe our babies with our words and actions: "I know you're sad, let's get this burp out and help you feel better," we whisper, as we gently rock them back and forth. Yes, when it comes to babies, we are constantly labeling and soothing emotions.

But then they become toddlers and preschoolers, and suddenly parents shift gears. Gone are the days of labeling each cry to determine the cause. For some reason, when little ones shift from baby to toddler to preschooler and beyond, the expectations shift. Many parents become focused on behavioral correction instead of working through the emotions that triggered the behavior. Almost overnight, it seems, following a certain set of rules and "behaving" becomes the new norm for little ones. The priority shifts from "happy child" to "well-behaved child."

With most of our extended family on the other side of the country, my little family makes a lot of cross-country flights. While the thought of flying for six hours with little ones sends some parents into an understandable state of panic (my husband, the world traveler, worries more about long flights with the kids than just about anything else), I don't worry. My theory is that once you enter that giant metal tube, all bets are off. There is only so much you can do once the trip begins, so it's best to keep calm and color ten thousand pictures (give or take) along the way. More often than not, the flights are great and the kids are fine and we experience very little drama along the way. And then some well-meaning passenger in 21C turns around with a smile and says, "You should be proud of your kids. They are very well-behaved." I smile and nod and secretly cringe inside because what I want to scream is, "They're happy! These kids are happy! Childhood is short, happiness matters!" 21C would not likely, of course, understand or share that sentiment. So I express my gratitude and move on.

This is not to say that my kids are happy every single second of every single day. That's just silly. No one is happy all the time. Life presents obstacles and we have to learn how to cope with those bumps (and, okay, occasional unexpected manholes that we fall into) along the way. In our home, we talk about emotions a lot. As in every day. I began teaching them to identify their feelings when they were toddlers, and we continue to work on it as they grow.

Young children confront many of the same emotions that adults do each day. While most adults have the words to describe their emotions and the skills to cope with them, kids generally do not. Sure, they begin to learn a few social-interaction skills in preschool and they socialize more and more as they grow, but social development and emotional development are two very different areas of growth. And many schools do not have the time to focus on emotional development. It has to begin at home.

The other big difference between kids and adults when it comes to confronting and processing emotions each day is that while adults might encounter one or two events or triggers that affect their mood, kids are more likely to encounter several triggers that are difficult to process.

Kids experience shifting emotions throughout the day; that's perfectly normal. They might be elated over a new friendship one moment and hysterical about a small paper cut the next. It's all in a day's work when you're young. While the kids who don't have a clear understanding of their emotional process might get lost in the highs and lows each day, the kids who can label their feelings and find a solution are able to move on more quickly after experiencing difficult emotions and, in turn, be more open to happiness, even when the going gets tough. Understanding emotions, it turns out, is a critical first step toward taking charge of happiness.

That begins with identifying the various feelings they encounter on a daily (and sometimes hourly) basis. Young children experience anger, happiness, sadness, frustration, exhaustion, anxiety, embarrassment, and excitement at different intervals throughout any given day, but they don't necessarily have the words to describe those big emotions. So they do what they can. They kick, they yell, they laugh until their tummies ache, they stomp their feet, they go boneless in the middle of the parking lot—they use their bodies and the sound of their voices to convey emotion. This can really spike frustration, anxiety, or some combination of the two in parents. Because why oh why does it always seem to happen in public places?

I will never forget one spring afternoon when I brought my kids to the local mall to see the Easter Bunny. They've been Easter Bunny/Santa stalkers since I can remember—no interest in meeting either one, but they sure do love to sit and stare in wonder at these oversized magical beings sitting right in front of them in a tiny little mall in Manhattan Beach that they know so well. I don't ever recall my parents making a big deal of sitting on Santa's lap when I was a child, and I've never asked my kids to partake in these holiday rituals, either. How many times have we discussed strangers and checking with Mommy or Daddy *before* talking to a stranger . . . but go ahead and sit on that strange man's lap for a picture because, even though you've never met him and he looks a little different from the Santa in your favorite Christmas book, it's a moment we just really need to have? I still can't wrap my head around it. Regardless, many parents want those holiday memories.

On that particular day of Easter Bunny stalking, Riley and Liam enjoyed ice-cream cones at the closest table to the bunny house while a long line of well-dressed toddlers waited patiently for the Easter Bunny to arrive. He strolled in right on time, pausing to wave to the kids before taking his seat. Riley's jaw dropped at the wonder of the creature before her. Liam played with a Matchbox car. And as the photo ops began, toddler after toddler kicked and screamed with arms flailing as anxious parents attempted to coerce them to just take one picture. Nervous laughter filled the room and the meltdowns seemed to have a domino effect. Within minutes, it seemed, a chorus of anxious tots surrounded us. And yet the parents still kept at it. Phrases like "What are you so afraid of?" and "Don't be so silly" wafted through the air. A little bit of my soul slipped away with each screaming toddler until finally Riley broke my trance. "Mommy, why do those kids have to see the Easter Bunny?" As we walked away hand in hand I did as any mom would do, I eased her own worries about the situation and promised her that she would only ever do that by her own choice.

Those children didn't have the words to express the fear they experienced. They were terrified. Fears of people in costume are fairly common among toddlers and preschoolers. If you really step back and think about it, it makes sense. In pictures, rabbits are cute and small and hop around on all fours. They are playful and seem to love carrots. This is the image that young children have burned in their minds when it comes to rabbits. Why wouldn't a life-size rabbit wearing glasses and a striped jacket scare them? They have every right to feel afraid in that moment! And they have every right to say, "No thank you." Sadly, many parents want the memory no matter the hysteria, so they keep pushing until exhaustion sets in and the puffy-eyed child sits still long enough to get the shot. And then they fire those pictures off to Jimmy Fallon in the hope of fifteen seconds of late-night fame.

Feelings are everywhere and feelings tend to be easily hurt when it comes to young children. A friend who won't share might trigger a few tears of sadness. A denied request for a new toy is likely to incite anger or frustration. More attention paid to a sibling is a likely cause of jealousy. And exhaustion can trigger a mixed bag of emotions when the day finally comes to a close. Imagine running through a laundry list of emotions each day without the words to describe them. How would you feel under similar circumstances? It's overwhelming, exhausting, and frustrating. Because what happens, of course, is that adults treat the behavior symptomatically. They address each behavior that arises without pausing to consider the underlying feelings. In the moment, it's perfectly reasonable to grab for the quick fix to end the meltdown, but that doesn't help kids process and understand their emotions long-term. It's crucial to teach kids how to identify and cope with their feelings.

Charlie is the perfect example of a child caught between feelings and actions. At seven, his father moved out of his home. His parents said all the right things. They worked together to create a schedule that wouldn't disrupt Charlie's normal schedule. They agreed to attend school functions together and remain equally involved in extracurricular activities. They thought they covered all the areas that would cause concern for Charlie. But they didn't prepare for the emotional upheaval that Charlie would experience when his father finally moved out.

Although Charlie saw both parents most days and they continued to plan family outings on the weekends, Charlie's behavior began to change. Despite their best efforts to normalize the transition for Charlie, his parents were under stress. They were short with each other when they thought Charlie wasn't listening, and they were short with Charlie when the constant questions got the best of them. Internalizing each little negative interaction along the way, Charlie began to project his internalized emotions onto other kids at school. He teased his friends. He yelled. He struggled to focus. His anger bubbled up here and there until his teacher began to lose patience each day. He struggled to identify and cope with his emotions, and that made each day completely overwhelming.

I get a lot of questions about emotional regulation from concerned parents. Parents worry about tantrums that continue beyond the toddler years or how much anxiety is too much anxiety. When emotions seem just a little too big, parents react. It can be stressful for a parent when a child appears to be in a near-constant state of worry or shifts from calm to super-angry in a moment. It's only natural to think about what might be going wrong or if there is a different way to handle these situations.

Emotional regulation is a fancy way of saying that a child can express his feelings in a constructive manner, without being hurtful or overreacting. In essence, teaching children to regulate their emotions means teaching them to express their thoughts and feelings instead of acting on impulse (as many youngsters are prone to doing).

The trick is that emotional regulation has to be taught. Kids are naturally impulsive and they tend to be fairly egocentric as well. It's not a great combination when emotions run high. When parents shush them and tell them to calm down, it can actually exacerbate the emotions because they really don't know how to calm down. Imagine, for a moment, how it might feel if you accidentally fell into an ocean full of huge waves and the bystanders along the shore repeatedly shouted, "SWIM! SWIM!" when all you could think was, *I don't know how to swim. I never learned.* It's vital to teach your kids how to swim in the sea of emotions, and that begins with throwing them a life jacket. Whether it's worry, anger, or some other feeling causing the reaction, they feel out of control and they don't know how to turn it off. They don't mean to upset you. It's generally not their intention to make the situation worse. They don't know how to cope or how to draw the connections between their thoughts, feelings, and behaviors. So they yell until someone takes notice.

Kids want their feelings to be heard and appreciated. Emotional regulation isn't about stopping a tantrum or controlling anxiety. Emotional regulation is about teaching kids to understand what triggers those very big feelings and what they can do in the moment to work through them without projecting them onto others. We want our children to have their feelings throughout the day. When kids learn to stuff their feelings, they internalize every negative emotion experienced during the day until they finally explode. Teaching your children to regulate their emotions means teaching them to express and cope with their feelings using healthy strategies. It's more than okay to cry when you're sad, and once you finish letting your sadness out you can brainstorm ways to cope with it so that it doesn't follow you around all day.

Emotional regulation plays a critical role in the emotional well-being of children. Kids confront a lot of obstacles each day and they need to learn how to cope with their emotions instead of letting their emotions take control of them. When kids learn that they can choose adaptive coping strategies to confront intrusive thoughts and emotional triggers, they free up space to focus, interact in a positive manner, and resolve conflict independently. They are also more likely to exhibit fewer physical signs of stress (those headaches and stomachaches can be debilitating for stressed-out little ones).

Parents can do a lot to help kids label, understand, and find solutions to cope with their feelings each day. It's tempting to think of emotions in black and white. We want to experience positive emotions (which might include happiness, love, elation, empathy, and excitement) and we will do just about anything to avoid negative emotions (including sadness, anger, worry, frustration, disappointment, and jealousy). But like most things in life, it isn't that simple. When we label emotions as good or bad, we inadvertently send a message that some feelings are acceptable while others are not. That's not the lesson we want our children to learn. While positive emotions feel good, we can also learn from negative emotions. It's important to send the message that all feelings are useful, even if some of them lead to discomfort.

That very first step to helping kids regulate their own emotions is building a feelings vocabulary. Children are far more likely to use language to express their emotions if they have a strong vocabulary of feelings words from which to pull. Most kids know happy and sad by the time they are toddlers. They might even add excited, worried, and mad to the list when they get to preschool. But it's not just about words. It's about understanding the *meaning* of the words and knowing when they feel that way. Your child probably knows, for instance, that happiness is most often depicted by a smile. But does your child know what happiness *feels* like on the inside? Does your child know what kinds of things trigger that internal feeling of happiness?

Building a "feelings vocabulary" means giving your children the language to express their feelings *and* teaching them the visual cues and internal feelings (e.g.: can't sit still, racing heart, tense muscles, gritting teeth) that accompany each feeling. It also means spending a lot of time talking about the people, places, events, and other things that trigger specific feelings. It's a process, and it isn't one that can be accomplished in a single sitting. It takes daily practice and reinforcement, even as children grow. Stressors and obstacles change as children get older, and so does their experience of feelings. It's a good idea to make the feelings vocabulary part of your daily routine in a way that best fits your family, because having the words is a very important step toward using them in a meaningful (and hopefully calm) way.

Once your children have the words to describe the various emotions that rock their little worlds each day, you can help them connect the dots independently. While we spend those early years commenting on their feelings and connecting the dots for them ("Tommy grabbed your toy and you feel sad and mad"), we tend to stop doing that once kids have a greater grasp of language. It's important for kids to make the transition from parents talking on their behalf to expressing emotions for themselves, but they do need a bridge to cross along the way. They need us to provide the cues to help them locate those feelings words and make sense of the triggers that leave them overwhelmed with emotion (both positive and negative).

Providing a description of how your child appears in the moment is a great way to cue your child to consider her emotional state. It's hard not to notice giant tears streaming down the face, but many kids don't realize it when they tense their muscles, appear hot and sweaty, or bite their nails and twirl their hair. Providing a detailed description of the emotional state and asking open-ended questions ("Why do you think you might be feeling this way?") helps your child stop and think about how she's actually feeling in response to the trigger.

As adults, we encounter plenty of stressors that cause us to pause and regroup throughout the day. Sometimes we even express those feelings of frustration or sadness without taking the time to stop and think. We might even walk away and give ourselves a break, a parental time-out to make sense of the stress. But for some reason, we hold children to a higher standard. We expect them to stop yelling, stop crying, or stop acting upon whatever emotion seems to be the loudest. But those loud moments, when the tears are huge and the primal wails seem never-ending, are exactly the moments when parents need to stand by and allow the feelings to exist. Only after we let kids vent can we help them identify the feelings and connect the dots to help them discover how they got there.

Somewhere along the line, frustration and sadness exhibited by young children, commonly referred to as "temper tantrums" and "meltdowns," became behavioral issues. Instead of looking at these moments from an emotional standpoint, parents began to see them as defiance. And while a meltdown in response to a child being told no to the lollipop might look defiant on the surface, when you peel back the layers and begin to consider the emotional perspective, the response doesn't actually seem that outrageous given the developmental level of the child. Does that mean that you appease the child by handing over the lollipop? Of course not! But acknowledging the child's feelings and working through the emotional upheaval together helps your child learn to cope with big feelings and frustrating situations so that huge meltdowns become a little less huge over time.

The key to helping kids learn to identify and cope with their feelings is not overparenting or underparenting. The key to helping them with these very necessary skills (big feelings arise during all stages of life, after all) is to support them, guide them, and help them begin to draw their own connections and problem-solve independently while adhering to the boundaries and limits that already exist within your family. When kids learn that they don't need to scream in order to be heard and understood, tantrums become less intense and kids begin to utilize adaptive coping strategies to seek help from their parents and other trusted adults.

Learning to regulate emotions and knowing that the parent-child relationship is blanketed in unconditional love and support plays an integral role in increasing childhood happiness. To raise happy kids, we have to give them the tools they need to work through negative emotions and difficult situations *while* loving them all the way.

Tips for Teaching Feelings Identification and Understanding Emotions

Mirror, Mirror

Many kids struggle to decode feelings by looking at facial expressions. They are likely to get the most common ones, such as happy and sad, but facial expressions can be confusing at times. Children have a tendency to exhibit opposite emotions when under stress. Nervous laughter hides anxiety. Tears convey both sadness and anger (and even pride and happiness), but anger can also manifest as uncontrollable laughter or a blank stare. There are a lot of mixed messages when it comes to facial expressions, and it helps to practice during a moment of calm.

Write down various feelings (remember to consider age and developmental level here) on index cards and place them in a hat. Sit in front of a large mirror with your child and take turns choosing feelings from the hat and acting them out in the mirror together. Although this little feelings exercise can be fun and lead to lots of silliness (which is a very good thing, by the way, as you want kids to feel comfortable and not threatened when working on difficult topics), try not to exaggerate your expressions too much. The goal here is to help children learn to decode and recognize the subtleties in expressions of feelings.

Have you ever had someone ask you if you're okay when you're actually feeling perfectly fine? Like Riley, I have a rich internal world. I have a tendency to zone out while I replay thoughts through my mind. I've learned over time that these little moments of internal regrouping are difficult for others to decode, particularly people who don't know me well. I've also learned to take those moments when I'm alone or respond with a cheery, "Just lost in thought!" Even as adults, it can be hard to decode facial expressions.

When kids learn to look for facial cues early on and to understand how their own facial expressions convey emotion, they have a better grasp of how people feel in various situations.

The Homemade Feelings Chart

A feelings chart is another great way to match facial cues to emotions. Kids can visit the feelings chart regularly throughout the day to choose their own feelings or simply talk about the various feelings on the chart.

Sure, there are countless feelings faces posters available online and in stores, and you can download smaller templates free of charge. But if you want your child to get attached to and use the feelings chart regularly, it helps to have your child create a chart that holds meaning for him.

A fun way to do this is to practice making various faces to depict different feelings together. Be sure to point out how different parts of the face appear when experiencing different emotions (e.g.: "down eyes" = angry). Talk about what it means to feel happy, sad, surprised, overwhelmed . . . You get the point. When your child has it down (can make the various faces and understand what they mean), snap a few pictures of him making those faces. Print those pictures and paste them on a large poster board, with the feeling written underneath. Have your child visit the chart regularly throughout the day, not just when he's upset. Over time, he will begin to make the connections between how he feels and what that feeling looks like. Once he can pick out his emotions on the chart, you can start talking about what to do with those emotions.

Bonus lesson from Liam: It also helps to use familiar characters that have meaning for the child. He uses the characters from the Disney *Cars* collection to identify emotions. We often hear him describing Chick Hicks as "mad with down eyes and a mad mouth" and Luigi as "happy with a big smile." Don't be afraid to snap a few pictures of cars, animals, or any other toy your child is drawn to and make a chart from those!

Feelings Buckets

Even when they can read the facial cues, older children sometimes struggle with understanding cause and effect when it comes to emotions. For instance, they are likely to blame another person for hurt feelings versus blaming the actual scenario (e.g.: "I missed the shot and I'm mad" versus "You made me miss that shot"). Kids need practice when it comes to learning about cause and effect. Once they learn to accurately identify what causes their feelings, they can learn to rely on the things that cause happiness.

While sitting down and talking about feelings isn't always considered "fun," making a game of it can get the job done while having a little fun. "Feelings buckets" helps kids talk about what sort of actions and scenarios result in different feelings. Label five to seven white buckets with the feelings that your child most often encounters. Happy, sad, scared, and angry are always great starting points, but remember to keep your child's needs in mind. Have your child stand behind a line and give her a few beanbags (you can even make your own with Ziploc bags and dried beans). Describe a typical scenario that your child might encounter throughout the day (e.g.: Sarah forgot her homework and doesn't want to enter class. How is Sarah feeling?) and have your child throw a beanbag into the feelings bucket that she thinks best describes the situation. Talk about possible solutions (e.g.: Sarah can ask to speak to her teacher outside and explain that she forgot to pack her homework in her bag) before moving on to the next scenario. *Note: The Happy Kid Handbook provides numerous scenarios to get parents started, but children are often the best source when it comes to reality-based situations that they are likely to encounter in their daily lives.*

Feelings Games

Understanding emotions takes time. Kids need a lot of practice and reinforcement so that they can understand and internalize the various feelings they encounter each day. A really fun way to achieve this, particularly with school-age children, is to slightly alter some fun games to include discussion of emotions.

- **Feelings Tic-Tac-Toe:** Customize a tic-tac-toe board instead of using blank boxes and suddenly an old favorite game holds a new meaning! Draw or paste (don't you just love old magazines?) a picture of a different feelings face into each box. As you and your child place an X or an O in each box, take a moment to describe the face and name a time that you felt that way.

- **Feelings Memory:** Memory is always a crowd-pleaser in the kindergarten crowd. Their development is such that they can actually recall where the cards are when placed face-down. Square index cards are perfect for making your own version of the game, complete with feelings faces. Draw one feelings face per card and be sure to make two cards for each feeling. (Better yet, let your child do the drawing.) Shuffle the cards, place them facedown on the floor, and discuss each feeling when a match is made. This is a great time to share stories of your own childhood. Remember, a little bit of empathy goes a long way.

- **Feelings Jenga:** Jenga is a great family game because it requires patience, turn taking, and planning while sitting around the table together. With a few small adjustments to the wooden blocks, it can also be a great game for older children working on emotional regulation. With a black permanent marker, write one question or sentence starter along each block. Examples include: "Talk about something that frustrates you," or "What should I do when I'm angry about something at school?" Have each player answer the question or finish the sentence as they pull a block from the tower. I've used this game for years with eight- to ten-year-old kids in my office. It's a great nonthreatening way to help kids open up while spending time together.

- **Feelings Chutes and Ladders:** This one is great for young children (preschool through first grade) who are beginning to understand emotion but still struggle to connect the dots between triggers and expression of emotion. You don't even have to alter the game at all to engage in this fun discussion of feelings. When your child climbs a ladder, ask her a question about positive emotions (e.g.: "What is something that makes you feel proud?"). When your child descends a slide, ask a question about negative emotions (e.g.: "What is something that makes you feel really, really mad?"). Try to take a moment to follow up each answer with some empathy and understanding, and share your own answer if you have one. At this age, normalizing children's feelings really helps them make sense of emotions. Be sure to have them ask you questions when you climb and fall, too!

Feelings Balloons

Young children learn the most when they are engaged in hands-on activities. Although it might seem like games and art projects can't possibly lead to meaningful discussions about emotions, that's actually the best way to engage young children in these conversations. The added bonus here is that the visuals created during these projects stick with the children long after the game is over or the artwork is complete. They can revisit each activity in their minds and process what they learned.

There are two ways to use feelings balloons. Many younger children (particularly preschool-kindergarten) fear the sound of a balloon popping. It's loud and shocking and often triggers fear and tears. For younger children, I recommend a soft approach to this feelings activity. Blow up a bunch of balloons in various colors. Using a marker, write a feelings word (sad, mad, happy, etc.) on one side of the balloon and draw a face to match the feeling on the opposite side. Toss the balloons in the air and try to see how many balloons you can keep in the air at once by tossing them back and forth. After a few minutes, ask your child to catch one balloon and freeze. Have your child identify the feeling on the balloon and talk about a time when she felt that way. *Bonus tip: This is a GREAT activity for classrooms!*

For older children who genuinely enjoy the thrill of popping balloons, you can add a little fun to this one. Instead of writing the feelings on the outside of the balloon, write the feelings on small pieces of paper and stick them inside the balloons before you inflate them. In doing this, each balloon contains a hidden emotion. Play the game as described above or use one balloon at a time and put up a barrier to create a "balloon tennis court" in your living room. Ask your child to stop and catch the balloon and use a pencil to pop it. After the thrill of the pop, unfold the feeling and discuss it with your child. *Note: This version of the game is not suitable for children with a sensitivity to sound.*

Feelings Masks

Got an artsy kid on your hands? No problem! Some kids prefer crafty projects over games, and feelings masks are a great project for hands-on learning when it comes to identifying and understanding emotions. Riley is the art director in the house, and she finds ways to make just about anything into masks. She has used everything from paper bags to paper plates to cereal boxes to create funny masks and robot faces, and her love of mask making inspired me to give feelings masks a try.

Paper plates are always great to work with because they are easy to cut and glue adheres to them well. Together with your child, create several masks to convey positive and negative emotions. Hang them on the wall to create a wall of feelings or put them on and act out the feelings. These are great props for creating a play about social stories that elicit emotions. Your child can switch between masks as feelings arise and are resolved within the play.

Check-in Board

You know those days when you pick up your child from school and ask her approximately seven bazillion questions about her day but she just stares out the window and doesn't say much? While those moments can be disappointing for parents who are eager to hear about the child's day, sometimes kids need time to zone out and process the events of the day before they start talking. It's important to respect that need for quiet reflection after a busy day of school. (Remember those little introverts? They *really* need this time to themselves.)

A family check-in board is a great way to ease kids into talking about their feelings at the end of each day. On a large poster board, create little "pockets" using construction paper. Paste one feelings picture on the outside of each pocket. Have a Popsicle stick for each family member (with their name or favorite color on it—or a picture of each person if you're really feeling crafty) in a blank pocket at the bottom of the board. Ask each family member to place their Popsicle stick in the pocket that matches their feeling at the beginning and end of each day.

This exercise gives kids (and parents) the opportunity to process and talk about the various emotions they encountered throughout the day. This kind of strategy encourages kids to think about how they actually felt during the day, instead of simply listing the events that occurred while at school.

Stories of Emotions

Once kids have a firm grasp on identifying feelings and are beginning to understand what triggers different emotions, it's time to
work toward emotional regulation. Like any other skill development
with young children, this takes time and practice. A great way to get
started is to create a series of books about the emotions they experience most often.

Stories of emotions move beyond simply drawing pictures to
match the emotions. In creating stories about emotions, children are
asked to write one "book" for each emotion. Very young children
should be encouraged to tell their stories in pictures. Picture books
are every bit as powerful as the written word when it comes to kids.
Older children might want to combine drawing and writing to tell
their stories.

Begin by talking to your child about the emotions he experiences
most often throughout the week. When feeling calm, children have a
tendency to identify only positive emotions. That's okay, books about
positive emotions are equally as important as books that address negative emotions. Help your child think out loud about some of the
negative emotions he's likely to encounter at school, at the park, at
home, etc.

Make one blank booklet for each feeling identified. (You can also
purchase premade blank books at many craft and office supply
stores.) Try to keep the books small to avoid making your child feel
like he needs to fill every page (ten to twelve pages is plenty). Ask
your child to write a story about one emotion at a time. When does
he feel that emotion? What triggers those feelings? What can he do
to cope with that feeling? Who can he talk to?

This exercise is a great tool for children. Take it slow. They don't need to complete every book in one week. It can be an ongoing project that you work on together. In writing these stories with words and pictures, kids learn to stop and think about how they can take control of their emotions and how they might avoid stressful situations that result in negative emotions.

Zoom Lens

A large part of the struggle to regulate emotions is that children tend to zoom in on one aspect of the problem without looking at the big picture. A child might hyperfocus, for instance, on the fact that a best friend wouldn't play with him at lunch without considering the fact that he wasn't friendly to his best friend earlier in the day.

Kids love cameras. They love to take pictures from their own perspective and they love to look back and see what they captured. The zoom lens is a great metaphor when it comes to teaching kids to consider the big picture before reacting to a situation. I often let my kids zoom in and out on pictures and ask them to describe the differences. When they zoom in, they notice every little detail. When they zoom out, they find hidden objects that they didn't know were there.

To make the jump from camera lens to emotional regulation, all you need is a pen and a piece of paper. Draw a large circle on the paper. In the very center of that large circle, draw a much smaller circle. Ask your child to repeat the story that caused him to feel upset. In the small circle, write or draw the event that your child sees as the problem that triggered big feelings. After you've identified the stressor, ask your child to take three deep breaths and then zoom out. What else was happening at the time? What happened earlier in the day? Are there any hidden objects that didn't make it into the smaller circle?

Clearly this exercise is more appropriate for children old enough to see the differences between the two "pictures." This works well for eight- to ten-year-olds, as it helps them move beyond one specific moment and evaluate the entire situation. After discussing the various issues at play in both circles, it's useful to brainstorm places where your child can do something differently in the future. How can he avoid becoming overwhelmed with emotion? At what point should he stop what he's doing and seek help? With practice, you can simply cue your child to "zoom in" and "zoom out" in the moment.

Puppets

Never underestimate the power of puppet play. Young children, particularly the preschool to second-grade crowd, often work through their emotions using play. You don't need a puppet theater and fancy scenery to tap into the imagination and make puppet play work. In fact, creating the scenery from scratch and setting up a makeshift theater is part of the process.

Whether your child comes to you with a specific problem in mind or you just want to help your child work through something that happened, puppets are a great way to connect and process big feelings in a fun and nonthreatening manner. When kids feel like they're being put on the spot, they tend to shut down and avoid talking. When kids engage in an activity that is fun and meaningful, they work through their feelings. Puppets provide just enough distance to work through challenging topics with ease.

The key to using puppet play to work on emotional regulation is that it can't be forced. You need time and patience. Children play through their feelings and emotions at their own pace. You can't make them talk and process simply by forcing the subject on them with puppets. You have to let the play evolve in a natural way.

From feelings tic-tac-toe and other games to art projects and homemade books about feelings, adding a little fun to the process takes the pressure off your child and helps her work through various emotions. Once your child begins to understand that experiencing many feelings throughout the day is perfectly normal, and that she has the power to restore feelings of happiness to her day, your child will experience greater overall happiness.

4

The Art of Forgiveness

Forgiveness is the fragrance the violet sheds on the heel that has crushed it.

—MARK TWAIN

BY NOW YOU PROBABLY know that the best way to start an argument between your kids is to take a shower. You can turn on the TV, set them up with a time-consuming craft, or leave them playing quietly (okay, maybe not quietly but happily), and the minute you step into that little slice of steamy bliss, something goes awry. Best parenting advice ever: Never take showers.

I was almost finished. I stood under the hot water thinking about the day ahead as my hair soaked in the conditioner. Perhaps I was stalling for time a little bit. Just as I began to rinse my hair I heard the crash of falling blocks followed by sobs. I heard my daughter running up the stairs, hysteria lining her voice, coming to tell me about her brother's latest infraction. I can almost guarantee that it wasn't intentional—that he simply didn't look where he was going—but that doesn't erase the hurt of hard work knocked over in an instant. She wanted me to see it first. And then, just behind her, her brother came barreling in. "Forgive me! Forgive me! You have to forgive me!" Tears streaming down his face, he glanced back and forth between the two of us before finally collapsing in a sobbing heap at my feet. "I didn't mean to wreck it."

Children are often asked to forgive other kids and adults for little things that happen throughout the day. Forgive him for wrecking your castle. Forgive me for being late. Forgive your friend for hitting you at recess. When kids are asked to forgive—to say, fine, I accept that, sorry—it's important to make sure that they understand what forgiveness really means, instead of simply repeating a script provided by a parent.

Forgiveness isn't about excusing or condoning a negative behavior. Forgiveness isn't about forgetting, which might cause the fear that it will happen again. Forgiveness means working through the situation, telling the other person how you feel about it, and then letting go of negative emotions. Teaching your children the art of forgiveness is an essential life tool that will help them avoid the anxiety and depression that occurs when people bottle up negative feelings and hold on to anger.

Forgiveness, at its core, is a shift in thinking. That hurt that caused you so much emotional pain might always be a part of your life, but letting go of the feelings associated with it can bring you internal peace. What kids need to learn from an early age is that forgiveness is a conscious choice to reframe the thought process. No one can force you to forgive someone who wronged you (although they might coerce you to utter words of forgiveness), but in making that choice to be forgiving, you free yourself from negative emotions. When you choose to let go of feelings of ill will, you can move forward with a positive focus. You might or might not choose to include the offender in your life moving forward, but you no longer have to hold onto the feelings that dragged you down.

Jamie was always at war with his emotions. He wanted to be

forgiving when he felt that his friends had wronged him, but at age eight he had a very strong sense of justice. He liked rules and order and he did his best to follow them. When others didn't, he was deeply hurt. Normal childhood interactions that most parents would wave off without a hint of concern left Jamie rattled to his core. He felt a powerful combination of anger and anxiety when teasing occurred, and he didn't see any possibility of forgiving a teaser. No matter the circumstances. Teasing was against school policy, and teasing couldn't be forgiven.

I once returned from a meeting to find him sitting in my office during snack time, silently fuming. A girl in his class had used a word that he felt was "bad," and he was angry, embarrassed, and anxious. (It was actually a very benign word, but he was adamant that the girl had used the word in an inappropriate way, to reference "private parts." It was the first I heard of such a reference.) He worried that his peers would tease him when he returned to class and he felt that the girl should be consequenced, despite the teacher's assessment that the word was not used in a negative manner. Arms crossed, head down, and tears lining the corners of his eyes, Jamie sat on my couch demanding justice.

The problem with this scenario was that there would be no justice. The girl didn't break any rules. Whether or not she intended that word to refer to something inappropriate, the word she used was not actually a "bad" word. But Jamie felt wronged and he couldn't move on.

What do you do when there is no justice? You work on letting go. And that begins with freeing yourself from negative emotions. I asked Jamie to pound on some clay for a while to release his frustration. When his body relaxed and he appeared calm once again, I asked him to write down all the feelings that bubbled to the surface in response to the situation. He took his time and made sure to write down every single feeling that crossed his mind. And then we played a little trashcan basketball. Crumpling each feeling into a little ball gave him a second opportunity to release any remaining anger, and shooting each ball into the basket enabled him to throw away his negative feelings while moving on with a positive attitude.

Jamie continued to go head-to-head with that girl as they grew. They were oil and water, for sure. And we continued to practice forgiveness. Over time, he learned to let go on his own. He established mantras that helped him talk his way out of his negative emotions and into a more peaceful state. As a result, friendships became easier and his feelings of anger and resentment became less frequent. He learned to let go so that he could be happy.

There are lifelong benefits to forgiving, including improved physical health, reduced stress, and better interpersonal relationships. In fact, researchers at Hope College in Michigan found that forgiveness yields both physical and emotional benefits, including reduced stress, less negative emotion, fewer cardiovascular issues, and better immune system functioning.[6]

Being forgiving boasts many benefits. People who let go of grudges and practice forgiveness experience healthier relationships and psychological well-being, exhibit fewer symptoms of anxiety and depression, experience decreased stress and hostility, have lower blood pressure, and have a lower risk of alcohol and substance abuse.

Being forgiving gives children the opportunity to move on and enjoy positive emotions. It gives them the power to break free from anger and hurt. In essence, forgiveness opens the door to happiness.

Forgiveness, however, is a skill—a learned behavior—and it takes practice. Simply telling your child to get over it and move on won't get the job done. The art of forgiveness requires guidance, patience, and repetition. And forgiveness isn't always easy. Sometimes life is beyond hard and people make choices that trigger emotional turmoil in others, and those instances can be very difficult to forgive.

It was the stomachaches that brought Henry to my office. At just six years old, he complained of stomachaches almost daily, beginning two months into kindergarten. His mother often referred to him as "gifted" and offered this as an explanation for his lack of social relationships: Other kids just didn't understand his complex thinking, or so she thought. She hoped that kindergarten would provide enough of a challenge to keep him engaged, as his play-based preschool lacked structure and therefore triggered behavior issues. That was the script she repeated over and over during his first few months of treatment.

It's almost never that simple, and Henry's case was anything but simple. Because they viewed him as "gifted" from the moment he could string words together, Henry's parents spent the majority of his toddler and preschool years drilling him with facts and information. He didn't spend much time with other kids until he entered preschool, and by then he was lost in a world of facts and numbers. Whether or not Henry was academically gifted didn't really matter. The problem was that he didn't know how to interact with others.

Henry was big on long monologues about topics that interested him and showed very little patience for interruptions or short attention spans. Two very common behaviors among the kindergarten crowd. Most of the kids learned to walk away when Henry insisted on teaching them one thing or another. But one child, the one Henry identified as a friend on the first day of school, turned on him. He would listen to Henry's speeches with feigned interest, and later tease him on the playground. The teasing was subtle and consistent with the developmental level of a kindergarten student, and the teacher intervened as much as possible. Henry took it very hard. He couldn't let go of the friendship, but he couldn't forgive his friend, either. He was stuck smack-dab in the middle of anger and hurt and he didn't know how to cope. And so the stomachaches began. Long story short: He was holding a grudge.

Holding a grudge is bad for the soul. If you've ever carried hurt around for any length of time you know how debilitating it can be. When you can't let go, you get that drowning sensation somewhere deep in your soul. It takes time to get to that point, of course, but it can happen when you least expect it. You try to tell yourself that you don't care. You try to tell yourself to move on and focus on the positive. But if you haven't given yourself the opportunity to forgive the person who hurt you, then it's all just words and empty statements. The resentment and negative emotions build up over time until you feel like you can't escape them for another minute.

Holding a grudge allows negative feelings to crowd out positive ones. Instead of thinking about what's right in your life, holding a grudge forces you to think about what's wrong. Holding a grudge can unknowingly cause you to bring bitterness and resentment to all of your relationships. When you don't take the time to forgive and move forward, you can get stuck in a negative loop and project that negativity on everything around you.

People like to think of children as being more forgiving than adults, and often that does prove true. But not all children are the same, and some struggle to forgive. Sometimes young children squabble, tease one another, and ignore each other for a day or two, but then they laugh at the same joke and suddenly all is forgiven. Other times kids hold on to the feelings that resulted from negative interactions. They internalize the feelings and struggle to let go. They hold those feelings close as a reminder that sometimes other people aren't nice. They wait for concrete evidence that the incident has been dealt with and they expect justice. Or at the very least, an apology.

The intense need for an apology can be a significant roadblock to restoring happiness when a child has been hurt. From the beginning, we teach kids to apologize when they hurt someone, even if it's accidental. It's the right thing to do. They take that in and bring it with them as they grow, as we hope they will. So when they are hurt by another child, they want that apology. They want to hear the two little words that mean that the other child admits to the behavior. They want "I'm sorry." Sadly, apologies don't always happen when kids argue.

It's important to teach kids that apologies don't necessarily provide closure. An apology is always a nice gesture and sometimes it opens the door to forgiveness, but we can't place our happiness in the hands of another. Part of being forgiving is understanding that closure often comes from within. Sometimes we have to find ways to come to terms with the hurt even when the apology doesn't come. Although this sounds like a difficult concept for young children, often it isn't. Kids can be very introspective and their ability to think about themselves in relation to others can help them find closure. It takes time for children to find their own closure when they've faced difficult emotions in response to another, but it can be done without an apology.

The problem, naturally, is that kids are impulsive by design and they tend to want that closure to happen on a more immediate basis. Although Henry eventually came to recognize that the boy who teased him early in the year really wasn't a good match for him (they had almost nothing in common and couldn't even agree on a topic of conversation), he struggled to let go of the anger because he simply wanted to replace the relationship instead of working through the hurt feelings that triggered the stomachaches in the first place. This is a common occurrence with kids. In the race to move forward they fail to address the present tense. Those feelings later become history that repeats itself.

Teaching children that forgiveness is a process, not an event, reminds them to allow their feelings in and to work through them at their own pace. There is a tendency to tell kids to just move on. *Don't worry. Stop being angry. Get over it.* Sometimes parents become frustrated with the complaints of a child and utter these phrases not to hurt but to speed up the process. It's hard to listen to the same story over and over again. Parents want closure on childhood hurts as much as children do. But forgiveness can't be rushed.

When a child is hurt by a friend, that child has a right to feel sad, anxious, angry, or any other feeling that might arise. As adults, we carry around any number of feelings on any given day. Time and practice give us the advantage of being able to cope with our feelings internally, but kids don't have that skill. They need to talk it out. They need to retell the story over and over again. They need to vent their feelings until the feelings are gone. It's up to us to let them do it.

Happiness is more complicated than people think. You can't just plaster a smile on your face each day and expect to feel sunny and happy in return. Bad moments, bad days, and bad weeks happen. Sometimes people disappoint us, even when we really, really wish they wouldn't. We have to work through the complicated moments to find our way back to happiness. The good news is that this is actually in our control.

Kids often feel a lack of control when other kids aren't being nice or something specific happens that leaves them with hurt feelings. Part of learning to forgive is taking back that control by making the choice to find closure and move forward. When we teach children that they can make the choice to forgive, we restore a sense of control over negative situations. We show them that they are not helpless, even when life isn't going the way they want it to. In practicing forgiveness, kids are no longer victims of their circumstances. Forgiveness gives kids the power to choose happiness over anger and sadness.

It would be foolish, of course, to pretend that learning to forgive is a one-time life lesson. While some children are more likely to forgive quickly, others get stuck in the moment and repeat the same behavior many, many times before finding their own way to forgive. And while some parents credit their children with being forgiving by nature, often those kids have been raised in a forgiving environment. Sure, personality plays a role in the ability to forgive, but so do environmental factors.

When Liam came running after Riley demanding forgiveness during the morning of that ill-fated shower, what he really wanted to communicate was one of our family mottos: Forgive easily.

Oftentimes teaching forgiveness begins with an apology. I am not afraid to admit to my mistakes. In fact, I do so often. I admit to and apologize for mistakes, big and small. Sean and I decided long ago to put perfection in its place. We didn't want our kids to grow up worrying about making mistakes. You're nodding your head, I'm sure, because what parent would *want* their kids to fear mistakes? But it isn't that simple.

Parents send mixed messages with their words and actions, often without intent. When you're exhausted and the milk spills and you just don't want to clean one more thing, maybe you snap just a little bit. Perhaps your voice takes on a negative tone while your eyes work to avert the gaze of the tear-rimmed eyes of your child who didn't mean to knock that glass over. It's okay. It's normal to have these moments. It's normal to feel frustrated at times. And although it's best to avoid crying over spilled milk as much as possible, sometimes you will cry. And your child will react. Apologies are important.

When parents apologize to their children, they teach their children that mistakes happen and apologies help. When parents are willing to admit to their mistakes, no matter how small those mistakes might seem to an adult, they teach children that taking responsibility for behavior is important no matter how old you might be. When we apologize for our mistakes, what we are really saying is this: "I messed up and I didn't mean to hurt your feelings. Please forgive me." When the seeds of forgiveness are planted early on in the home, children internalize the benefits of being forgiving. They learn to work through things and find peace with the moments that cause them emotional turmoil along the way.

The minute we send our kids out into the world, we can no longer coach them through every little hard moment that comes up. For some parents, that's a scary thought. It's hard to think of your child being sad or angry and left to deal with his feelings independently. That's exactly the reason parents need to work on skills like forgiveness at home.

Preparing your child to enter the world is less about the ABC's and more about emotional well-being. Your child will learn to read, write, and solve equations. Apparently your child will even learn geometry in first grade (who knew?)! Your child will learn more than you can possibly remember learning as a child, that's for certain. But your child won't learn how to cope with emotions at school. Your child won't learn how to let go of negative emotions, how to release a grudge, and how to forgive. That is something your child has to learn at home.

In order to raise a generation of happy kids, we have to teach those kids how to restore their own happiness in the face of pain and frustration. We can't simply throw a bunch of clichés in the air and hope one resonates (Don't cry over spilled milk! That's the way the cookie crumbles!). We have to give them the skills to forgive and seize the opportunities to talk them through the process of forgiveness as they arise.

Sometimes it seems as if the world of parenting contains opposing teams. On the one hand, you have people whispering, "Don't coddle them. Let them make their own mistakes. Step back and let them be." On the other hand, you can find advice on just about any aspect of parenting with a few taps on the keyboard. "Do this and you'll get it right," so say the experts. There is a happy medium in there somewhere, I'm sure of it. Yes, your kids will be faced with pain, frustration, and failure at times and you won't be there to help. But if you've nurtured them along the way—if you've given them the skills to cope with these situations, they will be able to handle most things that come their way.

It doesn't matter how old your children are right this very moment, and it doesn't matter how much you've worked on teaching them the art of forgiveness up until this point. The nice thing about forgiveness is that it can be learned and practiced at every stage of life. It is never too late to learn how to forgive.

Tips for Teaching Forgiveness

Release Frustration

When we run in with a quick fix for the problem or try to dismiss it in order to keep the peace at a playdate, we don't allow our children to express their emotions. When children are forced to bottle up their negative emotions, they experience stress. And there is nothing happy about living with stress.

Anger is a perfectly acceptable emotion and there is no harm in expressing that anger in an appropriate way. Getting nose-to-nose with a friend and screaming for all to hear won't help the situation, but pulling your child aside and encouraging her to clap her hands, stomp her feet, or yell into a pillow gives her a moment to release those feelings of frustration.

Once that initial moment of anger or frustration passes, kids feel calm and are more open to working through the actual situation. When kids are allowed to experience, rather than stifle, their feelings in response to stress, they feel heard and understood and experience greater happiness as a result.

Acknowledge What Happened

When parents dismiss a problem as no big deal or say that their children are simply being dramatic, kids feel sad and frustrated as a result. What parents often describe as overreacting is a child's way of letting them know that something isn't right. They've been wronged, and they want their parents to know. Just like adults, kids crave validation when their feelings are hurt. They need to vent their emotions and receive understanding in return (sound familiar?) so that they can open their hearts to forgiveness.

Instead of downplaying minor infractions or relying on distraction to put an end to the upset feelings, show some support. Talk about what happened and label your child's feelings. Provide some much-needed empathy by telling your child that you understand. Share a story about a time when you felt the same way.

Model Forgiveness

Children internalize a lot of what they see and hear in the safety of their own homes. When parents are short-tempered with one another in the face of frustration, for example, children are likely to repeat that behavior with siblings and/or friends. If parents exhibit good listening skills during times of frustration, however, children learn to listen first and respond later. While we can't make the generalization that parental behavior in the home causes all negative behavior seen in their children, we do know that children of all ages soak up our behaviors and take their cues from us.

With that in mind, it's essential to practice forgiveness in our own lives. We all do our best to shield our kids from grown-up stuff as much as possible, but the truth is that kids are listening even when we think they're not. In fact, sometimes their ears seem to perk up when they sense even the slightest hint of stress. It's not that they thrive on drama, mind you. It's that they don't even want to consider anything going wrong, and if something seems upsetting they want to jump in and fix it. Many kids are pleasers by nature and they get involved not to be nosy but to be helpful.

Show forgiveness with your partner, your extended family, and your friends. Talk about the times when you have felt hurt and what you did to let go of the negative emotions that resulted from that experience. A little bit of honesty with an age-appropriate spin can go a long way toward normalizing the process of forgiveness for your children. Forgiving your partner for a mistake made during the week shows your kids that yes, people mess up sometimes, but that doesn't mean that the relationship is negatively impacted for life. It simply means that you need to hit the reset button once in a while.

When something happens that can't be repaired, it's still important to show your children that you can find forgiveness in your heart.

Sometimes you have to forgive the ones you love for little things. Other times you are forced to forgive complete strangers for big things. Either way, making the choice to forgive and let go frees your soul to get back to the good stuff that awaits. And that's a lesson worth teaching.

Fly Away Feelings

It's easy for adults to recommend unleashing your feelings and letting them go. We know what it means to vent frustration to a friend. We know the power of a letter that never does make it to the mailbox or a journal kept in a secret spot. But kids don't necessarily know these strategies. In fact, more often than not, kids are taught to keep their voices calm and use kind words and never ever throw a tantrum (even if that's what adults do when they're "venting"). If the first step toward forgiveness is releasing frustration, we have to teach kids how to do that.

"Fly away feelings" is a great strategy for younger kids, who typically respond well to visuals and hands-on learning. Talk about what it feels like when someone hurts your feelings. Help your child identify the various emotions that he might experience and make connections between the actions of the offender and the resulting emotions. Help your child write down each feeling and a few words about what triggered that feeling on individual pieces of paper. They might even want to draw a picture or cartoon of what happened. Fold each paper into a paper airplane and line them up on a table.

Now it's time to fly! Encourage your child to yell out each feeling as he throws it into the air to send his feelings away. One client liked to yell, "I don't want to be mad! I don't want to be sad! I want new friends!" while he released his feelings. Encourage your child to throw them as many times as he needs to, until he feels at peace with the feelings. Then cuddle up and talk about how it feels to finally let those emotions go.

Unsent Mail

Older kids might laugh in the face of paper airplanes containing feelings, but they still need to release their pent-up emotions if they want to move forward and avoid getting stuck in a negative loop. Often a solitary activity helps older kids who want to handle things independently.

Unsent mail is a great way to vent emotions in a safe space. Encourage your child to write a letter to the person who hurt or wronged her. The letter should include details of what specific behaviors were hurtful, how she felt in response, and how she felt even after the initial heated emotions faded. The beauty of unsent mail is that no one will ever read it, not even you, if she so chooses. It is an opportunity to say all the things that she might want to say but probably never would. Sometimes kids keep things in because they're afraid. Other times they keep things in because it wouldn't be appropriate to say them out loud. Unsent mail is a great way to release those frustrations.

Once the letter is complete, encourage your child to rip it to shreds. She should tear it into hundreds of tiny pieces and throw those pieces away! This activity is cathartic. It helps kids release the emotions that are dragging them down and verbalize the words that replay through their minds each day. It's a great way to help kids work toward closure.

Trashcan Basketball

As we saw with Jamie, sometimes releasing negative emotions can be accomplished with a game of basketball. In fact, I once worked with a high school student who had his best therapy sessions on the basketball court. Free from the restrictions of a small office and couch and given the opportunity to play while he talked, my high school client vented hours of frustration while beating me on the court. But Jamie responded well to my trashcan version, and this strategy has worked well for many kids over the years.

To prep for trashcan basketball, you need to spend a little time helping your child identify his feelings and the triggers that set those feelings in motion. If your child can write well and likes to write, have him write one feeling with a short description of the event on each piece of paper. If he doesn't like to write, have him draw pictures and sequence the events. The point is to say the feelings and triggers out loud while getting them down on paper. Sometimes releasing negative emotions is best done in two ways. Once the feelings are on the paper, have your child crumple them up into basketballs. He can even color the crumpled feelings orange, if he so pleases. Have your child shoot those balls into the trashcan one at a time while saying the feelings out loud (e.g.: "I'm not mad anymore!").

Play as many rounds as your child needs to let those negative emotions go.

Sinking Ships

Sometimes kids don't understand what it means to carry around feelings. Because their emotions shift throughout the day, they don't always recognize the old emotions that stay with them. A child might attribute a feeling of anger to an unfair call in a kickball game during PE, for example, completely dismissing the fact that it was called in favor of the friend who had hurt his feelings by excluding him just days before. We have to help them break down and make sense of their feelings. And if they happen to be carrying around unresolved feelings, we have to start there.

My kids love to make boats in the kitchen sink. They tape together all sorts of interesting items (corks, cardboard, felt), tack on hand-made sails, and set sail in the sink. Some of them float and some of them don't even come close. So we reevaluate, decide what went wrong, and brainstorm alternatives. They keep trying until they get it right. The sinking is what points them in the right direction.

"Sinking ships" came to me during a frustrating boat-building experience. Nothing seemed to float. They tried and they tried, but the boats just kept flipping and sinking. Something was dragging them down. Much like holding a grudge can do to your soul.

Get your crafty hat on for this one, parents, you're going to need it! Help your child construct two small boats. I have found that cutting small paper cups down to size generally works and a toothpick makes an excellent mast. But let your kids get in on the building part of this strategy, that's the fun part. Once the boats are ready to sail in your sink full of water, place a coin or two (depending on how sturdy your boats are) in one of the boats. The boat with coins will sink to the bottom while the lighter boat continues to float.

Talk to your child about how anger and resentment can hold you down if you don't let go of them. Like the coins on the ship, anger and resentment push you toward the bottom while the other ship, free from those negative emotions, sails away to the next destination.

The Unforgiving Brain

Sometimes kids get stuck on certain negative emotions and can't find a way to shift toward positive emotions (sometimes adults do this, too, if we're being completely honest). When something feels really unfair or hurtful, it can be hard to let go. Believe it or not, sometimes kids aren't ready to let go. Sometimes they want to hang on to that feeling a little bit longer, even if it's negative, as they work through it.

Getting stuck in a negative cycle can affect social relationships, academics, team play, and family life. When kids internalize feelings like anger, frustration, and helplessness for too long, they start to project those feelings onto those around them. Emotions are powerful, and it can be very difficult to make it through the day without blowing up when you feel anger bubbling inside.

"The unforgiving brain" provides a visual that helps kids see how much space negative emotions can take up, and how those negative emotions crowd out positive ones. Draw or download a picture of an outline of a brain (it's actually best if it's completely blank inside). Have your child choose crayons in colors that represent a variety of emotions (this is an excellent time to revisit "The color of feelings" in Chapter 1). Using a pencil, divide the brain into several small boxes. Ask your child to think about all the things that currently cause her to feel angry, frustrated, sad, hopeless, or any other negative emotion that typically arises for your child and have her color one box per trigger in the appropriate color. Repeat this process with the positive emotions.

Once the brain is colored in, step back and look at the colors. Are there more negative colors than positive? Are the negative emotions crowding out the positive? Talk about how that affects the way we think and feel in all areas of our lives, not just related to their specific triggers. Ask your child to think about ways to increase the positive colors and shift the brain to a forgiving brain.

Change Faces

A large part of practicing forgiveness is choosing to let go and move on. We might not get the apologies we feel we deserve, but we can still choose to move forward, with or without the offender in our lives. This can be a difficult concept for kids to understand because it's hard to move on from hurtful situations and it's very difficult to give up a friendship, even if it's not working. Often, they end up somewhere in the middle. That's okay. That's part of the process of forgiveness. It's important to help kids understand that it's perfectly normal to experience a wide range of emotions when working toward forgiveness, and that feelings can change frequently.

"Change faces" is a great activity for kids who like to get creative and are more likely to express emotion when involved in creative activities. Using a stack of plain white paper plates and various crafting materials (glitter, buttons, feathers, felt, foam, cotton, etc.), ask your child to create masks to represent the different emotions she has experienced while dealing with this difficult and painful situation. Try not to lead your child when doing this exercise. If you want an authentic expression of emotion, you need to trust your child to choose the emotions that she feels. Talk with your child as she creates. What specific thoughts or events triggered sadness? What has her feeling hopeful?

Once the feelings masks are complete, use them to act out the events and issues that are preventing your child from resolving her feelings. Talk about how faces change in response to specific triggers, both happy and sad, and it's up to your child to move toward the triggers that result in positive faces and away from the ones that are laced with negativity. Discuss what your child needs to do to move from an angry, unforgiving face to a happy, peaceful face on a more permanent basis.

Recycled Emotions

Believe it or not, some kids don't actually want to let go of negative emotions. It's not that they want to walk around thinking about bad feelings, it's that they don't want to dismiss those feelings. Those feelings are real and powerful, and part of moving forward includes making different choices based on previous experiences. Revisiting the hurt from time to time helps some kids process their emotions on a more global level. They can see how far they've come, what changes have worked, and what might help as they grow.

"Recycled emotions" is a strategy I have used with kids for many years. It's important to help kids understand that sometimes feelings come back to us without warning. Sadness about the loss of a friendship might fade into memory as new friendships emerge, for example, but that initial pain that the child felt when the friendship first came to a crashing halt won't disappear entirely. As new stressors crop up, old feelings can come back. That's okay. That's how we learn to cope with and manage emotions as we grow.

Give your child a small box with a lid or a brown paper bag and ask him to decorate it to make it into a mini recycling bin. Talk about the meaning of the recycling symbol. Discuss things that we recycle each day and ask your child to think about what other kinds of things might actually be recyclable. Ask your child to think about feelings that come back even when they refer to things from the past. If you can, share one of your own examples.

Have your child write or draw (or tell you and you do the writing) scenarios that have caused hurt feelings. One by one, put those feelings into the recycling bin. Explain to your child that these feelings can be revisited by pulling out a slip of paper and talking about it, and that the more he revisits them, the better he will be able to cope with them over time.

I had one little boy who loved this activity so much that he kept one recycling bin in my office and another by his bed. When he felt that he was truly ready to move on from a scenario, he tore up the piece of paper and threw it in the trash so that it would not come back again. Some kids will want to keep their feelings forever as they learn to find forgiveness, while others will want to put them out with the trash at some point. Either way, giving kids a sense of control over the emotions that act as stumbling blocks to forgiveness can open the door to moving on.

Clean Slate

Guilt can be a significant roadblock to forgiveness for some kids. Although you might think that it is the offender who should feel the guilt in the situation, many kids are very sensitive to emotion and feel overwhelming guilt over their role in a negative encounter (no matter how small). Part of learning to be forgiving is learning to forgive oneself along the way.

Liam tends to hold onto feelings of guilt, even over the most minor events (sometimes events that aren't even on my radar). While Riley likes to forgive and forget quickly in an effort to get back to playing as soon as practically possible, Liam is known to send himself to his room (a consequence no adult has ever actually given him). With big tears and clenched muscles he will retell his version of events, complete with some infraction on his part that no one even noticed. I've learned that what he needs is a clean slate.

Wiping the slate clean is a powerful metaphor for kids. Sure, you made a mistake. You could have used better words, a calmer voice tone, or kept your hands to yourself. You could have listened instead of talking and you could have followed directions instead of goofing off in class. None of those things are the end of the world, but some kids are supersensitive to reprimands, redirects, or hurt feelings and they carry around guilt as a result. The good news is that with a whiteboard and a few dry-erase markers, kids can learn to wipe the slate clean.

Ask your child to identify the things that happened that he can't stop thinking about. Empathize with your child so that he knows that you understand why his feelings feel so big in the moment. Write down one action (as identified by your child) on the whiteboard (for Liam, "I should have used a nicer voice" might apply here) and hand your child the eraser. Tell your child to wipe that action away and let it go for good! You might find that the erasing is furious—that's okay, sometimes kids need a physical release with the emotional release.

Practice Forgiveness Statements

"I forgive you" are three little words that can mean a lot to some kids, but very little to others. Sometimes these words provide relief to kids and help them move away from the negative feelings they experienced. It can work well for both kids—the forgiver and the one who needs forgiving. But for some kids, three words aren't enough. Some kids need to go just a little bit deeper to forgive someone for hurting their feelings.

Practicing forgiving statements helps kids understand what it means to forgive and let go. When we use forgiving statements in their presence, we show them that even though the hurtful thing happened, we can find closure with forgiveness. I like to teach my kids to use "I" statements when working through forgiveness. Blaming others tends to inflame situations, but no one can take your feelings away from you. Start by having your child identify the situation that caused hurt feelings and how that felt, followed by a forgiveness statement specific to the situation. For example:

"I felt embarrassed and sad when you called me a name at school. I forgive you for calling me that name."

Or:

"I felt scared when you yelled at me today. I forgive you for yelling at me."

The more kids practice using "I" statements and using forgiving words, the more control they have over the situation. They can choose to find closure, with or without the person who hurt their feelings. The act of making that choice helps kids put their own happiness back on top.

Although some kids might appear more forgiving than others, forgiveness is a learned behavior that does require practice. From modeling forgiveness to using puppets and role-play to work through difficult scenarios, parents can help children learn to step back from anger and find forgiveness. When we validate the big emotions that children experience, we make them feel less alone. When children feel understood and know that others have walked in their shoes, they are able to calm down and feel happy again. While it's nearly impossible to forgive when you're stuck in a state of anger, it is easier to move on when you feel calm and happiness has been restored.

5

Empathy Matters

No one cares how much you know, until they know how much you care.

—THEODORE ROOSEVELT

AT EXACTLY HALFWAY THROUGH Liam's first year of preschool, a new student enrolled in his class. He came home bursting with excitement about a new friend who seemed to like trucks and cars and playing tag. He couldn't wait to go back and see his new friend again. Until he did. Let's just say that it was a quick honeymoon period.

In fairness, my son is *very* introverted, which often comes off as aloof to those who don't know him. If you happen to want to join him while he's playing trucks, drums, or tag, great. If you don't, you won't catch him crying about it. He'll simply move on to the next point of interest. In that way, it can be hard to get to know him.

But as much as he seems impervious to the antics around him, his feelings are very easily hurt. Translation: He cries. A lot. And he doesn't like it when he's falsely accused of things (although I'm not sure anybody really does). On their second encounter, the new kid teased him. First, he made fun of his long, shaggy, curly hair. Then, he told him he would tell the teacher that he was playing in a forbidden area. (I'm not even sure such a place exists.) After the third meeting, my son sobbed all the way home and said that he never wanted to return to the preschool that he loves so much.

So of course I went into mama bear mode. I decided to hang around for a while at the next drop-off. And sure enough, the minute I looked away, this little (actually he was quite tall for preschool) boy was nose-to-nose with my sweet little boy. I crouched down next to my son and wrapped my arms around him to provide support. With that, the boy hit me on the head and walked away. My mind racing, I searched for the teacher, the director, anyone who could help. I found the aide. He agreed to shadow my son and help for the day.

For a moment, I thought everything would be okay. But something didn't feel right. What kind of a kid hits an adult who also happens to be a complete stranger? So I went back to the school and met with the director. It was then that I learned that although the boy was five years old, he had never been in a preschool environment or socialized with other kids. He was struggling.

When I picked up my son that day, I decided to reframe the situation for him. We talked about what it might feel like to be new to a school when the rest of the kids have been there all year. We discussed ways that kids try to get attention and why he might be interacting that way. I chose to focus on empathy instead of repeatedly discussing the negative because sometimes it's hard to relate to others, and empathy can make a difference. The following week, I walked in to find my son playing quietly with that very boy on the rug. A little empathy helped him step back and give the new student another chance. I breathed a sigh of relief as I stood back and watched them interact.

Some people think that certain kids are simply more empathic than others, while others believe that empathy is a skill that can be taught. The research shows that both are true. Empathic children are aware of their own feelings, can relate to common feelings, and can conceptualize how a person might feel in a given situation and respond in ways that might soothe that person (based on their own personal experiences).

Children who are empathic are better able to make independent decisions and avoid negative peer pressure. Empathy can shield them from things like bullying, aggression, and substance abuse because empathizing with and trying to help others makes kids happy. Research conducted by neuroscientists James Rilling and Gregory Berns at Emory University showed that helping others triggers activity in portions of the brain associated with receiving rewards or experiencing pleasure. In short, helping others brings us pleasure.[7] When kids are taught to empathize and help others, they learn to make better long-term choices.

Empathic children grow into adults who experience better social interactions, academic performance, and accomplishments at work. In fact, empathy is a key aspect in a successful learner. In their research on the relationship between student empathy and grade point average, T. Darlene Bonner and David Aspy found significant correlations between students' scores on measures of empathic understanding and grade point average.[8]

Research is great because it helps us understand what works. It gives us a rough guideline for this parenting gig. But in the real world, it can be hard to determine where your child stands in relation to all of this wonderful research. Are my children empathic? Do they have to help every crying child we encounter at the park to be deemed "empathic"? What if they just want to walk away sometimes . . . is that a sign of lack of caring and compassion? It's a lot to digest.

Kids first start to show signs of empathy at around age two. That's when they begin to realize that they are separate from others, with their own thoughts and feelings. Toddler empathy typically manifests in the form of the toddler attempting to soothe a family member with things that soothe the toddler. Your child might wrap you in a favorite blanket if you're not feeling well or bring you a special lovey if you appear upset. This is how toddlers communicate that they get it—they know how you feel and they know that it helps to be soothed by a loved one.

As children grow, they become more aware of the world around them and the people inhabiting that world. Although many young children become self-centered as they work to understand their worlds, this doesn't mean that they are incapable of or lack empathy. While some kids tend to take on the feelings of those around them, others simply get lost in their own experiences. They need help nurturing that empathic part of them so that they can be more aware of the feelings of those around them.

The benefits of raising empathic children reach far beyond shielding kids from the negative and better success in school. Empathic children are more self-confident and secure. They are better equipped to make the right decisions for themselves, without hurting others or seeking approval and acceptance from others. Empathic children are better able to handle setbacks and establish meaningful friendships, and they have a greater sense of emotional connection to others. Empathy, it seems, is one of the fundamental building blocks of raising happy kids.

So how do you know whether or not your child is empathic?

Don't stress, most kids already display a fair amount of empathy before you even begin to address it at home. Do you have a child who believes in a spider relocation program instead of squishing? That's an empathic child, right there. That child understands that all living things have the right to live, even if they send a slightly bug-phobic mother running for cover. Related: You'll be happy to learn that Riley's spider relocation program has desensitized me to creepy eight-legged beings quite a bit. So that's a win/win. The point is, you don't have to get caught up in looking for empathic responses to other kids to know whether or not your child is empathic. Opportunities for empathy are everywhere, and many children appear to have an innate understanding of this.

But information is helpful. And there are a few signs of empathy that stand out. Empathic children:

- Are aware of their own feelings.
- Can read facial cues (determine when others are sad, happy, angry, etc.) and body language, and react accordingly.
- Are aware of their individuality. (I feel this way, but that boy might feel another way.)
- Can distinguish their own feelings from the feelings of others, and will attempt to help a friend in a way that is meaningful to that friend.
- Can anticipate how others might feel in a variety of situations.
- Understand how their behavior affects others.
- Can be caretakers at times.
- Are more aware of feelings in the room, and sometimes carry the feelings of others with them.

Kids who lack empathy, on the other hand, are likely to show a few of these warning signs:

- Difficulty reading facial cues and body language
- Difficulty understanding how others feel when they show signs of distress
- Difficulty expressing how others might feel
- Struggle to validate the feelings and emotions of others
- Fail to anticipate the reactions of others in response to choices
- Lack understanding of how their behavior affects others, and how they come across to others
- Put their feelings and needs above others

Some argue that empathy can be taught; others say that empathy can be "caught" (you know, like the stomach flu). I would argue that empathy can be nurtured. If most kids come into this world with some level of empathy that emerges as they grow, nurturing that natural instinct to empathize with others is the key to raising empathic children.

Building an empathic parent-child relationship is an obvious first step when it comes to nurturing empathy. Our kids take their cues from us. When they cry, we help them. We attempt to understand what triggered the tears, and we respond accordingly. When they express emotions, both positive and negative, we listen. We cheer when they are in need of cheering and we soothe when they are in need of soothing. We provide unconditional love, and that sets the foundation for an empathy-based relationship. But nurturing empathy in young children is more than just bandaging boo-boos and drying tear-stained faces.

Listening plays a significant role in the development of empathy. In the words of the mighty Ernest Hemingway: "When people talk, listen completely. Most people never listen." What stands out about empathic children is that they have the ability to listen with understanding. There is a big difference between listening to craft a response to the person speaking and listening with the intention of truly understanding the other person. Empathic children listen with understanding. They don't simply nod their heads as they wait to plead their case or share their insights; they attempt to understand how the other child is feeling and what caused him to feel that way.

The key to teaching children to listen with understanding is to listen to your own child with understanding. All too often, parents respond to scuffles with other kids with some version of "How do you think he *feels?*" It's a natural instinct to jump to empathy for others in the moment, but what we should be doing is empathizing with our own children first. "You seem really frustrated" opens the door to an honest conversation about what went wrong, and signals your child to stop and assess his feelings. If we only cue our children to tune into the feelings of others when the going gets tough, we send the message that their feelings are not important. That's a mistake. We need to validate the full range of emotions that children experience each day. Even the ones that cause negative interactions.

Jonathan had a very difficult time empathizing with other kids. Placed in residential treatment at just eight years old for myriad reasons, he was angry on a good day. He was prone to taking that anger out on other children. As a result, he was constantly in some version of time-out during the school day. Staff members would ask him to think about how his words made other kids feel. Day after day it was more of the same. By the time our weekly sessions rolled around, he was amped up on anger and injustice, making meaningful work difficult at best. It felt more like troubleshooting than therapy . . . from my side of the couch, anyway.

Given his need for attention and flair for the dramatic, Jonathan began most of our sessions with some grand statement followed by several exclamation points. "Call the police to arrest me, Kate, I've done it again!!!" This was usually followed by a litany of complaints about the injustice of it all—from his placement there to the things the other children allegedly did to trigger his anger. Attempts to empathize were often glossed over as he yelled and cried his way through each session. We dealt with his triggers. We practiced coping strategies. We worked on understanding emotions. But still, we were stuck in a vortex of negativity.

Until one day, when I decided to speak first. I took him for a walk around the campus to break the cycle of explosive anger the moment the office door closed. For a few minutes, we simply enjoyed our surroundings. When it seemed as though Jonathan was sufficiently calm, I spoke the words that changed everything (at least for a moment): "I don't know what it's like to be away from home so young, but I imagine that it's really, really hard. It must be lonely. And confusing. I'm pretty sure I would be angry at everyone, too." He looked up at me, tears forming at the corners of his eyes, and nodded his head. And then he opened up. He talked about feeling like a disappointment to his parents, unparalleled loneliness at night, and how he never really felt like a kid.

When we convey understanding of emotion and give our children the opportunity to share how they truly feel across all kinds of circumstances, we show them the importance of listening with understanding. There are always ways to mediate negative interactions, but a crucial first step toward resolving the negative is understanding how each person feels—even the person in the wrong. In Jonathan's case, the angry behavior directed toward his peers was merely a symptom of countless other feelings boiling beneath the surface. He got so caught up in the cycle of negative behaviors and consequences that expressing his anger was all he could do. He needed someone to validate all the other emotions that he wasn't able to access when anger took over.

Accessing emotions proves a significant roadblock for many children. Many kids tend to live in the present. They focus on the here and now. When things are good and they feel happy, this serves them well. But when negative emotions crop up, unresolved feelings can intensify the situation and make empathizing with others a difficult task. Showing compassion for our own children by validating their feelings first helps them work through uncomfortable emotions in an effort to understand how the other person might feel.

As important as it is for parents to display empathy and compassion for their own children, it is equally important to shift the empathy to others in the presence of the kids. Belief systems and attitudes are passed down from parent to child, beginning the moment children enter the world. If we consistently treat others with kindness and understanding, our children learn to account for other people's feelings before reacting. I don't know about you, but I have caught myself in moments of frustration and turned that frustration around under the watchful eye of my child.

It's not always easy to think empathically when it feels like the cards are stacked against you. Most children have a profound sense of justice, and this can lead to linear thinking in the moment. You wronged me and I want justice. In fact, adults even feel this way at times. To some degree, it's a fairly natural instinct. Something bad happens at the hands of another and that person should face a consequence of some kind. But in the real world, it's not always that simple. I find that self-talk helps me stay centered when I'm frustrated. Perhaps a customer service representative isn't handling a call the way I would like, but maybe that person had a really bad day. Maybe it's hard to field complaints all day and I was the last in a long line of complaints. Maybe that person isn't feeling well or has something else on his mind. I know my patience wears thin when I'm worried about one of my kids, so why shouldn't I give someone else the benefit of the doubt?

When parents display compassion without judgment toward others, they model the importance of thinking globally. We can't know what other people are feeling in every instance, and we certainly can't know what their lives are like, but we can stop and consider the possibilities before passing judgment or reacting in anger. When we lead with kindness, even if that kindness isn't necessarily returned, we teach our children to do the same.

The importance of empathy has gained steam in recent years as parents, educators, and professionals attempt to find ways to decrease bullying among students and increase kindness instead. Random acts of kindness movements have popped up all over the world, and across age groups. Doing something kind for another person, without the expectation of reciprocation or gratitude, inspires others to pay it forward. While these acts are generally well received and sometimes go viral (thereby potentially triggering more random acts of kindness), it is important to teach children to engage in deliberate acts of kindness. Buying a coffee for a stranger is a beautiful act of selflessness in the moment, but if we want to raise kind and empathic children, we have to teach them to choose kindness not just in random moments, but in every moment. We can't control how others will treat us, and we certainly can't control how others will respond to us, but we can control how we treat other people. And that is an important component of nurturing empathy.

The bottom line is that when we take the time to understand how others feel, when we put ourselves in someone else's shoes instead of rushing to judgments or reacting in the heat of the moment, we experience better relationships, a stronger sense of community, and a better sense of self. And that's a recipe for happiness.

Empathy, like anything else, requires practice and repetition. And empathy is best practiced in a way that is both meaningful and comfortable to each individual child. In short, choose the strategy that fits the personality.

Tips for Nurturing Empathy

Put on a Social Play

It's no big secret that young children love to dress up, act the part, and be someone else for a little while. Role-playing is an important part of figuring out how the world works and understanding the difference between fantasy and reality. It also helps kids master perspective-taking skills. When they try on a role, they have to think from a different perspective.

Parents can take this concept a step further by helping to incorporate lessons in empathy. Social stories really come to life when you add costumes, scenery, and lights. Write down a few prompts on some cue cards and have your child(ren) choose one (e.g.: A boy broke Timmy's truck). Ask your child to write, star in, and direct a play based on the prompt. Be sure to ask open-ended questions to get the kids thinking about feelings and solutions.

Use a "Talking" Beanbag

One of the most difficult parts of practicing empathy is relying on active listening. To truly listen to another person, you have to stop trying to talk over that person and stop thinking about what you might say next. You have to engage on the listening end by asking follow-up questions and understanding the concerns. Props can help.

Keep a small beanbag handy for those moments when you need to mediate a sibling squabble or help end a playdate standoff. It's a simple concept, really. The person holding the beanbag gets to talk while the other listens. The talker should be cued to verbalize his feelings, talk about what went wrong, and state his needs. The listener should be cued to ask follow-up questions and help identify solutions. Trade places.

Teaching kids to listen first and respond later helps them tune into the feelings of others instead of hyperfocusing on right versus wrong (a common childhood phenomenon). When they focus their energy on understanding how others feel and how they can help others feel better, they become confident and responsible. In the end, it all adds up to greater happiness.

Mixed-up Shoes

Parents often tell their kids to walk in someone else's shoes in an effort to encourage kids to try to understand how other kids feel, but that's no easy task. In fact, young children tend to be fairly literal thinkers. Combine that with the fact that they are also egocentric at times (ah, the benefits of being young) and that business of walking in someone else's shoes actually becomes quite confusing. What will wearing someone else's sneakers possibly teach me about under-standing others?

As it turns out, it can teach you a lot. "Mixed-up shoes" is a fun way to engage kids in a perspective-taking game. It's best played with a few kids (and even parents), be it siblings or friends. (Hint: great classroom activity!) Have all players form a circle, remove their shoes, and put them in a pile in the middle of the circle. One at a time, have players choose a pair of shoes that do not belong to them and put them on. Some will be huge, some might be too small, and some might be a different style. Part of the fun of this game is trying something new.

Once all players have on a new pair of shoes, have them attempt to walk around in them a bit. Kids get silly with this part of the game, but that's a good thing. They are literally walking in someone else's shoes, and that will open the door to understanding the other person. Return to the circle and have each player describe the shoes in detail. Cue the kids to notice everything from the colors and styles to how worn the toes and heels are. Have each child try to think about how the owner of the shoes plays, what he or she likes to do, and where the shoes might have traveled. In essence, each player should try to craft a story from the perspective of the owner of the shoes. Have the owner jump in and agree or disagree and share his or her own perspective before moving on to the next player.

Walking in someone else's shoes and trying to think like the owner of the shoes gives kids an opportunity to step away from their own feelings and needs for a moment and attempt to identify with someone else. This is an important life skill that will continue to help them relate to others as they grow.

Body Language Simon Says

Reading body language is no easy task. For instance, common wisdom leads people to believe that when people stand with their arms crossed, they are guarded or have something to hide. I find that I often cross my arms when I'm feeling nervous, or to avoid using my arms so much when I talk (I tend to be an animated speaker). Reading body language can't be simplified because all people are different and use their bodies to convey emotions in different ways. Riley twirls her hair when she's lost in thought, but many kids do the same when they're anxious. Not so simple, indeed.

"Body Language Simon Says" is a fun twist on an old favorite game and it helps kids think about how we use our bodies to depict emotions. It also helps them see how others experience and show emotions. Sad looks different on different people, and it can take time to understand what other people are trying to tell us with their facial cues and body language.

This game is as easy as its title leads you to believe! Play Simon Says as you normally would, but have the kids act out different feelings (sad, mad, loving, silly, etc.) instead of the usual directives. Be sure to describe how each child looks to cue the kids to look around at one another during the game.

Model It

I know, I know, you're tired of hearing about the fact that you have to set the best example. Because, let's face it, parenting can be trying and some days you probably set a better example than other days. Fear not. A few bad days (even more than a few) won't erase all the good days. Especially when you make your bad days into teachable moments and circle back to empathy.

In all likelihood, you probably do model empathy fairly regularly. Every time you encourage your kids to think about others, you plant the seed of empathy. When your child falls and skins his knee and you respond not just with a fancy Band-Aid but with soothing words about how much it hurts to skin a knee and maybe even a story or two about your own skinned knees as a kid, you're modeling empathy. When your child struggles in school and you respond with kindness and talk about your own ups and downs at school, you model empathy. When you respond to your child with kindness and consideration, you show them how to empathize with others.

There is a difference between helping children and running in with a quick fix to every problem and empathizing with them. When parents run in and fix problems as they occur, kids develop learned helplessness. Over time, they begin to think that they are incapable of solving their own problems. But when parents intervene by way of emotional support and empathy, kids learn that they can problem-solve and that their parents are there to support them in the process.

Beyond the immediate show of empathy within the family, it's important to extend empathy toward others within your community. When your children see you caring for others, and even help with the caring, they learn that helping others makes the world a happier place. Cook for a friend who is sick, drop off groceries to a neighbor in need, or help an elderly neighbor rake leaves or weed the garden. Small acts of kindness go a long way toward raising empathic children.

Change Makers

As much as parents need to model pro-social behaviors for young children, older kids can also inspire little kids. Older siblings and friends can act as empathy role models for younger children. Have you ever inspired your child to take on a dreaded household task simply by telling your child that the task at hand requires responsibility? I have. I recently handed over the power of the vacuum. That was a game changer.

Kids rise to the occasion when they feel like they are heard, recognized, and being treated in an age-appropriate manner. While it's tempting to try to make sure everything in the house is "fair," that practice is actually a little bit unfair to older children. The fact is that as kids grow, they become capable of greater responsibilities. If those responsibilities are framed in a way that helps the child feel confident and proud, the child is more likely to rise to the occasion (or the responsibility, as the case may be).

Inspiring older siblings and friends to act as change makers puts them in the position of helping younger siblings and friends while practicing empathy. When they shift into the helper role, older children look at social situations from a different perspective. The change makers become the ones asking the kids to verbalize their feelings, name their triggers, and brainstorm possible solutions. If two kids bicker over the rules of a game, for example, the change maker would help each child understand the situation from the other's perspective and find ways to solve the conflict together.

In helping younger kids, the change makers can also be taught to share their own similar situations and talk about how they felt during those times. Through this practice, the change makers model empathic thinking for the younger children. Children can learn a lot from their older friends and siblings, and this strategy helps all kids involved focus on positive social interactions.

Believe in Them

It almost seems as if this one needs no introduction. Believe in your children. Is it really that simple? Sometimes yes. Sometimes no. Of course we all believe in our children when the lights go down and the house is quiet and we have the time to reflect on the greatness of our little ones on any given day. We believe in the gymnast who didn't give up until she conquered that balance beam. We believe in the artist who created an underwater world so real and so mesmerizing that we are no longer worried about the paint on the wall and the glitter in the floorboards. And we believe in that little baseball player who finally, finally made it to first base. But do we believe in them during the difficult moments? If we're being completely honest, do we believe in them when it counts?

Children hear a fair amount of negative input throughout the day. *Don't climb on the couch. Don't talk when the teacher is talking. Don't be late for school. Don't get paint everywhere.* Childhood runs on trial and error and for every little success along the way, there is an error that stands out because of the negative input it earned.

We have to believe in our children when it counts. Not just when the lights go down. We have to believe in them when they're down. We have to believe in them when they're up. We have to believe in them when they don't know which way to turn. And we have to use our words, our actions, and our hearts to show them how much we believe in them.

There is a magnet on my filing cabinet, right next to my desk. Although I look at it at least once a day, I still tear up every time. It was given to me by an old supervisor, someone who helped me find my way. It's a simple quote, and yet the words echo through my soul each time I read them, reminding me that my journey to help kids might change course but it never ends. May these words from *The Talmud* remind you of the importance of believing in your children, even when it's hard: "Every blade of grass has its angel that bends over it and whispers, Grow, Grow."

Social Detectives

"Empathy" is a big word for little kids, and an even bigger concept, and kids don't always recognize an act of empathy when they see it happening. They might understand, for example, that a friend helping another friend when he's crying seems like a nice thing to do, but they don't necessarily draw the connections between reaching out to others and being empathic. They don't necessarily stop to think about how they can empathize with and help others in the moment.

"Social detectives" is a fun little game to play with your kids when you're out in the world. Kids are naturally curious about the people, places, and things they encounter in the community, and this curiosity provides a springboard for talking about how people interact. Instead of running right into the playground, sit back on a bench or in the grass with your child and watch for a little while. Ask your child to put on his detective hat and make a note of things that stand out. Some kids even like to bring a feelings checklist for the occasion. Point out (and ask your child to think about) how various kids might be feeling given their facial expressions and behavior. What might be making those kids feel that way? If they appear happy, is there a way to make them happier? If they appear sad, what might make them happy? If they seem lonely, what might they need to feel less lonely?

Encouraging kids to watch for clues and draw the connections between emotions and behaviors helps them take the perspective of the other kids and consider how they might help. It's great practice, particularly for quieter kids who aren't as likely to jump in with solutions.

The Gratitude Jar

Gratitude and empathy go hand in hand. When kids experience and express feelings of gratitude, they are more likely to show empathy and understanding toward others. By learning gratitude, young children become more sensitive to others around them (kids and adults). They learn to step out of their self-centered worlds and understand that others do things for them and help them along the way. Also? Grateful children are happier and more optimistic than children who are not raised with gratitude. (Sadly, ungrateful children seem to get stuck in a cycle of disappointment.) The only catch is that gratitude is a learned behavior. You have to teach it (and yelling "You should be more grateful" doesn't count).

The gratitude jar is a great family activity that is ongoing and helps each family remember to pause for gratitude. And all you need is a pretty jar, a stack of small slips of paper, and a pen (younger children will need assistance with writing). Place your gratitude jar in the most loved room of your home (for us, it stays in the combination kitchen–family room). Tell your kids that the jar will hold all the thoughts of gratitude that family members have during the week. Be specific here and provide concrete examples ("I'm grateful for my sister for helping me with my project"). Whenever a family member is feeling grateful about something (and it can be anything . . . sometimes I'm really just grateful for the smile that my rose garden brings to my face!), it should be written on a slip of paper and placed in the jar. Once a week (immediately following a family meal is a good time), empty the jar and read the thoughts of gratitude to the family.

Small exercises like this help ground us in reality. The gratitude jar helps kids remember to slow down and be thankful for the little things, and helps stressed-out parents find their center and take comfort in knowing that gratitude is all around them.

Change Places

Understanding how others feel can be a struggle for young children. They all live in these little one-person universes at times, and it isn't always easy to see beyond their own immediate feelings and needs. Adding a little fun to the task of learning about empathy helps kids absorb and internalize the information.

"Change places" is a fun empathy game for kids and parents. It's best played outside, where you have plenty of room to move. The first step is to come up with a list of social scenarios that apply to your kids and include opportunities for practicing empathy. "A friend is embarrassed because he was teased about his new haircut" or "A girl is sad because her dad is on a long business trip" might work in my house, but you need to come up with authentic scenarios that your child will encounter.

Write each scenario on a slip of paper and place them in a hat. Have your child choose one slip of paper and read it out loud. The child who picks the paper assigns a role to each player. In the case of the boy with the new haircut, for example, you need at least one person to play the boy and one to play the teaser. It's great to have a third person who can act as an onlooker who wants to help. Set a timer for two minutes and start acting out the scenario. Try not to place too many rules on the play. When kids play through these difficult scenarios without restrictions, they are more likely to gain insight and learn something meaningful. When the timer rings, yell, "Change places!" Each player rotates and switches roles for the next two minutes.

After each player has had a chance to play each role, stop the play and talk about how the various roles felt. Maybe being the teaser felt kind of powerful for a minute, but being teased probably felt pretty demeaning. Encourage the kids to talk about what it feels like to change places, and be sure to share your own thoughts and feelings about it with them.

Family Community Service

Working together as a family to help others is one of the most powerful ways to instill a sense of empathy in your children. Kids spend their days at school, in after-school activities, and playing with friends. As well they should. But because their worldviews tend to be a bit narrow when they're young (that's not a negative, that's simply a fact of childhood), they don't always have an understanding of the suffering around them. Getting them involved in helping others expands their worldviews, empowers them to make change, and helps them develop empathy and gratitude. Another added benefit of family community service projects? People who volunteer to help others experience greater overall happiness.

Opportunities to help are everywhere. After Hurricane Sandy wreaked havoc on large portions of the East Coast, my daughter collected sweatshirts from her kindergarten classmates to send to kids and parents in need. What started out as a little project and a few outgrown sweatshirts turned into two giant boxes containing over 150 sweatshirts! Whether you help play with dogs at an animal shelter, clean a local park or beach, or donate time and goods to families in need, working together to help others is good for the whole family. Get your kids involved in the process of choosing a project. When a project has meaning for them, they will take away more from the experience.

Plant a Tree

Did you know that gardening can actually help build empathy (along with responsibility)? It's true. Kids learn a lot from gardening projects. They learn that they are responsible for helping the plant thrive. They have to get to know each individual plant and find out its needs. Some need full sun while others need partial sun. Some need to be watered three times a week, while others need water every day. They have to pull the weeds around the plant and care for it. To help a plant reach its full potential, the child has to think about what the plant needs each and every day.

You don't have to plant a huge tree or a whole garden to help your child reap the emotional benefits of gardening. In fact, it's a good idea to start from seeds. When the plant starts as a seed in a little tiny cup, your child has the opportunity to nurture it and replant it as it grows. And that helps kids think empathically and beyond their own needs, which makes their world a happier place.

6

Speak Your Mind—
Building Assertiveness Skills

Don't be scared to walk alone. Don't be scared to like it.

—JOHN MAYER

THE THING ABOUT QUIET, mild-mannered kids is that sometimes they are quiet and mild-mannered to a fault. They struggle to assert their needs or seek help during a difficult situation. More often than not, they stand back and wait for the stress to pass.

Samantha was one of those kids. At eleven years old, she had been through enough. A contentious divorce, a close family member with terminal illness, and a brother who hardly gave her the time of day left her feeling alone in the world more often than not. You wouldn't know it, though, because she rarely asked for help. Quiet and creative (the drawings covering her notebooks were the envy of many girls in her class), she would often retreat into her own little introverted space when the stress became too much to handle.

She spent the majority of our therapy sessions lost in art while I gently probed her in an effort to help her understand that her feelings mattered, and that her needs were important. Creating elaborate mosaics using magazine clippings and construction paper, she opened up little by little as the months wore on. She was afraid, as it turned out, to assert her own needs because she didn't want to risk upsetting the family further or making her terminally ill family member more terminal. "I'm fine," she said, week after week, with tears rimming her faded brown eyes that had clearly lost their sparkle.

And so we used those mosaics to our advantage. We began piecing together assertive statements and feelings assertions. We worked quietly, side by side, comparing words and phrases and dissecting their meanings, until one day she pieced together the four words that finally opened the floodgates: "I am not fine."

Teaching kids to be assertive, to confidently state their wants and needs without imposing those wants and needs on others, can be a slow process. Some kids are more naturally assertive than others, but all kids can learn to stand up for themselves.

The first step to helping kids learn to be more assertive is to help them understand that they matter. It's not simply a matter of teaching kids to use their voices; it's a matter of showing them that they *have* voices and that their voices count. And that begins with parenting style.

In Chapter 1, we covered the importance of parenting the child that you have. Temperament is important, and paying attention to your child's personality will help you determine how to parent your child. Still, some days are wonderful and some days are trying, and most fall somewhere in between. And if we're being honest, parenting style likely changes from day to day based on any number of factors. After years and years of research into the matter of parenting, many experts rely on the four types of parenting styles that appear to emerge. And while it seems necessary to reiterate that there is NO SUCH THING as one-size-fits-all parenting, it can be useful to think about your go-to style and how you might tweak it to help your children thrive as individuals.

- **Permissive:** Permissive parents are the ones who get the reputation for always giving in. These parents want to keep things mellow and avoid blowups at all costs, so rules and schedules are not high on their priority list. More often than not, parents who fall into this category feel like they simply don't get enough time with their kids and they want time spent together to be happy. The downside, of course, is that kids might end up feeling entitled. When you never hear "no" and you pretty much get to run the show, it can be hard to enter the real world (school, camp, etc.), where "no" is part of daily living. These kids might even seem a little too assertive at times. On the flip side, permissive parents tend to be deeply aware of their affection for their children and truly want to help carve out happy lives for them. The solution: Find a happy medium. You can't say yes every single time. Kids need structure and limits. That's part of life. But focusing on both short- and long-term happiness will help your children understand the importance of making choices that work for them.

- **Hands off:** The hands-off parent is a fan of natural consequences. Let them learn from experience and they'll learn to be independent. It's a "teach a man to fish" kind of parenting style. On the bright side, these kids do learn to fend for themselves. They also learn to pick themselves up when they fail and try again. On the not-so-bright side, they might not learn to ask for help. They are so busy fending for themselves and being independent that they fail to learn that we all need help sometimes, and getting that help begins with asking for it. The truth is that kids need guidance. It's part of childhood. You know when your husband refuses to ask for directions because he's been there before and he knows he'll get there eventually? That's frustrating. Help is good. Let's make a pact to raise kids who aren't afraid to seek guidance, instead. The solution: Teach your kids to think for themselves, but encourage them to seek input and be available to help them when they ask. Be there now so that they won't need you so much later.

- **Authoritarian:** This fairly strict, rule-based parenting style demands respect. There is no democracy and no room for negotiation. These children know where they stand in the family, what they can and can't do, and what is expected of them at any given time. There is no room for error. On the positive side of things, these kids really come to understand rules and consequences at a young age. The negatives, however, outweigh the positives by far. Kids of authoritarian parents tend to be anxious, afraid of failure, and emotionally disconnected, and they are likely to engage in secretive behavior as teens. Remember Avery from Chapter 2? She began to travel that road the minute she hit middle school. The solution: Maintain your high expectations, but blanket them in love. Parenting involves a fair amount of give and take. To really meet your children where they are and parent them as individuals, you have to be able to bend at times.

- **Authoritative:** Often cited as the "most effective" parenting style (even though we all know there is no first place in parenting), authoritative parenting includes setting high (but age-appropriate) expectations for your kids, but also setting high expectations when it comes to your own choices and behavior. Kids of authoritative parents are said to perform well academically, have better social skills, and experience better overall emotional stability. These parents know when to say no, when to say yes, and when to throw the rules out the window for a minute. Is there a downside here? Parenting can be hard and no parent is perfect. Sometimes this style of parenting can lead to parents thinking a little too critically about their parenting decisions. The solution: Give yourself a break. Parenting is a marathon, not a sprint. There is no medal at the end of this journey, and you won't get it right every single time. Take the bad with the good and learn from your mistakes.

So if we're parenting the individual, why do we need to think about parenting style? The truth is that we all have our own styles of parenting, and the parenting style that we show to the world might look drastically different from the parenting style that we show in the privacy of our own homes. In order to parent children as individuals and raise them to be appropriately assertive, we need to think about how we parent and where we might need to make some changes. Knowing your own baseline will help you find the style, or mix of styles, that helps you raise confident and assertive children.

Assertiveness is closely tied to self-esteem. The need for belonging and the fear of rejection, criticism, and being seen as incapable often stop kids from speaking up. These kinds of fears can be paralyzing. When you're constantly worried about what others think or how you might be judged, the world can feel like an overwhelming place.

I would know. I was one of those kids. I was petrified of breaking a rule in school, so I didn't do a lot of talking in class in my early years. In fact, I still remember the day when I dared to let my feelings be known in second grade. I was bored with silent reading. We had been at it for a while. And although I have always loved to read, forced reading was never my favorite. So, in a move completely uncharacteristic of me, I raised my hand and asked how much longer silent reading would last. My teacher, a generally calm and motherly woman, stopped in her tracks and looked right at me. I felt all eyes on me as we waited to see what she would say. She put her hand over her face and said, "Katie, I am appalled and ashamed. Just ashamed." That was the end of speaking up for a while. Too risky.

Kids who learn to assert their needs in an appropriate manner experience greater confidence, bounce back from negative interactions faster, and generally feel good about the choices they make. They can stop a bully in his tracks (or aren't afraid to try, anyway) and seek change when something seems unfair. They navigate difficult social situations with ease because they know that while others have feelings and rights that need to be respected, their feelings and rights are important, too. They are happier in life because they aren't afraid to be themselves and speak their minds.

The trick is to teach them the art of assertive communication. Assertive and aggressive are two very different things, but sometimes they are confused in the mind of a child. There is a significant difference between speaking up and speaking over, and kids need help learning how to best assert their feelings and needs while keeping others in mind.

It helps to begin by teaching kids a little bit about different communication styles. Most kids don't know that they have choices when it comes to communicating with others. They've stumbled upon a certain style and stuck with it, no matter the natural consequences. As you teach your children about communication styles, it's helpful to have a few examples in mind (especially examples that have meaning for your child—skip the history lesson here and focus on people or characters your child knows).

- **Passive communicators:** Passive communicators tend to be quiet, mild-mannered, and accommodating. They get stepped on by others and fail to speak up for their rights. (They might not even know they have rights, truth be told.) They avoid disagreements and have trouble saying no, but often feel angry and/or resentful later.

- **Aggressive communicators:** Aggressive communicators are loud, loud, loud! They tend to dominate conversations and intimidate others. They like to get their way no matter what and react instantly (low impulse control here). They might violate the rights of others by using their power and position to get their own needs met.

- **Assertive communicators:** Assertive communicators are firm, direct, and honest. They are effective communicators, and are able to express their thoughts and needs. They make good eye contact and display self-confidence. They respect the rights of others but also recognize that they have rights and can make their own choices.

Most kids switch communication styles from day to day and depending on the situation. A child who is confident and assertive in the classroom, for example, might struggle to display those same traits on the baseball field. This is perfectly normal and to be expected with young children. All children have their strengths and it's natural to feel more confident and assertive in one setting than in another. It's important to talk about how they communicate in various settings, however, because it helps them learn to find their voices.

Believe it or not, it can be very difficult for kids to find their voices. Everywhere they go, someone has some list of expectations for them. They have expectations at home, expectations at school, expectations on the soccer field . . . you get the drill. When do they really have the chance to speak their minds? More often than not, the most vocal children in the classrooms are the ones being reprimanded. They are so eager to voice their thoughts, feelings, and concerns that they might not wait for an appropriate break in the learning to speak up. On the other hand, with academics becoming so very academic at such an early age, there probably isn't much time for verbalizing those thoughts, feelings, and concerns. But what the kids teetering on the edge of assertiveness hear in these circumstances (you know, the ones bored to tears with silent reading) is this: Keep your mouth closed to avoid public reprimand.

The fact is that from the moment our children learn how to talk, we teach them how to listen. We want them to follow directions, listen to and respect adults, and adhere to rules. The problem is that sometimes we forget to teach them how to speak up.

Helping kids understand that their thoughts and feelings matter is tricky. Young children are impulsive at times (sometimes even most of the time), and they don't always stop to assess the situation before making a choice. While some might blurt out their needs immediately, others might crawl into their shells and wait for the feelings to pass. They need help determining how and when to appropriately assert their feelings and needs.

The good news is that the parenting style we talked about earlier can really help with this. Being an assertive communicator is as much about listening and practicing patience as it is about verbalizing your feelings and needs. When parents rely on active listening skills and give their kids a chance to talk before jumping in with solutions or reprimands, they model assertive communication. Assertiveness is a learned behavior. When kids see assertive communication in action, they learn to speak their minds in a confident way. But if they see aggressive or passive communication in the home, they are likely to mimic those communication styles.

At ten years old, Maggie was quiet, reserved, and isolated. She preferred hiding under hooded sweatshirts and had difficulty speaking up. She talked almost nonstop with peers, but when it came down to interacting with teachers or seeking help of any kind, she put her hood up, sat in the back of the room, and fell silent. With one parent constantly traveling and the other in town but perpetually busy, Maggie retreated into her own little world more often than not.

Maggie could tell her mom anything. That was the good news. But her mom preferred to handle every little thing that went wrong along the way. She was always speaking for Maggie. And while this came from a place of love and loyalty (she wanted to help her little girl as much as possible), it had a negative impact on Maggie's self-esteem. It wasn't that Maggie felt entitled, or that she knew her mom would come to the rescue so she didn't bother handling her own stressors. It was that Maggie felt like she *couldn't* handle things. Her mom always knew what to say. Her mom always knew where to begin and how to keep fighting until the fight was won. Maggie was the opposite. And every time her mom asserted Maggie's needs (in a somewhat verbally aggressive manner) on her behalf, Maggie crawled a little bit deeper into her internal world—her safe place. What Maggie learned along the way was that she wasn't capable. It was my job to show her that she was.

The key to helping Maggie evolve from a child who frequently hid in the back of the room to a confident child who knew how to speak her mind was to go back to the very beginning. We crafted her very own "Bill of Rights" (see below) and followed that up with everything from lessons on body language to taking healthy risks to understanding the meaning of self-esteem. In fact, many of the tools mentioned in the next section played important roles in helping Maggie find her inner voice.

Assertive kids grow into assertive adults. Assertiveness fosters patience, insight, and acceptance. Teaching your child the art of assertive communication now lays the foundation for healthy and happy relationships in the future.

Tips for Teaching Assertiveness Skills

Craft a Bill of Rights

As parents, we spend a lot of time teaching kids how to be responsible. We set rules and limits. We create expectations. We tell them where they have to be, what they have to do, and sometimes even what they have to wear. When you stop and think about it, that doesn't leave a lot of room for kids to assert their wants and needs.

Kids respond well to visuals, and they respond even better when they get to create the visuals. Help your child create an assertiveness bill of rights. It might include things like: I have the right to say no, I have the right to disagree, I have the right to feel or express anger, or I have the right to recognize my needs as important. Teaching assertiveness skills can be tricky at times, and it is important to help your child balance her own needs with the needs of others. Part of assertive communication is listening to others and finding the middle ground. Be sure to let your child come up with as many rights as possible, as this is a great first step toward becoming more assertive.

Teach "I" Statements

It feels good to blame someone or something when you're stressed or angry. It might even feel good to lash out by way of a verbally aggressive statement . . . for a minute. But the minute kids start blaming others for their feelings—personal power is lost. There is a significant difference between saying "I feel angry when you ignore me" and "You make me angry when you ignore me." When kids learn to spot the difference and take ownership of their feelings, it puts them in control.

Practice using "I" statements at home. Use them when you're frustrated or upset by something to model a calm way to assert your needs as a parent. When your kids see that "I" statements help you remain calm and focused while asserting your feelings and needs, they learn that they can do the same with peers. They learn to shift the feeling from overwhelmed and out of control to calm and solution-focused.

Body Positioning

As parents, we are always teaching kids to listen. We teach them that eye contact shows attention. We teach them to stop what they're doing and keep their hands still to demonstrate good listening skills. But do we remember to teach them what assertiveness looks like?

An assertive communicator stands tall, maintains eye contact, and speaks in a clear but firm voice. Where a passive communicator speaks quietly and has difficulty maintaining eye contact and an aggressive communicator is too loud and possibly in-your-face, an assertive communicator knows when to speak, when to listen, and how to maintain a calm and clear voice tone.

Show your kids examples of assertive communicators throughout history. If you're up for it, consider running a family election. Come up with some fun positions that need filling (e.g.: light monitor or grocery list maker) and have everyone write and deliver speeches to earn the positions. Make sure to cue the kids to use assertive body language and voice tone at the podium.

Sales Pitch!

Selling a product is no easy task. I feel guilty every time I turn away a kid standing at my door trying to convince me to buy a magazine in support of the school band because I know that it takes a lot of courage to go door-to-door selling those magazines. And I can always tell which kids have been prepped, which kids have self-confidence, and which kids wish they could run away and hide.

A pretend sales pitch is a great way to practice assertive communication, and kids have a lot of fun in the process. Send your kids off in search of hidden treasures in their rooms and then have them prepare a sales pitch and attempt to sell you the product. Ask them follow-up questions to keep them engaged and give them specific feedback on their pitches, including praise for assertive communication.

Support Healthy Risks

This can be a hard one. Believe me, I understand. I have a daughter with absolutely no fear of climbing as high as humanly possible, and freakishly strong arms to get her there! It's difficult to step back and watch when you're not sure how the situation will end. But that's the thing about risk. To take a risk is to step off into the unknown and see what happens.

For some kids, climbing the monkey bars is considered a big risk while other kids are willing to try all kinds of physical and emotional tasks to see how far they can bend. Support healthy risk taking. No, you can't let your child jump into shark-infested waters at feeding time, but you can encourage them to learn how to surf. Help your child step outside her comfort zone at times. Praise efforts made to try something new, no matter the end result. When kids learn to push their own personal boundaries by taking healthy risks (making mistakes while reciting that poem in front of the class might not actually be that bad, you know), they become more self-confident and assertive along the way. Put your fear aside for a moment and let your kids try.

Resist Comparisons

It's only natural to draw comparisons between your children. But those comparisons should not be made public. Sure, Johnny learned to read at five but Sally is still struggling at eight, or Sam is an aggressive soccer player where Josh seems to hide behind the other goal whenever possible. Does it matter? Your kids are different. They are not like each other and they are not necessarily like you. They are individuals who need to find their own places in this world. In order to do that, they have to be encouraged to be who they are.

The truth is that most kids know exactly how they compare to their siblings. They might not say it out loud, but they know what traits they have that their siblings don't, and what traits they might be lacking. Many kids have a tendency to place undue pressure on themselves. Don't add to that by comparing them to their siblings or their peers. They need to be treated as individuals. They might need to work on a few things, but who doesn't? What your child is working on is between you and your child, and no one else.

Praise out Loud

There is a significant amount of backlash about praise these days. Some feel that kids are coddled and receive too much praise, that less praise builds more character. Some lash out about participation trophies, as if cheap plastic awards are creating entitled children who don't understand the value of hard work. Please don't crawl into this rabbit hole of parental negativity. Praise can do a lot of good. And when things like participation trophies are awarded to children at the end of a season, children have a transitional object to remind them of a great season working toward a common goal with a group of friends. Is that really such a bad thing?

The important thing about praise is that it should have meaning. When you praise your child's efforts rather than the finished product, for example, you teach your child that the hard work put into the product is what matters most. When you praise your child's character for acts of kindness, you teach your child that kindness matters. Be specific with your praise. Try not to overthink how often you praise your kids, as everyone enjoys positive feedback at times. I know I always enjoy a pat on the back, don't you? Doesn't it make sense to pay it forward and give our children the same?

Added bonus: When you praise your child's character to another adult within earshot of your child, your child will definitely take note. It's not about bragging about accomplishments to other parents, it's about sharing heartwarming moments in parenting. Those are the moments you want your child to internalize and return to at other times.

All About Me

Sometimes kids struggle to assert themselves because they fear what others will think of them. It can be easier to hide out in the back of the class than to show your true colors. For many kids, quiet is safe.

Creating an All About Me board helps bring kids out of the safety zone a bit. I can't tell you how many kids have sat on my couch and claimed they had absolutely nothing interesting to share, only to find out months later that they participate in junior guards, take fashion classes, or know a thing or two about computer programming. Many kids need a gentle push when it comes to describing their strengths and interests, but when they finally step out of that comfort zone and start sharing, they really begin to shine.

Help your child make a poster or a diorama that describes his personality, interests, strengths, dreams, and goals. Talk about it. Share it with family. The process of drawing out strengths in the safety of your home will help your child begin to share those strengths in more challenging settings.

Go on Record

Or video, as the case may be. Many kids truly don't know what it means to have an assertive communication style. As we established earlier, an assertive person stands tall but doesn't intimidate, uses a clear and confident voice tone, makes eye contact, and expresses his needs effectively. That's a tall order for little kids.

Kids love to make videos, both as the video stars and as the directors behind the camera. Together with your child, come up with a few scenarios that might require assertive communication. (A few examples include: choosing an activity during a playdate, approaching a teacher for help with something during school, or saying no to a peer who tends to be bossy.) Take turns both behind and in front of the camera as you attempt to use assertive communication to work through the various scenarios. Play back the videos and talk about things like physical stance, voice tone, eye contact, and word choice. Rate the performances and talk about ways to improve the next time.

Making video skits can be a lot of fun and can really help kids see themselves as others see them. When they realize that they have the power to change the way they communicate with others, they will be happier for it.

Tower of Self-Esteem

Given that self-esteem and assertiveness are closely related, it's important for kids to work on increasing self-esteem. Part of that includes recognizing what kinds of things increase their self-esteem and what kinds of things decrease their self-esteem. The journey to higher self-esteem doesn't happen overnight, and many kids take ten steps forward only to come to a crashing halt shortly thereafter. Helping them sort out the positives and negatives gives them the opportunity to evaluate and make better choices moving forward.

Self-esteem boosters are positive things kids can do or say to reach greater self-appreciation. Examples might include a positive mantra, choosing positive friends, seeking help when upset, etc. Self-esteem busters are negative things that lead to self-defeat or feelings of worthlessness. Examples of busters include intrusive thoughts, negative peer influence, teasing others, etc. It's useful to build a tower of blocks when talking about boosters and busters. For every booster your child names, a block is added to the tower. For every buster, one is removed. Work together to increase the boosters and build a supertall tower of self-esteem.

Teach Goal Setting

Learning the art of setting and attaining goals helps kids build self-confidence and begin to assert their needs and feelings. Many kids get a taste of goal setting at the beginning of the school year and around the first of the year. Teachers help them set personal goals in and out of the classroom and parents might help them set goals or resolutions at home. But those are easily forgotten.

The problem with long-term goals is that they tend to get lost in the shuffle of daily life. Sure, your kid wants to learn to skateboard. But first he has to complete piles of homework each week, get to all his baseball practices and games, learn to play the piano, and read a few books "for fun." Do you see where I'm going with this? Long-term goals are great, but without smaller, measurable benchmarks along the way it can be a setup for failure. Sometimes the end goal seems so overwhelming that kids abandon the effort before they've even begun. And that's not good for their self-esteem.

Goal setting is an important life skill, and working toward goals provides opportunities for assertiveness along with improved self-confidence as benchmarks are met and skills are mastered. In the case of the skateboard, for example, a child might try mastering a balance board first, then try the skateboard in the garage, then take it to the driveway, etc. As the benchmarks are met, the child asks for help moving to the next step and talks about how it feels to meet those benchmarks. As self-confidence increases, you might find that your otherwise quiet child suddenly has a list of challenges to conquer on that skateboard.

Ask your child to think about three big goals he wants to meet. It can be anything from painting a beach scene to Rollerblading to riding a roller coaster. Talk about the goals and why he chose those particular goals. (Is it something scary? Is he trying to make new friends? Is it something he doesn't have time for during the school year?) Have your child decide which goal he wants to work on first, and make a list of three to five benchmarks your child must meet in order to attain the overall goal. Make it into a checklist or a poster to place on his bedroom door. Highlight areas where he might need to seek help and be sure to practice ways to do just that. Establish a weekly check-in to review the goal and benchmarks and determine how things are going.

Road Race

For younger children, it helps to add a little excitement to the process of assertiveness training. A road race (or a silly obstacle course) is the perfect solution. You want to create a fun race or course that presents obstacles along the way where the child is required to verbalize his needs and feelings in the moment. This ensures that your child has to stop, think about the problem, verbalize what she needs, and then move on to the next obstacle.

Trike or scooter races are always fun for little kids, and you can easily create a "track" using chalk on your driveway or garage floor. All you need is a start and a finish and one rule: When you encounter an obstacle (like a suitcase in the way), you have to stop and assert your needs in a clear voice using good eye contact and body posturing (e.g.: "This suitcase is on the track. Will you please help me move it?"). In other words, to win the race you need to be assertive. You also might want to include fun checkpoints on the track (e.g.: "Tell me three interesting facts about you") and have a silly station (hop on one foot and sing "Jingle Bells" in a loud, clear voice).

No Regrets

You know those pesky negative, self-defeating statements that pop into your head when you feel regret after a particular interaction or situation that didn't go as planned? With adults, I refer to them as intrusive thoughts. It's the highlight (or lowlight, really) reel that gets stuck on repeat when you wish you could go back and change something to ensure a better outcome. Out in the world, we refer to these thoughts as "regrets" or remorse. With kids, I like to call them the "would haves, should haves, could haves."

We all have moments we wish we could revisit, and in hindsight we always have a much better plan. Once the event is over, we also know exactly what we would have, should have, or could have done. For kids, these thoughts can turn into self-defeating statements that they carry around with them, and they can cause kids to shy away from asserting themselves in the future.

Bad things happen and we don't always make the best choices. But living in the past and allowing those intrusive thoughts to permeate our souls doesn't do us any good. In fact, it can do us harm. (Hint: This is a great time to revisit empathy with your child and share a story or two.) The trick is to teach kids to boss back those intrusive thoughts by reframing them with positive statements. It doesn't matter what you could have done. What matters is what you will do the next time. Sometimes kids get so caught up in wanting to succeed that they forget that often we learn from experience. Sure, you could have studied for the math quiz instead of watching TV and you would have gotten a better score. But you didn't. So you learned that you need to plan your studies a little bit better and work on being prepared. Is that so bad? Did the world come to a grinding halt when you flunked that test? Not likely. Take the lesson and move forward. Talk back to those negative thoughts by asserting positive thoughts.

Building assertiveness takes time. Depending on the personality of your child, it can happen in a few months or it might take a few years. Patience is crucial. Because when they finally do find their voices, when they can finally assert their needs in a confident manner without stepping on the toes of another, a world of happiness becomes available to them. They feel confident, secure, and capable of coping with difficult situations. They take risks that they would have otherwise avoided and experience better relationships with others. They truly begin to thrive as the individuals that they are. And that makes for happier kids.

7

Embracing Differences

Every individual matters. Every individual has a role to play.
Every individual makes a difference.

—JANE GOODALL

I ONCE WORKED WITH a child so full of hatred, so consumed with revenge and anger that I had to debrief after just about every session. At just seven years old, Jason was lost in a sea of negativity. The hatred was a learned behavior, as you might suspect. But he didn't learn it from his parents. His parents were both humiliated and mortified every time a report of racist and hateful behavior came home from school. They attended meetings. They sent him to groups. They tried family therapy. They tried medication for his impulse control disorder, hoping that better impulse control would decrease the tirades. It didn't. And then one day he ended up in my office.

The hatred, it turned out, began in response to bullying. Scrawny, loud-mouthed, and exceptionally smart, Jason was an easy target, it seemed, for the kids in his class. He was always correcting them and shouting out answers, smirking when others got the answers wrong. Jason was two steps ahead of every teacher in the school, and he spent his free time memorizing history texts to prepare for the coming years. He didn't know how to relate to others, and he was constantly offending his peers. So they bullied him. A lot. And the school did little to help.

Over time, Jason's hatred became so overwhelming that he lost sight of everything else. He repeatedly yelled unspeakable words to his peers, which only intensified their responses. And although his tirades were challenging to process from my side of the couch, I quickly realized that Jason no longer had any control over his hatred. His hatred was who he was. At seven years old, Jason only knew how to hate. And that hatred was aimed at any person who looked, acted, or otherwise seemed different. (He lashed out at me many times during our sessions.) It wasn't one race or religion that Jason hated; he practiced equal opportunity hatred. And that was hard to undo.

Jason was caught in an endless cycle. The kids saw him as different and annoying, so they bullied him. He felt different and knew how to push their buttons and get (negative) attention, so he did. The teasing triggered feelings of anger and resentment, so he turned around and bullied others for being "different" in some way. He learned to look for differences and spot areas of what he considered to be "weaknesses" and his reign of anger and hatred continued. Jason needed to learn how to find the positives in differences, both his own perceived differences and the differences of others.

I've always disliked the word "tolerance." To tolerate something is to put up with it (like a traffic jam or baked chicken). It's akin to throwing your hands in the air and saying, "If I can't change it, I guess I should just accept it." Teaching kids to tolerate differences doesn't seem to make much sense. You tolerate things that you secretly wish you didn't have to deal with. But embracing, on the other hand, means opening your mind and your heart to something new and looking for the positive above all else. To embrace something is to feel good and happy.

The beauty of young children is that they truly are a blank canvas. If we lead by example and show them that everybody matters and everybody has unique talents, they will learn to simply embrace people for who they truly are. Children who embrace differences are better able to make and keep friends, more open to seeking and accepting help, and better equipped to stand up to bullying. When kids interact with and befriend kids from different cultures and/or religions or who have different abilities and/or interests, they expand their worldviews. They learn to identify with and understand all kinds of kids, not just the kids who share common backgrounds and interests. This understanding of others builds their social skills and teaches them to reach out to others. It also teaches them to care about the world around them. Imagine that!

Children begin to conceptualize differences at different stages. Toddlers and preschoolers, for example, are adept at noticing physical differences. Eye color, skin color, hair color, height, and physical abilities are always hot-button topics for these kids as they try to figure out how they are similar to and different from the people around them. They also tend to call these differences out. In public. In loud voices. Most parents have some story of feeling completely mortified when a young child pointed to a person with a cane or a wheelchair or a Seeing Eye dog and yelled something grounded in curiosity but possibly offensive to the stranger passing by. Although these moments might feel embarrassing for a minute, they are actually wonderful teaching moments. Toddlers and preschoolers call things out that seem different because they are busy collecting information. It's what they do. It's important to seize those moments and talk about the things they notice along the way.

Somewhere between the ages of four and six, most kids are able to identify their own racial or ethnic group. They continue to notice differences, but instead of just physical appearance they look for other clues. They notice the foods kids eat, whether or not their peers speak more than one language, and they start to tell each other about their own customs and traditions. And once they learn that word "ancestor"? Get out the family tree, parents, the discussions and questions about ancestry are endless!

This is an incredible period of growth and understanding for young children. They are hungry for knowledge about other cultures and how people differ from one another. They will ask thousands of questions, and some of them will be hard to answer. Resist the urge to change the topic. Exploring these thoughts and questions with your child increases your child's worldview. Go to the local library and take out books when you don't know the answers. Check in with your good friend Google when you don't have time to get to the library. Seek help from grandparents and other relatives who might have a few stories to share. This is the time to help your children feed their curiosity and understand the wonder that difference offers.

At seven, my daughter has a wonderfully diverse group of friends. Different backgrounds, different cultures, different ideas, different abilities, different strengths, different goals, different hopes, and different dreams. She learns bits of Mandarin from one friend and Spanish from another. She is fascinated by a boy who seems to know everything about laptops and wishes she could go to speech therapy with another friend each week.

Early on she forged a close friendship with a special needs child. They play together at recess a few days a week and yell hellos and good-byes from across the quad each day. It took her a good eight months to ask me why her friend has an aide and gets pulled from class so often. Having worked with kids for so many years, the response was at the tip of my tongue: "Her brain just works a little differently than yours, and having a teacher give her full attention helps her learn." She thought for a few minutes and replied, "She must be happy to get her teacher all to herself. That's something that's good about her brain." She is well aware of her friend's challenges. She helps her carry her things and opens her snacks at lunch, but she doesn't see any of her friend's differences as negatives. Most kids are hardwired to see the good in differences.

Between the ages of seven and eleven, kids have a better understanding of their own racial and ethnic identity and begin to explore what it means to be part of a group. They also begin to learn about how differences, and attitudes about differences, can make people feel included or excluded. They understand that being a part of one group might mean not being a part of another group, and that can be confusing and overwhelming. It is an important time to help your children explore what it means to live in a diverse population.

When children begin to form reciprocal relationships, they start to see the uniqueness of others. They might initially choose a friend because of common interests or classroom placement, but as they get to know their friend, they begin to uncover differences and interesting facts. They find strengths and information and they expand their global understanding of others. The attitudes and beliefs that children are exposed to in the home play an important role in whether or not kids will continue to explore these diverse relationships or shut them down.

Given that kids begin to form ideas about themselves and other people long before they even enter elementary school, it's important to teach them to embrace differences at an early age. Believe it or not, parents send subtle (and sometimes not so subtle) cues to children in both verbal and nonverbal forms (did you really think the eye roll went unnoticed?) each and every day. Your attitudes and beliefs might be confusing to your kids at times, but they hear them loud and clear. And they will internalize and repeat them. If we want to raise kids who find the good in others and embrace all differences, we have to talk openly and honestly about differences. And not just once a year because your child's teacher encouraged you to do so.

Sometimes kids ask difficult questions. Those usually come at the most inopportune moments and can completely catch us off guard. Sometimes silence or a quick topic change feels like the best way to get through these awkward moments. Here's the thing—kids often interpret silence or topic changes as a sign that they've touched upon a taboo topic. While your intention might have been to table the discussion until you're home for one reason or another, your child might internalize the message that it's not acceptable to discuss differences. Many children are literal thinkers *and* they think about things as they encounter them. They might not remember to revisit the topic of the man with a missing leg later in the day, so they seek answers on an immediate basis. It's important to answer all their questions, even if you need to save the specifics for later, so that they understand that differences are not taboo. Differences should be internalized as a welcome topic of conversation.

A large part of teaching kids to make the effort to understand others and celebrate differences stems from the behaviors we model and the expectations we create. Social interaction skills develop as kids grow, and those early skills such as sharing and making new friends evolve into people skills. Kids learn how to shape positive interactions with others by tuning into emotional cues, finding common ground, and extending kindness. Parents can help children learn and practice these important skills by modeling appropriate social interaction skills. Greet new people with a smile, kindness, and respect. Reach out to other parents at the park, at school, and in your community to show your children that friendships are always evolving.

I once had a mom pull me aside to discuss her worries about her son's ability to interact with others. A self-proclaimed "introvert who doesn't like to socialize," she was worried that her lack of social skills would rub off on her son. It's a legitimate worry for parents who prefer to keep to themselves. Although kids encounter other kids and learn to form friendships the moment they enter preschool, practicing social skills is a lifelong commitment. We can't expect children to learn and internalize social nuances during a few hours of school each week. They watch us to fill in the holes and understand how to shape positive encounters with others. When I asked this mom what obstacles crossed her path with regard to reaching out to other moms, she told me that friendships never really came easily to her and she didn't want to fail. As it turned out, she didn't consider herself particularly "likable" because of her quiet nature, and she preferred silence to the stress of working through her social anxiety. In avoiding socializing with others, this mom inadvertently instilled a negative core belief in her son. She taught him that friendship is hard and not worth the effort because not everyone is likable.

When it comes to modeling inclusive behavior and appropriate social interaction skills, we have to consider the messages our children might internalize along the way. It's essential to instill a positive core belief that your child is kind, respectful, and capable of empathy and understanding. Empowering kids to utilize their strengths and focus on the good helps them understand that they can make a difference just by being kind.

Racism and bullying are learned behaviors. Babies don't enter this world full of hatred for people who look a certain way, practice a certain religion, or wear a certain kind of clothing. Babies enter this world looking for love and comfort. As they grow, they begin to connect with those around them and learn how to interact with others. They say that sticks and stones will break your bones but words will never hurt you, but that simply isn't the case.

Words hurt. Words hurt the recipient of hateful tirades and mean-spirited thoughts, and they hurt the innocent bystanders, the children in the room, who learn to hate from watching others hate out loud. Sometimes things like fear, uncertainty, and discomfort prevent people from truly getting to know one another. Instead of reaching out and learning something new, people reach within and make assumptions based on past experiences, stories told by others, or tidbits from the nightly news. To generalize, to make assumptions about another person based on differences, is to teach young children that people are not individuals; people are simply part of a herd. If we want our children to thrive as individuals, we need to teach them to look for, and celebrate, the uniqueness in others.

Kindness Counts

At five, Timothy struggled to make friends. He attended kindergarten in a religious school close to his home. Many of his neighbors and friends from toddler groups attended the same school. His parents hoped that it would be a fairly easy transition for him. But shortly after his fifth birthday, Timothy began to change. He began wearing boas around town. (School dress code prevented him from wearing them to school, although he discussed the topic with his mother regularly.) He put all his creative energy into art projects that his father considered "girlie" in nature. He no longer wanted to play soccer, build with Legos, or learn to catch a baseball. He abandoned all play with his older brother in favor of playing dolls with his sister. He was happy at home. His mother wasn't concerned about his preference for dolls and dress-up and he enjoyed time spent with his sister.

The problems began at school. The boys in his class took notice of his preference for playing with the girls and teased him. Upon paying closer attention to him for purposes of teasing, they noticed that he walked on his toes. They teased him for that, as well. They called him a girl. They made fun of his voice. When they saw him around town, they were certain to take note of his boas and outfits and discuss those at school the following day. Other than a few reprimands for teasing, their behavior pretty much went unchecked. And Timothy's happiness began to fade. The pep in his step was noticeably less peppy and he pushed the boas to the back of the closet. He tried to act more like "a boy" in an effort to fit in and stop the teasing. But the damage had been done.

It's hard to know what to do when kids present as "different" from other kids, particularly when those differences appear to be conscious choices on the part of the child. Parents and teachers alike struggle to find the best way to handle such situations. In Timothy's case, it wasn't a matter of race, religion, a medical condition, or special needs; it was just a boy who gravitated toward things traditionally considered "girlie." Does wearing a boa at age five mean a child will struggle with gender identity later in life? No. It means a child is exploring roles and ideas through play and trying to figure out where he fits in the world at age five.

It should be noted that Timothy's teachers did correct the teasing when it occurred. The boys were asked to apologize each time they teased and the teachers discussed classroom rules regularly. What they didn't do was talk about differences. They failed to take advantage of a teachable moment that was presenting itself over and over again. They ignored the content of the teasing, citing rules and regulations instead. That was a missed opportunity.

Some people prefer to think that teasing is simply part of childhood, that kids should develop a thick skin to handle the teasing and this will help them cope with negativity later on in life. I disagree. Yes, we will all encounter people who appear to lack kindness and moments that rock us to our cores, but that doesn't mean that we should throw up our hands and take a "just deal with it" approach to life. In fact, we should do the opposite. We should take a proactive approach to teaching kindness, empathy, and understanding. We should, from the moment they are born, teach children to find the good in differences.

As a parent, you are your child's intermediary to the world around them. If you feel like your behavior is constantly under the microscope of your child, that's because it is. The way you interact with and treat the people you encounter each day becomes a springboard for your child. Yes, you will see your child's personality emerge as she grows and begins to understand herself in relation to others, but she will take her cues from you. If parents treat people with kindness and respect, even under stressful circumstances, children learn to do the same. If parents exclude or judge people based on differences, children also learn to do that. As parents, it's up to us to embrace differences and teach our children to do the same.

Diverse child-rearing practices across the globe should be a great platform for thinking about and discussing differences in a respectful way. There are endless possibilities when it comes to raising infants, toddlers, young children, and beyond. Even if you're not looking to change your parenting style, there is so much to learn simply by listening to others! Sadly, child rearing has become a constant source of judgment and arguments in recent years. Whether it's on the playground or on the Internet, negative remarks about child rearing are made and hurtful comments are posted. You can trace it back to self-doubt. You can delve into the psychology of judging other parents. And when a celebrity decides to pen a parenting book, you can even find these debates all over the nightly news. But in all the judgment and either/or debates, you rarely see input regarding what this mentality does to the small children caught in the crossfire.

When parents become stuck on one way being better than another (whether it's parenting style, race, political views, teaching style, etc.), children grow up with tunnel vision. They begin to believe that there is one right way to approach life, that life really is black and white. Not only do they fail to see the shades of gray that exist in this world, but they are also likely to miss out on the bright, bold colors that add so much depth to our existence. Teaching children to embrace differences isn't just about raising kind kids who choose not to exclude and/or hurt others, after all, it's about expanding the worldviews of our children and enriching their lives. Diversity enriches.

When children are able to embrace differences, to really connect with different people on a deeper level, they learn so much about the world around them. And when they learn to embrace their own differences as well, they truly begin to thrive. Happy kids are kids who seek the good in all people, including themselves.

Tips for Teaching Kids
to Embrace Differences

Talk About Differences Respectfully

How many times have you quietly hushed your child for asking a blunt question that seemed inappropriate? We all do it at some point. In an effort to protect the feelings of the innocent stranger, we silence the questions of our children. We should be doing the opposite.

Teachable moments are everywhere and it's important to take them as they come. This can be a difficult task, particularly when a toddler points out a person in a wheelchair while strolling through the mall or an older child begins peppering you with questions about a special needs student when that student's mother is standing nearby. Despite the embarrassment that can occur when kids ask difficult questions in public places, the best course of action is generally to stop what you're doing and give an honest but age-appropriate answer. In the case of the wheelchair, for example, you might say, "Sometimes people use a wheelchair to help them get around when their legs are not working well. Some people need them only some of the time, and other people need them every day."

Talk openly about the differences among family, friends, and complete strangers, and use the opportunity to talk about why it's good that people are different. (Imagine how boring the world would be if everyone was the same?) Acknowledge their questions and concerns as they arise and validate their confusion. It's okay to have questions. And those questions deserve answers.

Apple Picking

Believe it or not, fruit can be a real conversation starter when it comes to describing differences. Trying to find a pair of identical apples in a barrel is a useless task because all apples are unique. A larger apple isn't necessarily better-tasting than a smaller apple. A deep red apple might be a favorite of one family member, while another prefers the tart flavor of the green apple. Some are badly bruised, some are lightly bruised, and some have tiny holes. I could go on, but I think you get the point. All apples are unique.

"Apple picking" is a great game to play as a family or with a group of children. The goal of the game is to notice and think about differences so that children can understand that each apple is an individual. Have a bowl of apples ready, including one for each player. Ask each player to close their eyes and choose an apple. Once the apples have been chosen, take a few minutes to study the apples. Cue each player to get to know the apple by studying it. They might want to think about size, proportion, shape, color, marks that stand out, and length of the stem.

One at a time, have each player describe their apple in detail. Draw comparisons and point out differences. Once each player has had a turn to present their apple, place all the apples in a bag. Shake it around (okay, maybe do this lightly to avoid unnecessary bruising). Pour all the apples back into the bowl and ask each player to find their individual apple. What was it that stood out? How did they pick theirs out of the crowd? What makes their apple unique?

This game helps children focus on the small differences that make us all unique. Once the game is finished, the group can discuss their own differences. They can talk about how they stand out and how they see others as individuals.

Color Your World

In books and on computer screens, the world is often painted in green and blue. Land and water. Two colors that differentiate two things. The basics, I suppose. My daughter asks the same question every time she sees such an image: "Where are the flowers?" She prefers to see the world in color, and for good reason. The world is full of color.

It's important to talk about the world around us in fine detail. Children learn to soak in differences by acknowledging the little things. When was the last time you stopped to describe the color of a rose that you passed or to look up at the sky and discuss the nuances in color as day fades away to night? These kinds of conversations might seem to lack depth or meaning, but in the mind of a child these are the conversations that help them begin to understand the world. To reach children and help them learn larger concepts, we have to meet them where they are.

"Color your world" is a great activity for helping children notice the details that surround them. Give your child a printout of the world in black and white. Ask your child to think about what the world would be like if it only came in two colors. Would it be fun? Would it be boring? Would it be hard to find your way? Discuss what the world actually looks like. What colors does your child encounter in your community? How many colors might lurk beneath the surface of the ocean? What might it look like in the desert?

Once you've discussed the colors of the world for a few minutes, ask your child to color their world. They can color the world as they see it day by day, or they can color it the way they would like it to be. When the picture is complete, ask your child to tell a story about it. Have your child describe the colors and what they represent. Listen carefully as your child speaks. Chances are, she already has a very diverse thought process. Sometimes listening just for the sake of listening is the best way to help kids learn to think outside their immediate worlds.

History Lessons

My grandfather was the king of history lessons. Some lessons were more interesting than others, but the sparkle in his eye as he weaved his tales kept me coming back for more. Shortly after he died, my mother told me that I was his favorite. I would love to say that it had something to do with my unique personality, but I suspect it was largely because I sat on his lap and listened to his stories over and over again. There was something about the stories of family members I would never know combined with his descriptions of the places he had traveled that left me hungry for more details about my ancestry.

Grandparents, older neighbors, and extended family can be great sources of historical information for children (even if some of the stories aren't exactly historically accurate—my grandfather always managed to leave out the part about being a clerk in the army. I was sure he saw battle). Kids love to hear stories and extract details about history, both their own family history and stories of the past. They can learn a lot about culture, religion, and differences just by chatting with a trusted source. These relationships also provide a safe space for kids to ask difficult questions. When kids feel comfortable talking, they open up about their questions and concerns. That provides a starting point for addressing differences.

Helping Hands

When kids are put in a position of being a "helper" to a peer in need, they display empathy and understanding toward that peer. A large part of instilling positive core beliefs in children is communicating that you understand that they are capable of helping others and making responsible choices. You know that they are kindhearted and empathic. You believe that they can make a difference.

"Helping hands" is a project that helps kids make connections between the people in their world. Differences exist, but differences shouldn't stop people from forming positive connections and learning and growing alongside one another. When kids see problems arise at school or on the playground (or anywhere else, really), they can think about how they can use helping hands to resolve the conflict and work together.

Trace your child's hand several times and have your child cut out the hands and glue them to a piece of construction paper in the shape of a circle or a heart (it should look like the hands are holding hands). Ask your child to think about a group of peers (it might be friends from school, a team, Boy Scouts, etc.). Have your child use one hand per peer and write down one similarity (we are in the same class, we both like baseball) and one difference (we practice different religions, we have different hobbies) on each hand. Your child should also complete one hand to represent himself.

When the hands are complete, step back and look at the finished product. Discuss the similarities and differences between all the peers and where they all meet in the middle. Ask your child to think about how peers can help each other out when a disagreement erupts. For example, if a group of kids is tasked with a building project but they can't agree on how to start, asking a child who has an interest in building and/or organizing to share his opinion first might be useful (e.g.: John is really great at puzzles and putting things together, so he might have good ideas about how to begin). When we take the time to find the differences, we actually uncover strengths. "Helping hands" encourages kids to find the hidden strengths and become a helper by pointing out those strengths.

Strengths Board

Children with greater self-confidence are more likely to embrace differences and see the value in others. They understand that everyone has strengths, and they look for the good in others. To that end, it's always a good idea to work on self-confidence. (Added bonus: When children can label and celebrate their own strengths, they feel happier.)

A strengths board is a great way to help children understand the unique strengths of those around them. Using a large poster board, create columns for each family member, close relatives, and even some close friends. Have your child write down a list of strengths for each person on the board (this can be anything from "tells funny jokes" to "makes the best cupcakes"). Add things to the list as new discoveries are made. Ask your child to think about how others can use their strengths to help him, and how he can use his strengths to help them. Over time you will find that knowing that differences are everywhere but that everyone can make a difference puts a smile on your child's face.

Attend Cultural Events

If there is a holiday to celebrate or a parade to attend, my daughter is in. She loves celebrations, both big and small, but probably not for the reasons you might think. Sure, there's always a glimmer of hope that candy or balloons (or both—jackpot!) might be involved, but that's not the real reason behind her zest for celebrations. Really and truly, she wants to understand why the celebration exists.

From street fairs to exhibits in museums to informational sessions and musical performances in public libraries to religious events, the possibilities for learning about other cultures are out there. And, more often than not, they are kid-friendly. The best way to celebrate diversity and model an appreciation of cultural differences to your children is to immerse yourself in it. When you attend local events, listen, ask questions, and try new things, you open your child's world to new and exciting possibilities.

Embrace Ideas

I can't speak for you, but my kids have BIG ideas. From transforming the backyard into monster truck jams to taking trips to Africa in search of wild animals to taking the one clean room in the house and making it into a submarine for underwater exploration, they constantly amaze me with their imaginative ideas.

But sometimes I want to say no. Maybe it's ten minutes until dinner and I know the interruption of play will leave them unsettled (which is therapist-mom speak for "cranky"). Perhaps I just really want to have that one room remain clean for one more day. We might even be desperately in need of milk and bread from the grocery store. Whatever the trigger of my hesitancy, I take a few very deep breaths, smile, and watch as they execute their plans. And I'm always glad that I did.

Kids are faced with "no" on a fairly regular basis. Even if the dreaded word isn't actually spoken (I once went five days without using the word "no" but I didn't say "yes" to everything, either), there are rules to follow, expectations to meet (both in school and at home), and voices of reason chiming in regularly. Even though many kids have very big ideas, often those ideas are squashed before they even find an opportunity to voice them.

When we embrace our children's ideas and provide the opportunity to try, we encourage them to think beyond their own immediate needs and feelings. We give them the proverbial blank canvas—the chance to try something new and different. And what our positive responses tell them is this: You have interesting ideas and your ideas matter. I believe in you. That's a powerful message for little kids, and one that will encourage healthy risk taking and exploration of differences in the future.

So go ahead and look the other way while your freshly mopped kitchen floor turns into a worm racetrack. Your children will be better for it (and so will you).

Look for Clues

My daughter recently learned one of those facts that are utterly fascinating in the eyes of a child. She learned that all fingerprints are unique. She didn't learn it from a police officer visiting her school, as I did as a small child. She actually learned it on her own. Ever on a quest to figure out how things work, she was delighted to completely dismantle a marker and find that she could repurpose the ink into her own little ink pad. Naturally, this discovery led to fingerprinting and little brother joined the fun. It was when she stopped to look at the lines that she noticed the differences.

Fingerprints are a great metaphor for kids when it comes to

understanding diversity because they are proof that we all make our own unique marks in this world. No matter where we feel we belong in relation to others, we are all different.

Kids love to play detective. Armed with a notebook and a glitter pen, my daughter started listing likes and dislikes, strengths, favorite things, and other points of interest for our family. Noting that Liam likes to do puzzles while she prefers to draw but they both feel calm while doing those things helped her think of ways to help him when he's sad or frustrated.

Playing detective, by uncovering differences, helps kids get to know people on a deeper level and increases empathy and understanding. In the classroom, it's a fun way to learn more about cultures and personalities—to uncover the details that make up the whole. Too often we gloss over the details in favor of pushing life along, but when we stop to truly connect with others, we learn and grow as individuals.

Help your child learn to uncover and embrace differences by making fingerprints, asking detailed questions, and taking the time to get to know someone on a deeper level.

International Collage

One of the fun things about having a husband who frequently travels the globe is that he shares little cultural tidbits with us along his travels. It's never quite enough, though. Little kids tend to be hungry for information and they genuinely want to know what kids in other countries like to play, eat, and watch on TV. They want to know how they learn, what they do on summer vacation, and how they sleep at night. While it's hard to answer *every* question that comes my way (Do kids in Germany sleep with a lovey?), I do my best to research different countries and provide them with some information.

An international collage is a great way to help kids learn about different cultures while making comparisons (Hey! We love soccer, too!) and learning about differences. Cutting and pasting pictures into categories of interest (food, clothing, hobbies, music, etc.) helps kids learn about and understand different cultures around the world. It also opens their eyes to the power of differences. They might feel envious of some things and empathetic about others. It's another way to connect and understand other people.

Open an Airport

Working in groups always helps children understand others and embrace differences. When a small group of kids works toward a common goal, they have to put their heads together and use all their strengths to succeed. Tapping into the imagination of children through group play is a great way to open their minds and their hearts.

Airports are busy places. They require a lot of people to keep things safe and running on time. It's not just about stamping tickets and boarding a flight, after all. There are bags to check, accommodations to consider, time frames to adhere to, and food to purchase. An airport is like a small city, when you stop to think about it. Which is what makes opening an airport an excellent group project for little kids.

Whether this task is done in a classroom environment or among a small group of neighborhood friends, kids will work together to imagine and create a functional airport! Help the kids think about the must-haves when flying (tickets, luggage, seat belts, etc.) and create a punch list for them to get started. Then step back and watch them divide and conquer tasks to get their airport up and running. You will be amazed at how quickly they divvy up tasks based on interests and strengths to get the project started. When problems arise, they will have to work together to resolve them in the best interest of the group.

Discover New Roles

Although they don't always articulate it, kids do spend a fair amount of time thinking about who they are. Part of figuring out where you fit in is understanding where you come from. Kids tend to focus on who they are right here right now, so helping them investigate the many roles they play helps them see the bigger picture.

During my first week of graduate school, I was asked to write down all the roles I played in relation to other people, and then rank them according to order of importance. I remember it clearly. I began scribbling without much thought and the result was a longer list than I would have guessed: daughter, little sister, big sister, grandchild, friend, cousin, support system, student, coach, Catholic, American with Irish ancestry, neighbor, nanny, niece, and social worker came to mind. When I was tasked with ranking those roles, I froze. I was a daughter to both my mother and my father. I was a sister to my sisters and my brother. I was a friend to many and a support system to quite a few. How could I choose one role as the most important? I couldn't.

The experience stayed with me, and more roles crossed my mind as I went about my day. The exercise succeeded in opening my eyes to the many roles we all play, and how we choose to play them.

Engage your family in this simple exercise and help your children brainstorm the many roles they play each day. It will help them gain greater understanding of their own uniqueness, and it will also help them see how others affect them along the way. There are two sides to every relationship, and understanding how both sides work is an essential component of embracing differences and relating to others in a positive way.

8

In Support of Passion

One can never consent to creep when one feels the impulse to soar.

—HELEN KELLER

FOR HIS FOURTH BIRTHDAY, my son had just one item on his wish list: a set of cymbals for his drum kit. I should back up. For starters, I begged (BEGGED) my husband not to bring a drum kit into our home. Bring any other instrument home, I said, but please not the drums. There isn't enough Advil in the state of California to counteract two toddlers and a drum kit. Claiming it would be fine in the garage, he did it anyway. So then I begged him not to buy cymbals.

For his fourth birthday, my son received a set of beautiful cymbals that professional players everywhere bring from gig to gig. You might think that I caved to the pressure or couldn't stand the constant requests (for the record, he didn't ask very often). I didn't. I caved to passion. My son might not actually grow up to be a drummer, and right now he's pretty certain that driving a logging truck is the way to go, but he is passionate about playing. He sits at his drum kit and plays along to Coldplay and John Mayer. He listens to the beats and counts along. He is free, expressive, and happy. Where my daughter needs to write, draw, and live in an imaginary world, my four-year-old son needs to play the drums. But it should be noted that he recently developed a new passion—piano. You see what I did there? I allowed passion to shift (more on that later).

Lately there is a push in the world of parenting to raise the perfectly well-rounded child. Some of this is the trickle-down effect of the college and private school admissions process. Depending on where you live, the pressure to raise the kid who can do everything and get a community service project off the ground is enormous. But the truth is that it's nearly impossible to be good at *everything*. Sure, there are athletes who also excel in academics, actors who sing, and artists who write. But the push to excel at all things leaves little room for passion.

In fact, we've really gone off course when it comes to developing passion. Peter Gray discusses the importance of self-education in his book *Free to Learn: Why Unleashing the Instinct to Play Will Make Our Children Happier, More Self-Reliant, and Better Students for Life*. In exploring the importance of allowing adequate time for children to play without pressure or judgment, Gray explains: "That time is needed to make friends, play with ideas and materials, experience and overcome boredom, learn from one's own mistakes, and develop passions."[9] Bottom line: We can't push them toward one passion or another; we have to give them the time to figure out what drives them.

Some people equate passion with excelling above and beyond. They feel that knowing your true passion will guide you to the career that best fits you. But passion is simply a strong emotion, or excitement about something. Cultivating passion doesn't mean forcing your kid into one particular activity or overwhelming your kid with several activities until you find his ultimate strength—the one that will get him into college. Cultivating passion means allowing your child to truly enjoy something (or a few somethings), even if it is time-limited. It means supporting your child's interests and getting to know what really makes your child happy. And sometimes that means driving in the slow lane even when everyone around you appears to be in a high-speed race to the finish.

"College-ready" and "career-ready" are the current buzzwords permeating the world of education. At some point, it will be something else. But for right now, educators are determined to ensure that all children are college- and career-ready when they finish high school, and that begins in kindergarten. While long-term goals are great and planning for the future never hurts, all this talk about the end result increases the pressure for parents. If a five-year-old is working on college and career readiness in his kindergarten classroom each day, what should he be doing *outside* the classroom to be meeting the same goal? And what does all this really mean?

The reality is that passion shifts as kids grow, and that's a good thing. They discover new areas of interest and begin to understand that you can't place a limit on possibilities. But it's still important to support their passions along the way. My son might very well walk away from both the drums *and* the piano in the next few years, and that's okay. For right now, learning about music is a source of self-confidence, interest, and focus. Kids who have a couple of areas of passion and focus have a better sense of self (they know who they are and what strengths they have), are more engaged in school (sometimes one interest sparks another and another and . . .), and enjoy a variety of peer relationships (refer back to Chapter 7 for more on embracing differences).

Passion, however, is not to be confused with specializing. I've helped countless parents cope with their anxiety regarding kids who seem to lack any passion at all. These days, if a child doesn't show an aptitude for something by age six, many parents fear an aptitude will never develop. Imagine putting a cap on passion at age six? This fear can cause parents to force kids to choose a focus early on or, even worse, to choose a focus for them.

Specializing often comes up in the world of youth sports, but it can just as easily emerge in music, art, math, science, or any other area of interest. My daughter currently has an intense love of Irish dance. She loves the moves, she loves her teacher, and she seems to enjoy pushing herself to reach higher with each competition. But she also loves soccer, drawing, playing pretend, writing, and swimming with equal amounts of passion. I've had other parents of Irish dancers encourage me to enroll her in multiple classes each week to hone her skills at an accelerated rate and other parents of soccer players hint that skipping out on spring soccer now can be a real career killer down the road. While I'm sure that some of this well-intentioned advice has some glimmer of merit behind it, I refuse to force my seven-year-old daughter to specialize. The best way to extinguish passion is to burn out your child.

When kids are forced into a singular area of focus at the expense of free time, play, and even boredom, the result can include feelings of resentment and loss of control, anger, lashing out at others (frequent recipients include the parents who insist on the daily dance practice prior to anything even remotely fun), poor school performance (see Chapter 9 for more on childhood stress), and symptoms of anxiety and/or depression. While supporting passion enables children to discover areas of interest and open their eyes to new possibilities, specializing closes the door on future areas of interest.

The thing to remember about passion is that passion is individual in nature and often very personal. While I have a love of reading and creative writing, my husband is always thinking in musical notes.

Where my daughter can create something out of nothing in a matter of moments, my son loves the order he finds in puzzles, math, and memorization. You might think that baseball is the very best sport in the world and that the benefits of playing a team sport will help your child find his way in the world, but your child might really, really, really want an ant farm. He might prefer studying nature to organized sports at the moment. That might very well change as he grows, but extinguishing that spark of interest so that he might find a new passion that matches yours is a mistake. Kids need to find out what makes them tick. Kids should be encouraged to follow their own interests as they grow.

Nicole was the daughter of a former dancer. She was eleven years old when she first entered my office. Enrolled in ballet since the age of two, Nicole knew that she was a skilled dancer for her age. Some days, she felt good about it. Other days, she felt like she would never quite measure up to her mother's legacy. In moments of complete honesty, she admitted that dance wasn't really her thing. A skilled artist (although self-trained because her dance schedule didn't allow room for formal art instruction), she secretly dreamed of a career that included drawing in some way. She didn't have a specific job in mind, but she desperately wanted to explore her options. Her mother disagreed.

For a while, Nicole remained focused on her dance. I had the opportunity to see her do a brief performance once. I could understand why her mother was so intent on her continuing with dance. She was graceful and appeared confident while dancing—a big change from her demeanor in school. But the constant pressure to perform and excel left Nicole feeling frustrated and angry. She had no control over her life. She couldn't even choose to take one art class.

Eventually her self-confidence began to fade and Nicole gave up on her dream of studying drawing. When I saw her last (just before she turned thirteen), she had finally taken a break from dance and replaced it with time spent alone in her bedroom, drawing all over her notebooks. To this day I wonder if she ever did follow her heart and enroll in some art classes at the college level. It's a sad thing to see passion fade away in a child simply because the parent had different plans.

On the other end of the passion spectrum, of course, are the parents who feel that more is better. Forget specializing, these passion chasers want their kids to have an intense love of and excel in a little bit of everything. This tends to manifest as kids playing multiple sports per season, learning an instrument, and taking an extra class or two just for fun. These kids are stressed out, exhausted, and constantly feeling the pressure. When every moment of your life is accounted for either by learning in the classroom or finding your strengths outside the classroom, how can you ever truly know who you are and what makes you happy?

While there are kids out there who truly enjoy playing team sports and seem to want to play as many sports as possible, it's important to help those kids learn to slow down and appreciate what they're doing. When kids are constantly running from one thing to the next, it's difficult to enjoy any one thing. Where is the passion in that? The thing about supporting passion is that it means supporting your child in the activities of their choice by way of providing encouragement and praise for effort. Often, the kids running from team to team are the ones who feel that they won't make the cut if they don't keep playing. That's not passion. That's feeding into external pressure.

Our culture provides children with so many options and opportunities that, frankly, it's a bit overwhelming. It's no surprise that many kids struggle to find what really motivates them. As parents, it's up to us to help maintain forward movement with our children. So soccer didn't turn out to be the thing that your child couldn't stop talking about—that doesn't mean that your child lacks passion or drive. It simply means that your child hasn't found her passion(s).

The only thing parents seem to dislike more than participation trophies is quitting. Quitting a sport or activity is often seen as giving up, and parents who allow their children to quit are viewed as passive or overindulgent. But where does the child fit into any of this? Childhood shouldn't be about learning difficult life lessons around every corner. Life is hard enough as it is without that kind of sentiment. Sure, if a child commits to a team for a ten-week season, the child should honor the commitment. But I've seen more parents bribe their children into playing soccer year after year just because they think that child will eventually grow to love it, despite ample evidence to the contrary. I've seen parents offer five-year-olds a Matchbox car for every goal in noncompetitive AYSO soccer. I've seen parents of seven-year-olds offer a dollar per goal, per kick, per touch . . . just to get the child to play another season. I hate to be the bearer of bad news here, but if you have to pay your child to play a sport, your child isn't passionate about it. Your passion isn't your child's passion. Let your child move on. She'll find her purpose. And when she does, you won't even have to open your wallet.

So how do we help our children find their areas of interest and what does it really mean to support them? It's tricky, that's for sure. The mom pushing the child to win every gymnastics competition might appear to be overdoing it to an outsider, but she might very well feel like she is simply supporting her daughter's dreams. I know what it's like to have a child with big dreams, and sometimes supporting those dreams means teaching her to slow down as much as it means encouraging her to work hard. Supporting our children as they reach for their dreams (their dreams of the moment, anyway) is a balancing act. It's up to us to establish healthy boundaries so that our kids don't burn out before they accomplish their goals. Although being passionate is sometimes equated with diving in headfirst and giving 150 percent at all times, often success takes time, practice, and patience. There's something to be said for supporting passion, but taking the slow road to the finish line. Remember the story of the tortoise and the hare? Slow and steady does, in fact, win the race.

As for those kids who seem to lack any passion or drive, think twice before you throw up your hands in defeat and assume that they only want to play video games all day long. It can be hard to find your thing, and some kids just need a little help figuring out what drives them. And who knows? Maybe that love of video games will one day shift into a love of video game or app development! The best way to help your child find his passion is to listen to him.

Every child has a spark, and you don't need to focus on what you perceive as your child's talents to find it. Your child might be very interested in basketball, for example, even though he has yet to sink a shot. Or perhaps your daughter constantly asks questions about sewing, despite the fact that she can't thread a needle. Finding passion and moving forward with it shouldn't be about playing to strengths. Kids should be encouraged to try things that interest them, even if some other talent seems to lurk beneath the surface. If you provide the opportunity to explore areas of interest, your child just might find a strength you didn't even know existed. (My daughter recently discovered that if she plants random seeds, we end up with beautiful flowers.)

Attentive listening plays an important role in helping kids figure out what makes them tick. Unstructured one-on-one time is a great way to get to know what interests your child. If the answer to "What do you feel like doing today?" always seems to be "Put on a puppet show," you'd have to be asleep on the job not to consider looking into theater or creative arts classes. Does he like to make the puppets or create the voices and story line? That's all you really need to know. If your child wants to try new recipes in the kitchen every time you have a free moment, it's time to find a cooking class for kids.

One of the problems parents face is that it's easy to get stuck in the loop of sports and musical instruments. It makes sense. Traditionally, that's what kids do after school. They play on a team, they practice an instrument, or maybe they attend a scouts meeting. The upside of all the opportunities presented to kids these days is there really is something for everyone. Your little fashionista can learn how to make clothes, your little builder can learn about architecture, and your budding pastry chef can learn how to bake. Sometimes parents need to step away from tradition for a moment to find something that truly interests their child.

I once worked with a mom who was determined to find the "right" sport for her son. After suffering through two seasons of soccer (where he spent most of his games picking dandelions), she finally let him quit. Baseball was up next. You can only imagine the tears every time the ball came his way. Sensing that team sports weren't working out, she tried tennis, karate, and swimming. Each one resulted in stress, anxiety, and tears. Week after week I asked her the same question: "When he has free time, what is it that he really likes to do?" Legos was the answer. As it turned out, he spent his nights building intricate Lego buildings and vehicles without any directions. At last, she enrolled him in a building/technology class for kids.

There, he found friends, self-confidence, and happiness. Doing the thing that he loved the most was the key to reducing his stress and anxiety.

We tell kids to think outside the box. We encourage them to problem-solve from multiple angles so they will learn that life isn't linear and there is more than one solution to any given problem. But then we sign them up for soccer or football against their will because that's what "every other kid" is doing. If you want to help your child find her passion and support her as she reaches for her dreams, you have to be willing to think outside the box.

There is a strong correlation, it seems, between doing what you love and living a happy life . . . even when it comes to young children.

Tips for Cultivating Passion

Know Your Child's Interests

We live in a world driven by competition. Kids today face high expectations when it comes to involvement in extracurricular activities. Part of the problem is that the options are endless. Why not raise an expert gardener who plays the trombone and wins an MVP trophy each season? And what if he could also be published at age twelve? Wouldn't that be great? Harvard, here we come!

In the race to nowhere, children's unique interests and needs are often forgotten. It's easy to get caught up in what everyone else is doing. Children have a natural tendency to want to be with their friends, and will sometimes ask to participate in sports or classes simply to be with friends.

It's important to help kids find their strengths and passions so they can experience greater confidence and happiness (versus struggling to keep up with the crowd). Get to know what makes your child tick. Is art what brings your child to life? Does your child love to learn words in different languages? Start there. Listen to what excites your child. Observe as your child engages in various activities to determine what brings her the greatest happiness.

Try to consider one important fact: Not every area of passion requires a class or structured activity. Your little writer only needs journals, fun pens, and a quiet space, after all.

Baby Steps

Many parents feel that the best way to figure out what their kids are good at is to enroll them in absolutely everything. Kids can quickly become overwhelmed by choices and agree to everything without really understanding what that means. What parents fail to realize is that this often leads to burnout, and it is very difficult to find even a hint of passion when a kid is utterly exhausted and longing for a break. An activity a day means no free play, after all.

The nice thing about kid world is that it's essentially broken down into seasons. You've got four seasons per calendar year to fit in a few activities and figure out what makes your child happy. Aim for one to two activities per season. When kids have manageable schedules, they are better able to tap into their strengths and find their passions. When they find what excites them the most, they find happiness.

Ask, Don't Tell

As tempting as it is to watch for clues (or better yet, strengths) and gently nudge children in a certain direction based on your detective work, it won't necessarily inspire passion in your child. If the key to finding passion is self-discovery, your child needs time and space to make his own discoveries. But conversations can be useful. Sometimes kids need to think out loud to figure out what inspires them, and asking open-ended questions can help young kids explore their areas of interest. Examples include:

- What makes you happy?
- If you could play only one thing from now on, what would you play?
- What do you love learning about in school?
- What's important to you?
- What's missing in school? Is there something you wish you could do there but there just isn't time?
- What's your favorite TV show right now? What do you love about it?
- If you could live somewhere else, where would you live? What do you like about that place?
- What's your favorite book right now?

Giving your child the chance to share her likes and dislikes in a relaxed atmosphere (that's important—firing off questions under stress doesn't help with self-discovery) gets kids thinking about their interests. When they feel empowered to show their true colors, kids are more likely to discover their passions.

Watch for Sparks

As I mentioned earlier, every kid has a spark. Every child has at least one thing that generates excitement and happiness. While some kids are big talkers and enjoy lengthy conversations with their parents, others rely on one-word answers. That can make it hard to find the sparks, and searching for clues becomes more about observation.

If you were to watch my son closely on any given day, you would find that his play always centers on a few themes: African animals, ocean animals, cars, and building. Day after day he returns to his favorite play scenes whenever he has a moment. These are the sparks in his life (at the moment, anyway). While his piano class excites him and gives him purpose, learning about animals is what gets him up in the morning.

Your child's play is like a window to his soul. Stand back and peer through the window as much as possible to get to know your child's inner world. During stress-free, self-directed play, children discover their passions and show us what matters to them the most.

Think Outside the Box

When the vast majority of kids in the community seem to be involved in a select few activities, it's easy to follow the herd and register your kids for those popular activities. But not all kids are athletes and not everyone enjoys music instruction or drawing classes. If your child is struggling to find her calling, it might be because she doesn't fall into the usual stereotypes. The trick to helping your child find her passion is to think outside the box.

I once worked with a young boy who was desperate to learn needlepoint. With a quick trip to Michaels and a few needlepoint kits, this little boy found a new passion and learned a new craft. Having passion doesn't have to mean joining a team, taking a class, or joining a group of other kids. There are plenty of solitary activities that inspire passion. I spent years hiding away in my bedroom writing stories on yellow legal pads pilfered from my father. Consider things like knitting and needlepoint, building model cars, writing, drawing cartoons, gardening, ant farms, coin collecting, and more. Are you thinking these things don't translate into those superimportant catchwords "college-ready" and "career-ready"? Think twice. Supporting their interests now, no matter how small they might seem, will encourage your child to find the subjects and activities that move them. Besides, your little coin collector might one day become an executive at Citibank. Think outside the box now so that they will hone the skills they need later on. And, more importantly, so that they will be happy.

Follow the Rule of Three

Sometimes less is more, and when it comes to extracurricular activities for kids, less is definitely more. Yes, there are those kids who genuinely *want* to play two sports at once, participate in a theater group, take a cooking class, and join a writing seminar all at once. And on paper, that might even look like the beginning of an exceptionally well-rounded childhood. But there's a catch: Running around from activity to activity and trying to do absolutely everything is stressful . . . for kids and parents. What about that crucial unstructured playtime that we talked about in Chapter 2? What about playing with friends after school with no particular activity in mind? There's an old saying about the jack-of-all-trades, and for good reason. If you're always doing everything, how can you ever focus on one thing?

Follow the rule of three. School takes up a good chunk of your child's life, so you can go ahead and consider that one thing. If we're being honest, the added homework could actually be considered an extracurricular, but that's no fun. Two after-school activities (be it team sports, Cub Scouts, or any other extracurricular) at any given time is a good limit. If your child decides that the cooking class wasn't that great and a drawing class sounds better, make a change. Piling on activities will only increase stress and internal chaos. It won't help your child find a focus or inspire passion. Healthy limits help kids focus and pour their hearts into the things they love, even if those things change over time.

Recognize Success, Not Winning

Overzealous sports parents take note: Scoring goals and winning games is not actually a measure of your child's success. Many kids are naturally competitive and find ways to compete in just about anything. It doesn't help that they are constantly presented with opportunities for winning or losing. *Enter the school art contest for a chance to be featured on the cover of the Spring Sing booklet!* Kids compete over things large and small, and that's part of growing up. But when parents compete? That's a whole different story.

If your children are only recognized for scoring and winning, they become fixated on those two things. It's one thing to be passionate about a sport, but being passionate about playing to win shuts the door to learning and growing. Whether it's on the field, in the classroom, or on the playground, make it a point to recognize your child's successes, big and small. For a child who struggles with spelling, completing spelling homework independently is a big deal. Recognize that. For a child who struggles to relate to others, meeting a new friend at the playground is huge. Talk about it.

When parents take the time to identify and talk about what's going right in various areas of a child's life, they help the child see that hidden talents and areas of passion are everywhere . . . just waiting to be discovered.

Avoid Judgment

So you secretly hoped that your seven-year-old daughter would enjoy softball as much as you did as a child, but she's determined to spend the bulk of her free time working on her stamp collection instead. Or maybe you tried to encourage sailing for your nine-year-old son but he won't stop riding his skateboard. Sometimes our children follow in our footsteps (willingly), but sometimes they don't. It's best to avoid judgment.

It's crucial to stop fixating on the future for a moment so that we can allow children to live in the present tense. In all likelihood, the stamp collection will probably come and go and the skateboard will be replaced at some point, but right now these things might be very important to your child. Let your children be little. Let the scent of Strawberry Shortcake fill the air and let all cardboard boxes be converted into makeshift racetracks for Matchbox cars.

When parents judge their children based on their interests, their children feel rejected. They also begin to develop negative core beliefs. Negative input is hard for little ones to shake. If, on the other hand, parents support their children in their interests, areas of creativity, and pursuits, children begin to develop positive core beliefs. Sure, those interests and pursuits will shift over time, but with positive core beliefs in place, kids feel confident in their choices and are more likely to follow their dreams.

Dial Down the Pressure

More often than not I find that parents carry around a fairly significant amount of anxiety about their children. Parents worry about getting them into the best school, and then about securing the best teacher. Parents worry about enrolling kids in extracurricular activities at an early age to begin building their childhood résumés. (Seriously, apparently that's a real thing now in some places.) Parents worry about how their children perform in the classroom, on the field, and just about everywhere else, and what they can do to improve that overall performance. And therein lies the pressure component.

Yes, we live in a competitive world and future-oriented thinking can help you prepare your child for some of the obstacles along the way to adulthood. But it can also place undue stress on your child. You have to put your own worries and anxiety into perspective and shove them to the back of the filing cabinet when you're engaged with your child. Pushing your kids to play harder or better on the field or micromanaging their extracurricular activities to ensure that they get the most out of them meets your needs, not the needs of your child.

Kids enroll in a variety of activities, and sometimes try new hobbies and activities at home, to learn more about themselves, to figure out what talents they might possess, and to understand what kinds of things make them happy. They find their hidden passions by throwing themselves into new things. Sometimes those activities inspire lifelong goals, other times kids realize that they don't actually want to continue. That right there is the essence of childhood: trial and error. When parents pile on the pressure to succeed, kids feel anxious and disconnected, and fear disappointing their parents. Childhood shouldn't be about attempting to please parents every step of the way; childhood should be about finding what makes you happy and pouring your heart and soul into that thing.

Nurture Optimism

Popular opinion dictates that optimism is a genetic trait. That you either have it or you don't. That's a nice excuse for relying on pessimism during the low moments that life sometimes has to offer, but the truth is that optimism is learned early in life and is primarily the result of experiences. Optimism acts like a shield to help buffer kids as they work through difficult situations. And optimism leads to better problem-solving skills, better relationships, and greater success. Optimism is one of those essential traits that we can nurture in our children to help build their resilience and guard them against things like depression.

Popular opinion also dictates that optimistic people have their heads in the clouds and aren't grounded in reality. The power of positive thinking gets a bad reputation in some circles. But to be optimistic is to understand the realities of any given situation and think about what you can do to make that situation better. In other words, optimistic kids learn how to flip the script. When you take control of a negative situation by reframing it and finding a positive solution, you get to write your own ending. That's a powerful lesson for little kids.

So how do you nurture optimism in your child?

- **Start each day on a positive.** I know—I'm not much of a morning person, either. But I do find that when I ask each person in the family to name one thing they're excited about for the day, the demeanor instantly shifts to happy and excited kids. Starting the day out on a stressful note (rushing to get ready, arguing about homework, etc.), on the other hand, can really drag kids down and increase negativity within the family. When you start off each day with a declaration of excitement, you approach the day in a positive light.

- **Put a cap on complaints.** Some kids do complain more than others. Particularly when they're under stress. Allow your child three complaints each day, and follow those with three positives. In doing this, you validate your child's feelings and help him learn to shift the focus.

- **Laugh more and join the fun.** Savor the moments of laughter to decrease family stress. When you see your children erupting in giggles over something, get in there! Add your own silly spin and a big smile.

- **Lead with optimism.** If you're always stuck on what's wrong in the world, your child will follow your lead. If you choose to pick out the positive moments and place your focus on those, your child will learn that the good holds more importance than the bad.

- **Confront negative self-talk.** If your child makes negative self-statements (e.g.: I'll never be good at soccer, I can't do this homework, I'm not smart enough), it's important to discuss the feeling behind the statement and encourage your child to replace the intrusive thoughts with positive self-talk (e.g.: With a little help, I can do this puzzle. Soccer is fun and I feel strong when I play). Negative core beliefs can and should be reframed early and often so that children develop and internalize positive core beliefs.

- **View setbacks as temporary.** Kids can be all-or-nothing thinkers. Sometimes a poor grade on a spelling test feels like a life sentence for little ones. Help your child put setbacks into perspective. We all have bad days once in a while, and one low grade isn't a game changer. When kids learn to view failures as temporary, they begin to focus on the positive and what they can do to overcome those failures.

Let Them Walk Away

Winners never quit. Quitters never win. These are misguided statements people throw out there in an attempt to inspire perseverance. But sometimes closing a door on something that isn't working opens a door to something new and exciting. Don't let your fear of having a child who is perceived as a "quitter" guide the choices you make for your child. Be realistic. Make a pros-and-cons list with your child. If something isn't working, or is causing stress for your little one, let him walk away. It might just change his life.

The day that I finally walked away from my college hockey team was the day I began the internship that set the course for the rest of my life. I've never experienced a single moment of regret about that decision. Don't be afraid to walk through new doors. A fresh perspective can be life-altering, and help a child find her true passion in this world.

Go ahead and support those passions, big and small. When kids have a passion for something, even if that passion changes over time, they put their heart into it. They learn, strive, push, and work. They feel confident and competent when immersed in their passion. They feel free to be themselves. In short, they feel happy.

PART 2

LESSONS IN COPING

Wouldn't it be great if kids were just happy every second of every day? There would be no tantrums, whining, or sibling squabbles. Days would be marked by laughter, cooperative play, and manners worthy of a royal tea party. Sadly, the real world of parenting is a little less rainbows and butterflies. Stress happens. Some kids are natural worriers and others are stubborn beyond what you can even comprehend. Life throws obstacles at parents and kids alike, and it isn't always easy to get around those obstacles.

Part 2 of *The Happy Kid Handbook* takes parents through lessons in coping with the ups and downs of childhood. With specific strategies to target childhood stress, anxiety, and frustration, to meet the needs of high-intensity kids, and to cope with parental stress, Part 2 helps parents help their children handle the negatives in order to restore positive emotions and happiness.

9

Reducing Childhood Stress

*In times of stress, the best thing we can do for each other is to listen
with our ears and our hearts and to be assured that our questions
are just as important as our answers.*

—FRED ROGERS

MY DAUGHTER WAS JUST over three when I first noticed signs of
stress. My husband was midway through a yearlong tour with John
Mayer, and the separation was too much for her little soul. Although
it wasn't his first tour in her three short years, it was the first one
that she understood. It was the first time that she actually had to
miss him. Her baby brother, thankfully, was none the wiser.

Most tours follow a vague schedule of sorts—six to seven weeks
on and ten days off seems to be the norm. But this one was longer.
The eleven-week winter run was too much to take. Sean was only
home for about ten days, and we just weren't ready to send him off
again. Riley followed her daddy around asking him question after
question and trying her best to shadow his every move. It was clear
that she wasn't ready to say good-bye again. She had had enough.

Five days after he left, the stress set in. It began with nightmares.
My sweet little sleeper who was long past night wakings suddenly

woke with a scream every single night. She sobbed in my arms as I rocked and sang and did my best to calm her down. Most nights, she ended up cuddled with me. It was the only way for both of us to get sleep.

It wasn't long before the sickness set in. Sure, she was around other kids at times and germs were everywhere. But it didn't account for the string of colds, one after another, that kept us cooped up and cranky. The days felt long and the nights went by in a flash. And suddenly my happy little free spirit seemed a little less free. And a little less happy.

So I put on my therapist cap and got to work. We Daddy-tracked using a large wall map with guitar stickers to mark his path. We Googled each city to learn something interesting and tried foods that he might be eating. I let her choose one of my favorite hooded sweatshirts to sleep with at night so that she might feel a little less lonely. (She still sleeps with it to this day.) And we made sure to prioritize Skype chats with Dad in every hotel. Soon enough, her smile returned. She slept peacefully each night, which led to better health and happier days. And, just like that, our world was right again.

Childhood stress is very real and can cause significant emotional and physical problems. It can result in chronic illness, headaches (including migraines), sleep disturbance, high blood pressure, digestive problems, and back and neck pain. Stress can also exacerbate symptoms of allergies, asthma, and diabetes. And that's just the physical. Stress can cause anxiety, depression, problems with socializing, and poor school performance. It should not be taken lightly.

But it's tricky because it can be hard to spot. The symptoms often mimic common daily complaints and it can be difficult to know when to intervene.

Common symptoms of childhood stress:

- Complaints of stomachaches or headaches
- Sleep disturbance (difficulty falling or staying asleep)
- Nightmares or night terrors
- Changes in eating habits (eating more than normal, or less)
- Difficulty concentrating
- Behavioral changes (excessive crying, short temper, increased anger, withdrawal)
- Nervous habits/anxious behavior such as nail biting or hair twirling
- Refusal to participate in normal daily activities (school, camp, sports, art class, etc.)
- Decreased social interaction
- Regressed behavior

Childhood stress can be triggered by a variety of factors. Sometimes it's external stress placed on the child, such as big transitions or academic pressure; other times it's internal stress, such as the pressure to fit in with friends and please others.

Common triggers of childhood stress include:

- Transitions (new school, new teachers, a new baby in the family, moving, etc.)
- Separation anxiety (common in toddlers and preschoolers)
- Medical issues/frequent medical appointments
- Family problems (divorce, illness, death in the family, etc.)
- Parental stress (financial problems, job loss, fighting between parents, etc.)

- Overscheduling (too many activities = stress and exhaustion)
- Internal pressure (wanting to fit in, wanting to get perfect grades, fear of making mistakes or disappointing parents)
- Sibling rivalry/sibling bullying
- School stress (test anxiety is very real and very stressful, bullying, poor relationship with teacher, learning issues)
- Peer problems (shifting friendships and trying to establish friendships can be a significant source of stress for young children)
- Bad news (major world events can really shake up kids)
- Scary stories, books, movies, TV shows, games, etc.
- Extensive screen time
- Feeling pressured to behave beyond their ability/developmental level

Whatever the trigger(s), it's important to pay close attention to kids who appear to be under stress and intervene with help. Most children simply do not have the skills to cope with excessive stress. They need strategies, guidance, patience, and repetition. In short, they need you.

Eleanor was in fourth grade when the subtle symptoms of stress that had escaped her mother's watchful eye during the previous year finally became quite evident. The stress was beginning to affect her school performance. Where Eleanor once had jumped out of bed each morning to go to school, she was finding it nearly impossible to get out of bed in time for school because of her disrupted sleep. She ate less. She had headaches almost every day. And then she refused to go to school. It was the school refusal that prompted her mother to call me.

As it turned out, Eleanor was struggling in school. Although she didn't have any significant learning issues during her first three years of school, fourth grade proved to be a challenge. The homework was much more than her mother expected, and homework battles consumed many afternoons. By the time she finished her homework each day, there was little time for anything else. Three sessions into treatment, Eleanor broke down in tears and admitted that the reason the homework was so hard was that she felt lost in school. She was sure that she was the only one who couldn't follow the class lectures and she was mortified. She spent her school days holding her anxiety in, and she fell apart when she got home each afternoon. Her nights were filled with nightmares when she managed to fall asleep, after hours of thinking about her worry list. Eleanor was in a daze and overwhelmed with stress.

For Eleanor, identifying strategies to reduce her stress, both while in school and at home, was the immediate challenge. Although testing was needed to determine whether or not she had a learning disability and accommodations were put in place to help in the classroom while we waited for results, what Eleanor truly needed in the moment was a schedule overhaul. Eleanor was social and preferred to be busy after school. She took art and cooking classes, played sports, and crammed in as many playdates as possible. She didn't know how to slow down, so she simply kept moving. Assuming that this was a function of her personality, her mother went with it and loaded her up with teams and activities. Even playdates were structured with crafts and activities. The stress accumulated slowly over time, and by the time it hit critical levels, poor Eleanor was shutting down.

That's the most difficult part of childhood stress: It's very hard to spot and it does build up over time. People love to describe young children as "resilient." Kids can roll with the punches, so say the masses. While kids can be resilient at times, they can also be very sensitive. They can be internalizers (these kids direct their worries inward versus talking about them). They can be warriors (you know, the ones who never seem to react). They can hide their stress to please their parents, until they can't hide it anymore. And then they fall apart.

Many kids get to high school before they even understand the meaning of stress. They might experience it along the way, but because it isn't talked about frequently in elementary and middle school, they don't make the connections between what they're feeling and what's actually happening in their lives. They aren't likely to recognize, for example, that the headaches that seem to crop up every day right before recess are related to the fact that they are being teased on the playground. When we teach kids the meaning of stress and how it can impact them physically and emotionally, we empower them to seek help for stressful situations *before* they become overwhelmed to the point of avoiding school or experiencing multiple physical symptoms.

Stress, in isolation, isn't always a bad thing. Stress is the body's physical, chemical, and emotional reaction to any stimulus that is overwhelming, confusing, or even exciting. Yes, happy stress does actually exist in this world. Normative stress occurs when children encounter big transitions or adverse experiences that are mild and short in duration. In fact, when kids encounter stress they develop the skills necessary to cope with negative situations. Kids can and should learn to manage their own stress levels as they grow, but that begins with oodles of parental support and guidance. Kids aren't born into this world with coping skills; they need to learn them. When stress reduction isn't taught and stress builds up over time, kids can reach critical levels of stress. That is when kids begin to fall apart, both emotionally and physically.

The Centers for Disease Control and Prevention (CDC) identifies three categories of stress that children might encounter.[10]

- **Positive stress:** This kind of stress results from short-lived negative situations. A good example of this might be getting a cavity filled or having a fight with a friend. The child might clench her muscles and experience a racing heart for a minute, but this is a very "normal" stress reaction and won't cause long-term problems. With the support of parents, kids can learn to cope with this kind of stress.

- **Tolerable stress:** This kind of stress results from negative situations that are still relatively short in duration, but are more intense. The loss of a grandparent or a beloved pet or a significant family event (divorce or new baby) might trigger this level of stress. With unconditional love and support and assistance from parents, a child can learn to cope with and manage this level of stress. Without love and support, a child will struggle to overcome this level of stress.

- **Toxic stress:** This level of stress results from negative experiences that are sustained over a long period of time (this can range from weeks to years). An example of this is child abuse or neglect. Kids can't cope with this level of stress independently. It can negatively impact brain development if left untreated. Children need appropriate support and intervention to overcome toxic stress.

The average child is likely to encounter stress ranging from positive to tolerable as they grow. An abrupt change in preschool might trigger stress in the "positive" level while a diagnosis of cancer in the family would trigger a longer term and more intense stress level, likely in the "tolerable" level. When parents take a moment to sit back and consider potential causes of stress for their children, they increase their own awareness of what their children are up against at any given moment.

I often encourage parents and children to create stress lists when they're in my office. I ask parents to write their own stressors in one column and what they believe to be their child's stressors in a second column. I ask children to write or draw their own stressors on a single sheet of paper. When we compare the results, the parents are often surprised by what they hear. Kids will identify things like "Daddy works too late" or "I'm terrible at spelling" as significant stressors, where parents thought that their kids lived a fairly stress-free existence.

Understanding the triggers of stress for your children is the first step toward helping them learn to cope. The key to understanding your child's stress, however, is to really listen and focus when your child approaches you with concerns. It's easy to brush off "minor" issues as no big deal, but what seems minor to you might be fairly major to your child. A toy ripped away by another toddler, for example, feels huge to your little one in the heat of the moment. Will he get over it and move on? Sure. But validating his frustration in the moment helps him understand that his stress reaction is normal. It does feel horrible to have your favorite toy ripped away by a bigger, stronger sandbox buddy. And it feels good to have your parent recognize that and help you calm down.

Parents sometimes minimize stressors because we have the benefit of experience. We know that friends argue and make up and that school can be really hard or really easy or somewhere in between during any given year, and we can put things into perspective. Kids can't automatically do that. With practice, they can learn that something that feels *really* horrible right this very moment might not feel so bad three hours from now, but they need help getting there. Kids often come to me with the same complaint: Some version of "My mom always tells me to 'just stop worrying' or 'it's no big deal' but I can't stop worrying when it is a big deal" echoes through my office on a regular basis. Can you tell the earth to "just stop shaking" during an earthquake? Of course not. You can't just tell kids to stop stressing and walk away. That's meaningless advice. They need to talk things out. They need perspective. And they need strategies to learn how to cope with adverse experiences.

My mom was a big proponent of the "mental health day" when I was young. I wouldn't say that she let us off the hook at the slightest hint of stress, but she believed in the power of a day at home with Mom. In fact, the mental health day was such a normal part of my existence that I was shocked to learn that other parents didn't do the same. I didn't miss much school and I wasn't often under stress, but when I was I knew I could count on her to be aware of it before I even uttered a word about it. She always knew exactly when to intervene.

Parental support is critical when it comes to helping kids learn to recognize the symptoms of stress and manage their reactions. Helping children manage stress can be difficult at times, though. As parents, we are natural fixers. We want to intervene swiftly and resolve problems as soon as practically possible to ensure that our kids don't reach toxic stress levels. That can backfire. If you're always troubleshooting for your child, your child won't learn to cope. Like everything else in parenting, it seems, you have to strike the balance between being the fixer and being the one who brushes everything off. You have to acknowledge and validate the trigger(s) of the stress (reassurance that it's okay to feel scared, lonely, or nervous helps), help your child learn to cope with the stress reaction (calm down in the moment), and teach your child how to manage stress as they grow.

As important as it is to tune into your child's sources of stress, it's just as important to tune into your own. Children are quick to pick up on parental stress, and it's essential to create a buffer zone from adult stress. While we can't shelter our kids from every possible trigger of stress that exists in this world, we can avoid burdening them with our own adult worries. Kids don't need to be privy to every source of stress in the home. Kids don't need to know that the bills haven't been paid, the car needs astronomical repairs, or that your doctor wants to run a few tests. There is a time to give children information that directly affects them, and a time to let them be children. Things like terrorist attacks in other countries and natural disasters around the world are terrifying for young children. The combination of too little information and an active imagination can lead to significant stress and anxiety. Create a healthy buffer for your kids. Let them be children as much as humanly possible.

Triggers of childhood stress vary by age and stage, and some kids cope with stress better than others. But all kids need help learning how to cope with and manage stress. The fact is that stress always exists. We are constantly bombarded with stressors, large and small, as we grow. We can't escape it. If we learn how to manage it effectively, however, we can utilize adaptive coping strategies when stress begins to build, and that will guard us against reaching toxic levels. The best way to help kids learn and internalize adaptive coping strategies is to begin teaching stress management as early as possible.

If you want your little ones to experience greater overall happiness, you have to keep their stress to a minimum and make sure that they know how to cope should something unexpected arise. Happy kids are kids who are prepared to handle the ups and downs along the way.

Tips for Reducing Childhood Stress

Revisit the Schedule

I don't mean to hit on this again and again, but it seems like busy, action-packed days are the new normal for kids today. This kind of schedule comes with big consequences. Kids who are always on the go and lack downtime (including that coveted unstructured play-time) are at risk for emotional and physical exhaustion, increased illness, and excessive stress.

Sure, many kids *want* to play two sports per season and throw in some extra activities just for fun. One of the problems with the endless opportunities available to kids today is that it's nearly impossible to choose! We have to set limits for them. We have to teach them to make choices and say no along the way.

Given that many sports require multiple practices and at least one game per week, it's probably best to stick to one sport per season. Yes, there are travel teams and club teams and kids who play on four teams at once. But does that make it right? If you suspect that your child is under stress, you need to look at your child's daily calendar and see where changes can be made. Have an honest conversation with your child about it. Draw the connections between overscheduling, exhaustion, and stress. Involve your child in the decision-making process when it comes to decreasing after-school commitments. In general, two extracurricular activities at a time are plenty.

Prioritize Sleep

Sleep is just as important as food, water, and safety when it comes to a growing child. Uninterrupted, quality sleep resets children and helps their brains stay calm and alert during the waking hours. Sleep is linked to cognition, behavior, and mood. The way you feel when you're awake, in fact, is partially dependent upon how well you sleep. In short, sleep helps your brain function properly.

When children lack adequate sleep, they are likely to appear wired and hyperexcitable (the opposite of the lethargy you experience after tossing and turning). They lack focus and have difficulty following directions. Sound familiar? The behavior of a sleep-deprived child mimics that of a child with attention-deficit/hyperactivity disorder. It impacts learning, relationships, and social interaction skills. It can also trigger increased stress (it's hard to exist in a state of sleep deprivation).

It's important to prioritize sleep for growing children. Prior to age six, a child needs between twelve and fourteen hours of sleep (never underestimate the importance of naps). After age six, kids need between ten and eleven hours of sleep each night. I know, I know, kids fight bedtime and the nighttime routine can be incredibly stressful for parents. But it is essential for growing children. So it's important to create a routine that works for your family and gets the kids to bed at an appropriate bedtime.

- Establish a predictable routine (bath/shower, small snack, reading, cuddling, lights-out)
- Allow plenty of time for the child to wind down with relaxing activities
- Allow filtered light for children with nighttime fears

- Introduce security objects (like that old sweatshirt of mine that Riley loves)
- Consider relaxing music
- Develop positive associations with bedtime (never use bedtime as a punishment)
- Create a relaxing environment (no screens, decrease clutter, shut down loud toys)
- Keep bedtime consistent (even during vacations)
- Anticipate! (Kids always want "one more thing"—kisses, water, and extra stories generally top the list. Troubleshoot and be prepared.)

Body Mapping

Every once in a while I wake up with a very stiff neck. Or worse, a migraine. When one of those two things strikes, it takes me approximately thirty seconds to realize my stress level is too high and something needs to change. As adults, we know our limits. If we happen to push those limits a tad too far, we understand the messages our bodies are sending us. Headache? Get more sleep. Body aches? Slow down. Migraine? Take a day off. We know that if we don't listen to our bodies, our stress will reach critical levels (cue the high blood pressure).

Kids don't make those connections. Frequent complaints of headaches or stomachaches might sound like whining, but kids do experience psychosomatic symptoms when under stress. They just don't make the connection between feeling "sick" and being under stress. They don't understand the signals their bodies send them in the same way that we do.

Body mapping is a great exercise for kids of all ages. (I use this one with adolescents under stress on a regular basis.) It works because it helps kids make specific connections between sources of stress and physical complaints. Have your child draw the outline of a body (and, sure, go ahead and add hair and a face to jazz it up a bit). You want the outline of the body to cover most of the page, leaving plenty of room to fill it in as you talk. Give your child an age-appropriate explanation of how stress affects the body and what things people do when under stress. Examples:

- "When something makes you feel stressed or overwhelmed or upset, your heart might beat really, really fast."
- "Sometimes people feel really sweaty when they get stressed out, or their hands might feel cold and clammy."
- "Some people clench their fists and other muscles really tight when they're stressed . . . even their teeth and jaw!"
- "Sometimes kids feel dizzy or even like they might throw up when they get stressed and overwhelmed."

It helps to share your own stress reactions to help your children draw connections. For example, I grind my teeth at night when I'm under stress and that leads to headaches the following day. Once you've discussed how stress affects the body (the mind-body connection), have your child map her stress. Talk about specific stressors (being left out by friends, taking a math test, a parent traveling) and where it hurts on the body. Have her color those areas red and write in the stressors.

This exercise gets kids thinking about the connections between our emotions and our health, and it helps kids understand that a headache doesn't only come from the flu.

Increase Quality Time

"Quality" is the important word here. Many parents become stressed in response to the schedule of their kids. When you have multiple children, you have multiple schedules. Everything adds up and life seems to pass parents by. Suddenly, it seems, they are off to middle school and no longer interested in hanging out with the family. That's when regret sinks in. Stop obsessing about this hypothetical parenting moment! Repeat after me: I am doing my best on any given day.

One-on-one time with kids is beneficial for both the parent and the child. It strengthens the bond, provides opportunities for conversation, and improves overall communication. But before you get caught up in the stress of scheduling yet another essential parenting thing into your already packed week (which will be less packed next week now that you've read about the importance of slowing down), remember this: It's not the number of one-on-one hours that you spend with your child that counts, it's the quality of the time spent together that makes a difference.

Go ahead and sneak in a weekly date with each child. Go out on an adventure, play at home, or take a long walk around the neighborhood. Just be sure that you are present and attentive to your child during that time. That will help decrease your child's stress level and restore a sense of calm to the family.

Step Away from the News

I'm always amazed by the number of small children who seem to be exposed to the news on a daily basis. While we discuss current events in our house, we don't ever have the news on in front of the kids. I have to admit, this is partially because I don't enjoy watching the news. Yes, I check my CNN app to stay up-to-date on what's happening in the world, but I don't watch the morning or evening news. More often than not, I find it overwhelming. And if it overwhelms me, it will certainly be too much for my children.

The fact is that the news can be scary. Technology has changed the face of "live" TV forever, and we are now privy to car accidents as they happen, wreckage from horrible bus or train accidents that we wouldn't otherwise see, and turbulence on airplanes that would send even the toughest among us running for cover. People film just about everything with their smartphones these days, and it only takes moments for these horrifying images to hit the news.

Imagery is everything for children. The imagination can be a beautiful thing, but it can also be downright scary. That high-speed car chase resulting in a car in flames that your child watched out of the corner of his eye while he colored a picture the other night could potentially trigger fears and nightmares for months to come. We can't protect our children from everything, but we can shield them from scary imagery that they don't need to see. Those accidents might be few and far between in real life, but once you've seen the wreckage it can be hard to shake the imagery. Save the news for after the kids have gone to bed. Don't burden them with details. Give them the gift of ignorance for a little while longer and allow them to play in blissful happiness.

Monitor Content

You know your child the best, and you know what she can and can't handle. My daughter has difficulty with any content that involves death of a parent (thanks, Frozen, we're still working through that one) or harming others, so I'm very careful about the movies that I allow her to watch. I have learned the hard way that it's not enough to ask a few parents for reviews of content. Due to the fact that all kids are different, you won't necessarily get the review you're looking for. (Case in point: Not a single parent mentioned that the parents are killed off in *Frozen* early on and that the sisters are estranged.) You have to monitor the content on a case-by-case basis to know what will be a good fit for your child.

While movies can put specific imagery in your child's head, monitoring content shouldn't stop there. Books, games, movies, apps, and TV can all cause stress for young children depending on the content. Read the books, play the games, and watch the shows before introducing them to your child. And when you do introduce new content and themes to your child, be there. Read with her (*Harry Potter* is great fun, but that Snape sure is creepy), watch with her, and play alongside her. Be involved and help your child process what she's viewing and internalizing along the way.

Above all, limit the overall screen time for your child. Constant exposure to screens (even the "educational" apps) will deplete your child of energy, and that increases childhood stress. If you want your kids to experience greater happiness, you have to teach them the art of finding balance.

Tips for Teaching Coping Skills

Balloon Breathing

Have you ever told your child to take a deep breath in a moment of stress only to find him practically hyperventilating from taking giant, quick breaths? You're not alone. Many kids don't understand the concept of deep breathing, and this can cause them to breathe in and out quickly in a desperate attempt to calm down, only to find themselves more upset as a result. Teaching kids how to use relaxation-breathing techniques when they are calm is the best way to help them understand how to slow themselves down when they're upset.

Balloon breathing is a favorite technique in my house, and for good reason. The combination of positive imagery and deep breathing works for every single one of us (seriously, adults can use this, too) during stressful moments. And once kids really have it down, they can use this strategy anywhere—without anyone else even noticing.

Explain to your child that when you blow up a balloon, you have to breathe in very slowly to fill your lungs with air, and then breathe out into the balloon in a slow and controlled manner in order to fill it. If you blow too little, it won't inflate. If you blow too hard or fast, the balloon will fly out of your mouth. You have to use controlled breathing to inflate a balloon. Ask your child to think of his favorite color balloon (my kids also like to add designs to their imaginary balloons—often rainbows and fire trucks). Once he has a balloon in mind, ask your child to close his eyes and take a big, slow breath in (count to three and cue him until he understands how to do this), and then bring his fingers to his mouth to inflate his imaginary balloon and slowly let his breath out into the balloon. Once he lets his breath out, ask him to open his eyes, tie a string on his balloon, and watch it float away. (My kids like to make up destinations for their balloons, which helps distract them during times of stress.) Repeat as necessary.

Rainbow Breathing

Rainbow breathing is another strategy for teaching relaxation breathing, and often appeals to older, school-aged children. To benefit from relaxation breathing, kids need to learn to control their breathing. This slows their heart rate and restores a feeling of calm. Teaching your child to breathe in for a count of three, hold for a count of three, and breathe out for a count of three helps them learn to stay calm during moments of stress.

Deep breathing on its own can be boring for kids, and positive imagery helps. Have your child lie down on the floor with muscles relaxed and eyes closed. While she practices her breathing, guide her through the colors of the rainbow (you want to do one breath per color). Ask her to think about how a rainbow forms after a storm. First you see one color, then another and another, until finally all the colors emerge. As you cue her to breathe on red, have her think about her favorite red things (e.g.: strawberries, jelly beans). Repeat this through all the colors until she is left with an image of a rainbow full of her favorite things.

Practice Guided Imagery

Ask your child to name her five favorite places ever, real or imagined. They can be anything from a beach on Hawaii to a butterfly garden to a princess castle in the Land of Lollipops. Wherever they are, you want them to be places where your child wants to be.

Teach your child to use relaxation breathing. When she's flat on her back in a comfy place (a bed always works well), have her breathe in for a count of three, hold for three, and release for a count of three. Practice together a few times.

Once your child has learned to slow her breathing (which helps relieve stress), take her on a guided imagery adventure to one of her favorite places. In a low, even voice, describe the journey to the location in as much detail as possible. Point out the sights, smells, and sounds. Tell what happens once your child reaches her destination. Describe the journey home. Ten minutes of guided imagery per day helps decrease overall stress and trains your child to think in pictures to help relieve acute stress reactions to specific triggers. When children are under stress, they can revisit their guided imagery adventures in their minds while using relaxation breathing to help calm themselves.

Melt Away Stress

Although young children might not be able to describe the meaning of symbolism, symbolic acts can go a long way toward helping them decrease stress. Sometimes a small act of letting go can help kids feel relief from the triggers of stress that keep them up at night. "Melt away stress" is a relaxing ritual that can be done daily, weekly, or based on needs.

Draw a pillar candle on a plain sheet of paper. (You know what's great about the Internet? If you aren't much of an artist, you can download a printable of just about anything!) Talk to your child about the specific triggers of stress at that moment. Perhaps a math test didn't go as planned, or maybe friends aren't being very nice. Have your child write or draw her stress triggers on the pillar candle, putting the most upsetting ones at the top and working down from there.

Once the stressors are verbalized and written down, get out a real pillar candle (small ones work well as they burn quickly). Note: It *should go without saying, but never leave children unattended with candles and/or matches!* Explain to your child that as the candle burns, her stressors of the day will melt away with the wax. Some kids like to talk through it and take control by saying things like: "There goes that math test!" Enjoy the relaxation of the burning flame and quietly cue your child to let the stressors trapped in her body melt away with the candle.

Choose Your Own Ending

The tricky part of coping with stress is that people often feel completely helpless when they're in the midst of a stressful event. When kids are under stress, they feel like bad things are happening and they can't do a thing about it. They have no control over their lives. Everything is spinning and they're caught in the vortex. That's a terrible feeling.

Teaching kids that they can take control of their stress, even in small increments, helps empower them. When kids realize that they have the power to make a change, they no longer feel utterly consumed by the things that bring them down. The bottom line is this: You can't control how other people treat you and what obstacles you might face on any given day, but you can control how you respond to those things. There's a big difference between feeling overwhelmed and stressed out and experiencing a moment of stress but working through it.

"Choose your own ending" empowers kids to change the ending to their stress stories. Let's say, for example, that a child is being teased repeatedly by another child in his class. The teasing becomes overwhelming and the child can no longer focus in class. He spends his days reacting to the teaser and trying to get back at him in subtle ways. Sooner or later, the teacher will call home and the stress level of the child increases in response. Instead of getting caught up in the behavior (and that phone call), try asking your child to choose his own ending. Does he want to keep trading quips with the other child? Does he want to be friends with the other child? Does he want to avoid that child completely and find a new friend?

Kids get stuck in a rut when they think they don't have options. Have your child draw a picture to sequence the events (like a cartoon) and fill in the last box with a new ending. Let go of what did happen and replace it with a positive choice and a better outcome. Teaching kids to rewrite history gives them the power to get out of the negative loop and make better choices in the future. This reduces their stress because they feel empowered instead of helpless. And when kids feel empowered to conquer stress, they feel happy and confident.

Stress-Free Zone

I don't know about you, but excessive clutter makes me positively batty. Truly, I feel my stress go up in direct proportion to the amount of clutter in my house. I do have two small children, however, so I've learned to make peace with clutter. The things I might see as stuff, after all, are likely very important works of art in the eyes of my children. But even kids get overwhelmed by stuff.

Sometimes a stress-free zone, even just a small corner of one room, can really help kids cope during the overwhelming moments. My kids have comfy chairs and blankets near their bookshelves in their rooms. I also stashed a stress ball in each room and a few soft stuffed animals for snuggling. They enjoy relaxing music and will ask for it when they want to chill out in their stress-free zones.

Creating a small safe space for your kids to relax in (stocked with the things that help them relax) helps them learn to relax independently. When they're little, they need tons of hugs and kisses to get through the hard moments, but as they grow their emotions can stretch for longer periods and they need strategies to relax. They also need to learn how to cope with stress when they're away from Mom and Dad. Giving them their own space to practice stress relief independently helps prepare them for stressful experiences outside the home.

Helping your kids learn to cope with stress guards them against feeling completely overwhelmed when things don't go as planned. We all encounter stress in our lives, but when we feel confident that we can conquer those stressors we are more likely to get through the difficult moments with ease and find our way back to happiness.

10

The Anxious Child

Anxiety's like a rocking chair. It gives you something to do,
but it doesn't get you very far.

—JODI PICOULT

AT NINE YEARS OLD, Andrea had the weight of the world on her shoulders. She worried about little things (like not hearing the school bell or not having enough time to eat her lunch), big things (like plane crashes and natural disasters), and just about everything in between. Several times a day she wandered down the therapist hallway just to wave to me and double-check that I would, indeed, pick her up at the appointed time for her weekly session. Andrea was hardwired for anxiety.

There were few things that she disliked more than fire/earthquake drills. Sound-sensitive and quick to panic, the shrill fire alarm was too much for her to handle. And when she managed to recover from the sound of it, her anxiety-ridden brain went into overdrive thinking about what would *actually* happen in the event of an earthquake or a fire. But the drills were mandatory and she had to learn to cope. And so we practiced the art of self-talk. We came up with a list of counterstatements to address each fear and practiced them every week. It took *a lot* of practice, a lot of patience, and a lot of cueing, but eventually she was able to talk back to her anxious brain and regain some control during those drills.

Some kids are naturally more anxious than others. Anxiety and fears are perfectly normal, and most kids experience a little bit of each at some time during childhood. But some kids have excessive fears and worries. For some children, anxiety can significantly interfere with their daily lives.

When kids experience anxiety, even when it's fairly mild, they often have disproportionate reactions. Because their hearts race and their minds go into overdrive, many kids tend to have strong reactions to all worries, big and small. A spider sighting during the night can really shake things up in the house, right? Other kids might have equally strong reactions, but in a more internal manner. Kids who tend to internalize their fears and anxieties experience that same feeling of panic and excessive worry, but they keep it inside. These kids are more likely to "make themselves sick with worry" (as my nana used to say) or complain of stomachaches, headaches, and various other aches. While these disproportionate reactions to seemingly small events can cause distress for parents, symptoms of anxiety do not necessarily translate to an anxiety disorder.

Understanding common childhood fears and worries at different ages can help. Fears shift as children grow. While preschoolers are more likely to fear the dark, school-age children have a better understanding of the world and fear more global issues like natural disasters or death (this is why the news can be extra scary). Examples of common fears by developmental stage include:

Toddlers

- Loud noises
- Separation
- Transition/change (even changing the furniture can throw a toddler into a tailspin)
- Strangers
- Sudden movements

Preschoolers

- Monsters
- The dark
- Noises at night
- Ghosts
- Animals
- People in costume
- Masks

School-age children

- Storms and natural disasters
- Snakes, spiders, and bugs
- Bees and wasps
- Being home alone
- Scary TV shows, movies, or news
- Doctors, shots, or other medical appointments
- Fear of rejection (by peers or adults)
- Fear of failure
- Fear of a teacher who appears upset, angry, or disappointed

Kids work through fears at their own pace, and some fears might bleed into the next developmental level. That's okay. Kids need time to process their fears and worries. A particularly negative experience with one specific fear might make it difficult to move on from that fear. When Riley was three, she saw a dog attack Sean out of the blue as we were out for a walk one morning. For unknown reasons, the dog lunged at him and bit him twice on the hand. That moment caused significant anxiety for Riley, and only recently has she begun to trust certain dogs.

Animals, in particular, are unpredictable. Children like routine and predictability because they feel more in control when they know what's coming next. Resist the urge to force your kids to work through these fears before they're ready. Begin by using books and learning about the source of the fear. If spiders incite sheer terror in your child, for example, get some informational books about spiders from the library and learn about them. Did you know that some spiders are actually pollinators? I didn't, either. I try to keep this handy fact in mind when the kids implore me to save the spiders by relocating them instead of simply squishing them.

The active imagination during the preschool years can cause all sorts of fears and worries, and most of them come out at night. Ghosts and monsters are the most common fears, but some kids worry about strangers in their rooms and shadows on the walls. Believe me, I understand, once bedtime rolls around, you just want them to go to bed! Try not to minimize or brush off these fears. They won't last forever, and they are intense for children who experience them. If you don't deal with them, you might find that your child has frequent night wakings and nightmares. And then you just have an exhausted preschooler on your hands every day (read: no fun).

While the magical thinking of preschoolers (which, by the way, is a superfun stage) inspires parents everywhere to concoct quick fixes to fears, such as "ghost spray" or "monster spray," tread carefully. Monsters and ghosts aren't real. And I know, there's the whole issue of the big guy in the red suit and the flying fairy that collects teeth for a living, but the difference here is fear. Filtered light in the room and checking for shadows before bed (I have rearranged my daughter's furniture more than once to get it right) will help ease nighttime fears, as will loveys, frequent check-ins, and empowering your child to talk back to her fears. Grounding fears in reality, even for little ones, helps reduce those fears.

As kids grow, their fears become more based in reality. A child who witnesses a car accident, for example, might worry excessively about Dad when he leaves for work. If you live in earthquake or hurricane territory, you might want to educate your children about your safety plans so they aren't consumed with worry about what to do. School-age children are big on control, and having plans in place helps reduce fears. I know you know what to do in the case of a house fire, but does your child? Establishing and practicing family plans for things like natural disasters, fires, and even being separated in public empowers kids to gain control over their fears. If they know what to do, they are less likely to panic during an event and are more likely to feel confident in their ability to handle anxiety-producing situations in the future. This helps guard kids against persistent worry.

Symptoms of anxiety that cause excessive worry and interfere with normal daily activities (school, socializing, sleep, etc.) can be signs of an anxiety disorder. While you should never attempt to diagnose your child with anything (ANYTHING!) based on symptoms found in a book or online, it can be helpful to understand how severe anxiety manifests in young children. The earlier you get help for your child, the sooner your child will work through her anxiety and return to happiness. If you suspect persistent anxiety that affects your child's normal daily living more often than not for at least two weeks (without any specific trigger, such as grief), the best first step is to consult your pediatrician.

Symptoms of anxiety in children manifest in different ways depending on the child and on the nature of the anxiety. Knowing when to intervene can make a big difference for your child. *Note: The following brief list of symptoms is intended to help you understand common symptoms of childhood anxiety. It does not replace an evaluation by a doctor or licensed mental health professional.*

Generalized anxiety

- Excessive, unrealistic worry about everyday things
- Intrusive thoughts that signal danger
- Anticipate disaster
- Affect multiple areas of their lives
- Restlessness
- Poor concentration
- Frequent stomachaches
- Sleep disturbance
- Irritability
- Edginess
- Muscle tension (aches and complaints about sore muscles)
- Exhaustion

Separation anxiety

- Excessive fear about being separated from home or caregivers

- School refusal
- Frequent tantrums
- Symptoms of panic in response to transitions
- Nightmares
- Physical complaints such as headaches and stomachaches

Phobias

- Persistent, irrational fear about a specific thing or situation
- Might report feelings of imminent danger
- Feel like they need to escape
- Shortness of breath
- Dizziness
- Excessive sweating
- Heart palpitations
- Fear of losing control

Social anxiety

- Excessive worry about being negatively judged or scrutinized
- Fear embarrassment and/or teasing
- Avoid answering questions in class, oral exams, or even reading aloud
- Hesitate to start conversations or join existing conversations
- Avoid meeting new people
- Experience loneliness

Panic attacks

- A period of intense fear that usually begins suddenly and escalates quickly, with no known threat

- Attacks are unexpected
- Worry about impending attacks
- Physical symptoms can include: shortness of breath, chest pain, pounding heartbeat, feeling of being smothered or choked, nausea, light-headedness, trembling
- Child might fear he is losing his mind
- Can occur during sleep

Before you go running off to the doctor with a list of symptoms that have you concerned, it's important to remember that many children experience mild symptoms of anxiety at times. One panic attack doesn't mean that your child has a lifetime of panic attacks ahead. A fear of dogs at age six doesn't mean that your child will develop a specific phobia that requires treatment. Anxiety is a very normal part of childhood. Anxiety can play an important role in helping kids stop and think before talking to that stranger on the bus. In fact, many kids experience a mild form of social anxiety as they begin school and meet new people.

Kids have peaks and valleys as they grow. When anxiety permeates a child's life to the point where that child can't even get to school in the morning, the child needs help. But a mild level of social anxiety (quiet in groups, reluctant to approach new kids) isn't cause for alarm. Many kids go through phases where they don't want to go to school for one reason or another, and sometimes it's just plain exhaustion. That doesn't mean that you should Google "school phobia" and start compiling a list of experts in your area. Sometimes kids just need a little help managing their symptoms and gaining control over their anxious thoughts. And that can begin at home.

Natalie was in third grade when she started treatment. According to her mother, Natalie had always been a worrier. She was the kid who double-checked the locks and made sure the oven was off. Prior to third grade, it was never much of an issue. The family put her in charge of things (e.g.: turning out the lights before they left the house, bringing snacks for a long car ride, or closing the garage door) to channel her worries into something positive. With a list of jobs in place that would help the family, Natalie would remain focused. It seemed to work. Until it didn't. Suddenly, Natalie began reorganizing her bookshelves constantly, and thinking about organization while she was at school. She talked a lot about things like earthquakes and floods and worried about her future. Would she be able to keep up her grades in high school? Would she get into college? Her worries distracted her from her schoolwork, and she started falling behind. That's when her mother sought treatment.

As it turned out, Natalie had always worried about future-oriented things a little bit, but her worries began to escalate when her mom took a new job. Her mom had always worked part-time, but the changing needs of the family necessitated a shift, and her mother took a full-time job with a forty-five-minute commute. Natalie began attending the early-morning and after-school programs at school to work around her mom's schedule, and her mom had significantly less time to just hang out. The change in routine combined with longer separations from her mom triggered intense anxiety, and Natalie was consumed with feeling a complete lack of control over her life.

Natalie needed to learn how to take control over her intrusive thoughts. Her thoughts constantly sounded the alarm about impending danger, but the reality was that she just really missed her mom. We began by working on relaxation breathing so that Natalie would be able to calm herself down during moments of anxiety. Once she learned to regulate her breathing and slow down, we moved into self-talk. Describing intrusive thoughts as "bossy" and "often misleading," I helped Natalie learn how to create counterstatements to "boss back" her intrusive thoughts. With practice, she learned to stop her anxiety the moment it was triggered. Natalie learned how to gain control over the anxiety that once consumed her.

Managing anxiety and coping with negative input takes practice. Although it might seem like some worries don't make much sense, they can still have a powerful effect on young children. That's the thing about anxiety, after all; more often than not it just isn't rational. While living with a chronic worrier can be difficult on parents, it's even more difficult for the young child doing the worrying. Try to keep that in mind as you help your child learn to process and cope with a long list of worries.

It's difficult to find happiness when you live in a perpetual state of anxious thoughts (regardless of whether or not the thoughts and fears are rational). Anxiety and worry take up a lot of emotional space and generally leave kids feeling uneasy. While some kids might always experience low-grade anxiety or a propensity for worry (genetics can be strong, regardless of environmental factors), they can learn to cope with and manage anxious thoughts in order to increase happy thoughts and feelings.

Tips for Helping an Anxious Child Cope

Boss Back

It is positively essential for anxious kids to learn and master the art of self-talk. I know what you're thinking—what does talking to yourself have to do with getting rid of anxiety? A lot. As we saw with Natalie, bossing back intrusive thoughts by replacing them with positive counterthoughts empowers kids to take control over their anxious thoughts.

Although it sounds easy, it can be hard for kids to use self-talk effectively. Anxiety can be all-consuming, and once those intrusive thoughts spin out of control it's difficult to calm down. The trick is to practice self-talk when kids are feeling calm. I often ask kids to draw an image of the anxious voice in their brains. What would he look like? Is he big? What's his favorite color? Does he have hair? Having an image to talk back to help helps kids visualize the process, and that will stick with them when caught in an anxious moment.

Once your child has a face for his anxiety, ask him to tell you his biggest fears and worries. Make a list for him as he talks. Share some of your own worries so that he knows he's not alone. Once you have a solid worry list in your hand, help your child think of positive counterstatements to replace the intrusive ones. For example, a child who worries about making friends might replace "No one likes me" with "I'm really good at making friends because I'm kind and funny." When parents get involved in the process, it helps kids feel less embarrassed and normalizes it. Get in there and boss back your own worries to show your child that we all have to learn how to take control!

Create a Worry Box

Kids love concrete strategies. When they can see it, feel it, and keep it nearby, it gives them a sense of control over the situation. A worry box is a great way to help kids put their worries away for the night.

Give your child a small box to decorate any way he chooses. Be sure to provide plenty of stickers, buttons, glitter paint, magazine clippings, and any other items that might draw in your child and inspire creativity. Explain that your child is creating a worry box—a safe place to keep his worries tucked away at night so that he can drift off to sleep with fewer worries.

Ask your child to name his biggest worries each night. Write each worry on a slip of paper and have your child place the worries in the box. Be sure to talk about those worries as he labels them. Empathize. Try not to jump into problem-solving mode right away. Simply listen and convey understanding. Once the worries are tucked away, ask your child where you can keep the worries for him at night. Have him choose the location so that he knows exactly where they are. Control over those worries can ease an anxious mind and restore happiness.

Relaxing Stories

Many children, after holding in their worries all day, are prone to feelings of anxiety at night. You can keep yourself busy and distracted by day, but when the lights go out the anxiety creeps in. This can make for long nights and tired days. Guided imagery helps.

Please revisit Chapter 9 for a refresher on teaching your child how to use relaxation-breathing techniques. Adding guided imagery to deep breathing just before bed can help kids release any remaining pent-up tension from the day. Ask your child to think about her favorite place (it can be real or imagined, it just needs to be a happy place). Have your child provide a few details so that you can create a guided journey to that favorite place.

Ask your child to get comfortable in her bed and cue her to begin relaxation breathing. As your child relaxes her muscles through breathing, tell a story about a journey to her happy place. Use a quiet, even voice tone and take breaks between thoughts to allow for deeper relaxation. A five- to seven-minute journey provides ample time for kids to release their anxiety and settle into a peaceful sleep.

"Three Good Things" Journal

Journaling is another great nighttime activity for late-night worriers. Drawing pictures or cutting and pasting images is just as effective as writing down words, so even early learners can use this strategy.

The only downside to journaling is that kids can get stuck in a negative loop. They write out their complaints over and over again, without resolving the problem. You know those friends who only ever tell you the bad things happening in their lives? It's like that but with a younger storyteller.

While getting out the intrusive thoughts is important, it's equally important to replace those negative thoughts and feelings with positive ones. A "three good things" journal strikes a nice balance. Ask your child to write down (or draw) the three hardest parts of the day. It can be anything, and your child doesn't have to share it with you. Once she's released the negative thoughts and feelings, on a new page have her write down three good things that happened during the day. These can be small things, big things, or things in between. The point is to help anxious kids see that even when life feels hard and worrisome, good things still happen. Where there are good things, there is hope. Better days are ahead.

Happy Brain/Worry Brain

Sometimes natural-born worriers are so busy worrying that they start to lose track of what they're even worrying about. The older children get, the more their worldview expands. The more they learn, the more potential worries they face. It can be a never-ending cycle if kids don't learn how to talk back to those worry brains.

A lesson in self-talk and a visual aid that shows what fills a happy brain versus what fills a worry brain can really help kids gain some control over their anxious thoughts. Trace a large picture of a brain. (Smart mom tip: Google and download one—print several copies.) You will need two blank brains for this project.

Start with the "Happy Brain." Talk about the fact that the CEO (the guy in charge, that is) of the brain feels calm and in control when the happy brain takes the lead. Worries might pop up from time to time, but when the happy brain is in charge, the worries feel manageable and the worry center is small. Ask your child to fill her happy brain with all the things that make her happy (e.g.: family, riding a bike, friends, etc.). Help cue your child so that she really fills that happy brain with all the good thoughts.

Once your child finishes filling up and talking about her happy brain, ask her to think about her worry brain. Talk about the fact that the worry brain can be sneaky and often hits the panic button when a trigger arises, leaving her feeling scared, anxious, and alone. Have your child fill her worry brain with her most common triggers of anxiety (e.g.: separation from parents, homework, making friends, etc.). Tell your child that when the worry brain takes over, the CEO shrinks and the worry center expands. In fact, it becomes enormous.

Once your child has talked about and looked at the two different brains, discuss the concept of self-talk. In talking back to the worry brain, kids can actually shut down the irrational thoughts and regain control. By saying things like "You don't scare me, worry brain. I know I can make a friend," kids can learn to talk their way through their triggers. Gaining control over their worried thought process brings self-confidence and fewer anxiety symptoms, which ultimately leads to happier days.

Yelling Contest

Anxious kids hold in a lot of feelings during the school day. School is busy and there are a lot of rules. There generally isn't much time or space for releasing worries and confronting intrusive thoughts. But you already know this if you have a worrier on your hands, because your worrier probably comes home and takes his worries out on you. A good old-fashioned primal scream can go a long way toward releasing pent-up emotion.

The moment kids learn how to yell, we start discouraging it. Who in this world enjoys being yelled at by another? With that in mind, it can be hard to convince anxious kids to yell it out. But it can really help. When you stuff your feelings all day, you feel tense. You clench your muscles, you grit your teeth, and negative emotions simmer just below the surface. Left unchecked, those emotions will blow at some point.

Challenge your child to a yelling contest and get those feelings out! Scream into a pillow! Go into the bathroom, shut the door, and yell into the shower. Better yet, run the shower to drown out the noise and yell as loud as possible. Yell together. Yell in turns. Jump up and down, stomp your feet, and do anything else that helps get those feelings out. Then recover together with a big hug, some cuddle time, and a few favorite books. *Note: Yelling can be scary for some kids. Be sure to warn others before engaging in this game with your child.*

Controlled Venting

While stomping and yelling might help release pent-up emotions, many kids do need to verbalize their specific triggers. They need to talk about all the things that caused them to worry throughout the day. And they might want to talk about those things for two hours at a time.

Some venting is good. It helps kids get their feelings out and share their worries with someone who might be able to help. Too much venting, however, can have the opposite effect. Kids can actually vent their way into more stress and anxiety, and that doesn't help anyone.

Try controlled venting. Before your anxious child begins spewing negative thoughts at the end of the day, tell her that there is a time limit on venting. "I know you have a lot of worries to share and I really want to hear them, but I also want you to think about the good parts of your day. You have two minutes to tell me everything bad that happened today, and then let's talk about something good" is a great way to set the tone for your child. Set a timer for two minutes and hold her to it.

After a few hours of relaxation, revisit your child's worries and frustrations with her and share some possible solutions. Saying something like "I was thinking about what you said earlier, and I have some ideas for what you might do tomorrow instead. Before I share mine, do you have any thoughts?" empowers your child to step away from the heat of the moment and think about ways to resolve her worries in the future.

Regress!

You know that end-of-the-day, possibly insane cackling that sometimes occurs when your kids are ready for bed? The second wind, some might say? That kind of silly laughter can actually provide the same amount of emotional release as the primal scream or the controlled venting. Laughter can actually get your worries out.

Engaging in silly skills like making funny faces, juggling stuffed animals, playing balloon tennis, chasing bubbles, putting on funny skits, or singing nonsense songs can really get kids laughing and help them release those emotions in a positive way. Funny dress-up dance parties are always crowd-pleasers, as well. The options are endless when you give yourself permission to regress and simply have fun.

Mandatory Quiet Time

Anxious kids need quiet time to engage in relaxing hobbies (not to sit around and perseverate). Worriers tend to fill their days with busy-work in an attempt to avoid worrying, but that just stuffs the emotions down to save for a later date. The more you stuff, the bigger your emotions become. The volcano is always a great metaphor for little worriers. Your worries are like hot lava bubbling and growing until one day it all just erupts. Having a calming hobby helps anxious kids channel their feelings into something positive while learning to slow down.

The benefit of having a relaxing hobby is that you can think through your worries without becoming fixated on them. The hobby provides an outlet for the tension so that you can think clearly. Knitting, scrapbooking, and painting are always great choices when it comes to relaxing activities, but kids are different and those aren't for everyone. Some kids might enjoy building model cars or boats, while others might find stamp or coin collecting interesting. I once worked with a girl who made friendship bracelets to calm her anxious thoughts. Take your child to a craft or hobby store to help her decide what might work. Forty-five minutes of quiet time each day can really help kids reset their souls and prepare to tackle the next thing.

Relaxation Box

Do you ever find yourself staring out the window, dreaming of a long day on the beach in Hawaii? I do. As adults, we take little mini-vacations in our minds when stress and anxiety creep in. We check out for a little while to avoid becoming overwhelmed. Kids prefer a more concrete approach to checking out.

Kids love to hold things in their hands and look at objects and pictures that remind them of happy times. A relaxation box is a great tool for helping kids take those minivacations when the going gets tough.

Have your child decorate an old shoebox with her favorite colors and themes. She might want to cut and paste images that make her feel calm and happy on the outside of the box. Help your child fill the box with objects and images that evoke positive memories. A shell from a family trip to the beach, for example, might help your child escape to a sunny day playing in the waves. A photo of a favorite relative might conjure up memories of a fun family holiday. Let your child choose the items that hold meaning to her and create a box that helps her take a break from worries and think of happy memories instead.

Anxiety and fears can have a profound effect on the daily functioning of kids. When kids don't know how to channel their feelings and resolve their triggers, the worries grow in size and can affect sleep habits, eating, and school performance. Helping your child find a couple of strategies to ease her anxiety teaches her to take control of intrusive thoughts and replace negative thoughts with positive ones. Although anxiety will crop up at various points in life, a child who knows how to cope with it will be better prepared to work through it and return to a happier state.

Happy kids aren't kids who are free from anxiety every second of every day; happy kids are kids who are confident in their ability to work through anxiety-producing situations and find their own happy ending as a result.

11

When Frustration Strikes

When angry, count four. When very angry, swear.

—MARK TWAIN

FOR MORE THAN FOUR YEARS, my son never really threw a temper tantrum. Like any toddler/preschooler, he had his moments, but he never really had the *Oh my God we need to leave the mall right now* kind of temper tantrum that moms everywhere dread more than explosive diapers on airplanes. He was always just kind of mellow.

Until four and a half hit. Wow. Suddenly, my mellow little boy has very big ideas, and when those very big ideas don't work out in his favor, yikes. Truthfully, routine plays a huge role. His mellow demeanor stays very much intact when he has his perfect little routine, but he also has a big sister. Sometimes the routine has to change.

Recently, our family decided to spend the summer on the Connecticut shore—three thousand miles from home, but in a place where the kids could ride scooters in the street, spend long days on the beach, and see extended family almost every day. For the most part, they enjoyed every second, but their schedules were off—late-night family dinners and just a little too much excitement changed their sleeping habits radically. And the fallout was tough.

I heard the primal scream of frustration when I was in the shower. Please let this one end quickly, I thought, as I threw a towel around me and ran downstairs. Magna-Tiles littered the floor and my sweet little boy stood back, staring at the damage, as he yelled and screamed that he would never ever play with those again. Stomping his feet and lost in fury, he just kept yelling. Until he didn't. And then we got to work on dealing with those big and complicated feelings (again).

Kids get frustrated. From toddler temper tantrums to big-kid meltdowns, frustration is a normal part of daily life. But it takes a lot out of a kid. Explosive meltdowns can leave a child feeling physically and emotionally exhausted, and often they need a recovery period following the event.

While some parents worry that temper tantrums and meltdowns are indicative of a larger problem (such as ADHD, bipolar disorder, or some other medical condition), often they are just a cry for help. Kids are not born with frustration tolerance skills built into their brain structure; they have to learn how to cope. They have to practice getting their feelings out in a healthy way, and they have to practice calming down.

Anger and frustration are powerful emotions and reactions tend to be intense, even in the case of an otherwise mellow child. Common childhood reactions to anger triggers include yelling, screaming, kicking, hitting, biting, stomping feet, and sometimes falling to the floor in the process. Strong anger reactions can trigger any number of emotions in the people witnessing the event. Siblings or other young children might feel scared or worried. Parents might feel angry, overwhelmed, or embarrassed. The child caught in the middle of the meltdown is often impervious to the emotions and reactions around him, though. His emotions are simply too intense in the heat of the moment for him to have any awareness of what's happening around him.

More often than not, anger turns out to be sadness, fear, hurt, or disappointment wearing a different mask. Kids are little and their feelings tend to feel very, very big. They also struggle to differentiate between feelings and behaviors, which means that they don't realize that throwing a toy at someone's head is an inappropriate expression of anger. In the mind of a child, throwing the toy felt good and relieved some of the physical aspects of the anger. The child did what he felt was the only thing to do in response to his anger. And therein lies the problem: What children need, starting at a very young age (think toddlers and beyond), is an anger toolbox. They need to learn how to differentiate between feelings and behaviors, and how to channel those feelings of anger and frustration into a more positive outlet.

One common roadblock to implementing healthy frustration management skills is poor problem-solving skills. As a parent, it's difficult to watch a kid struggle with tasks (big and small). Given that, it becomes almost second nature to jump in and rescue the moment red flags are raised. Instead of rescuing, we should be teaching. Say, for example, your toddler is melting down because the Duplo blocks won't fit together correctly and stand upright. The natural inclination of the parent might be to jump in and reassemble the blocks with a giant smile to indicate that the frustrating moment is over. The better choice, however, would be to empathize with the toddler and then provide step-by-step help so that the toddler can learn how to solve a similar problem in the future. As children grow (and become more rational), parents should offer to help and work together to figure out ways to solve problems.

A key component of building problem-solving skills, of course, is increasing parental awareness of frustration triggers. Triggers change as kids grow, but there are a few common causes of feelings of anger and frustration worth noting:

- Change (transitions can be very difficult for reactive kids)
- Concealing other feelings (try to consider feelings of sadness, fear, etc.)
- Exhaustion
- Unexpected situations (surprises are not always fun when you're little)
- Feeling misunderstood
- Lack of control (kids get bossed around *a lot*)
- Actions of others
- Feeling left out
- Hunger

Kids develop patterns of behavior fairly quickly, and maladaptive responses to anger can become second nature when kids do not learn healthy alternatives. Over time, those negative responses are likely to escalate in intensity, leaving kids feeling overwhelmed and confused after an explosive event. In fact, many kids feel guilty about losing control of their behavior. The aftermath of a meltdown can be very emotional for young children. Many worry that they've caused irreparable damage to a relationship, even if the meltdown was triggered by something as benign as an ice-cream cone.

It can be tempting to jump into distraction mode when a child melts down, particularly when that meltdown occurs out in the world. I've been there, and I'm almost certain that I've used distraction at some point to calm a frustrated child (a particularly long and exhausting plane ride comes to mind). But letting kids experience and express their emotions is the first step toward helping them learn to cope. Teaching frustration management skills isn't about showing kids how to avoid or control their emotions; it's about teaching kids how to understand and cope with their emotions, instead of screaming, yelling, and melting down in the middle of the mall.

Kids can learn to recognize their red flag warning signs of anger. When you observe your child closely during moments of frustration, you will start to see patterns of behavior emerge. Perhaps your child becomes hot, itchy, and physically uncomfortable. Your child might clench her fists or jaw or become very stiff. Throwing something small or stamping feet might be a preliminary indicator of anger and frustration. Watch for clues so that you can help your child understand her patterns. Once patterns have been established, you can help your child identify when the red flags are being raised. When kids learn to recognize anger as it happens, they can replace maladaptive strategies with healthier choices.

Some kids are just more intense than others. They come out with a scream and they seem to react strongly to just about everything along the way. Intensity, when it comes to measuring emotions, describes how strongly a person responds to things, both positive and negative. It is a measure of the amount of energy children use to express their emotions. High-intensity kids are big reactors—they tell the world how they feel in a loud, clear voice. Whether they are mad, sad, excited, angry, or happy, high-intensity kids respond deeply and passionately. This helps them get their needs met quickly, but it also sets them up for a lifetime of overreacting. When their feelings are focused outward, they are loud and dramatic (in happiness and unhappiness), and when their feelings are focused inward, they are quiet, absorbed, and intensely observant.

Susie was the kind of kid who always seemed intense. She worked diligently in the classroom, erasing and rewriting over and over to get things right. She also played with enthusiasm at recess and during PE. She was loud and commanding in groups, and thought nothing of moving from group to group until her needs were met. At home, she was always on. Her mother came to me in tears one day, concerned about meltdowns that lasted an hour at a time (she would tear apart her room to the point where her parents removed everything but her bed from the room), laughter that seemed disproportionate to the situation, and behavior that required so much attention that her siblings were left to fend for themselves. She worried that medication would be the only answer, but she wasn't ready to travel that road with a seven-year-old. She needed help.

I asked her mom to keep a journal to track Susie's feelings, good and bad, small and big, for at least one month. She logged possible triggers, intensity of the reactions, solutions that seemed to help in the moment, and how Susie's behaviors affected the family. At the end of the month, I encouraged Susie's mom to compile the information into a checklist to establish patterns. What she found was that Susie's meltdowns in response to negative triggers most often occurred immediately after school and shortly before bedtime. Her excitability responses increased when she was exhausted, had to endure long waits for something positive, or when her routine was disrupted (on the weekends and during vacations). Holding Susie during meltdowns helped to soothe her, and giving plenty of warnings about transitions seemed to help Susie feel more secure in her environment.

High-intensity kids melt down with intensity when their needs aren't met. They are quick to react, and meltdowns can occur in a moment. (Parents tend to refer to this as "He just snaps.") High-intensity kids also shout with enthusiasm when their needs are met.

They are excitable, prone to rapid speech, and often present as the life of the party when they're happy.

Signs of a high-intensity child:

- Quick to react, both positively and negatively
- Explosive and loud
- Wail with frustration when confronted with something they do not like
- Express emotions in extremes (superhappy, superangry, superexcited, etc.)
- Parents report constantly asking them to calm or quiet down

High-intensity kids need help managing their very big shifts in emotions. While they do get their feelings out, all that verbalizing, yelling, high-pitched laughter, and nonstop going can be exhausting. It takes a toll on kids. Without adequate downtime, these kids can experience stress. Overreacting to everything from broken toys to unwanted dinners isn't a lot of fun, and it definitely doesn't make for happy days. Helping high-intensity kids maintain happiness requires teaching the symptoms of anger, paying close attention to environmental stressors, and providing consistent guidance. High-intensity kids need highly patient parents to help them stay in the happy zone.

Patience can be a tall order when high-intensity kids are constantly drawing energy from their parents and the people around them. It's essential for parents to work together to find strategies that work for the whole family. Experiencing exaggerated responses to emotions can be scary and exhausting for little kids. They might appear to be stable most of the time, but these responses are very draining. The quick reactions also leave kids feeling out of control. Imagine what it would feel like if you couldn't control your emotional responses, positive or negative.

Due to the vigorous reactions to all feelings, high-intensity kids endure a fair amount of negative input from adults, siblings, and peers. It's natural for parents to feel frustrated and exhausted in response to high-intensity kids at times, but this also occurs with teachers and other adults. Siblings are likely to become jealous of the attention high-intensity kids receive in response to their behaviors, or they might begin to lash out as a result.

Both being high-intensity and having strong anger reactions are functions of temperament. In Chapter 1 we discussed the importance of knowing your child's personality. Some kids are internalizers and direct their emotions inward, even when frustrated. They might run and hide out when angry or upset. Some kids are externalizers and direct their feelings outward, but don't necessarily experience emotions as passionately as high-intensity kids do. Many kids fall somewhere in between, directing some emotions outward while holding others in. And then there are the high-intensity kids who experience all emotions to an extreme. Paying attention to your child's temperament will help you determine the best way to help your child when frustration strikes.

Kids who tend to direct their emotions inward will need help expressing their emotions. These are the kids who complain of frequent stomachaches and various other ailments. Holding emotions in is a difficult task and can cause kids to feel physically ill. Although they might answer "Nothing" or "I'm fine" every time you ask what's wrong, this is generally a defense mechanism used to deflect and avoid verbalizing feelings. Changing the way you address them in moments of frustration can help. Instead of asking a generic question, for example, you might share an observation followed by a statement that cues your child to share one detail about the trigger of frustration. Example: "I noticed that you appeared frustrated when your brother changed the game without asking you. Tell me what you wanted to do instead." The kids who hold in their feelings tend to be the ones who don't like to be put on the spot. Making alterations to your conversational style can help your child verbalize and process her feelings in a more adaptive manner.

Kids who tend to direct their emotions outward, on the other hand, are more likely to need help calming their emotions before they learn to cope with them. Often children who externalize their emotions have a tendency to react first, think second. These kids express their emotions before they've even had time to process the situation. While it's important to allow your child to express her emotions when she's frustrated, it's also important to help your child slow down her reaction time by cueing her to stop and assess the situation before she responds. A simple cue to slow down your child will help her think things through before she melts down. Example: "I can see that you're really upset right now. Let's take three deep breaths together and talk about what happened first, then we can figure out what went wrong."

High-intensity kids are quick responders. This means that there isn't a ton of time to cue your child to slow down between a trigger and a reaction. As trying as big reactions can feel in the moment, it's essential to remember that when your child is at her most intense is when she needs you the most. Yes, that raging tantrum in the middle of the grocery store is frustrating for you, too, but she's not doing it to upset you. She's doing it to signal that she needs help.

Likewise, the cackling in church isn't meant to embarrass you or disrupt the service. Your child is simply responding to something and needs assistance managing her emotions in the process.

No matter the temperament of your child, the first step toward helping your child learn to manage her anger constructively is to create a home environment where anger is consistently handled in a calm and healthy way. The initial flush of adrenaline that anger triggers ignites the fight-or-flight response. Often, kids want to attack or fight against the thing that caused that anger reaction (like a big sister for taking a toy or a parent for embarrassing a child in front of friends). Between the ages of five and six, most kids can tolerate this fight-or-flight response without actually acting on the impulses. (They might yell or cry, but they won't hit someone for taking a toy.) Parental response to these emotions is crucial, however. If a parent jumps in and begins yelling at one child or another, the kids build negative associations with expression of feelings and internalize mixed messages. In essence, they learn that yelling regains control and resolves the situation. When a parent accepts the child's anger and remains calm and focused, the child internalizes positive messages. The child learns that anger is acceptable and that it's possible to cope with anger in a neutral manner.

Developing the emotional skills to calm down independently is a necessary first step toward learning problem-solving skills. While it's tempting to find a quick fix to get little ones through the hard moments, frustration management skills require years of practice and parental guidance. Although that probably sounds like a daunting task, for every anger event that you help your child through now, your child is one step closer to managing those very big feelings on her own.

Frustration occurs at every age and every stage clear through adulthood. We can't take the frustration out of life. But we can change how we react to it and what we do with those overwhelming feelings. When children learn to manage their frustration so that their meltdowns are a little less frequent and/or intense, they free up more time to enjoy their lives. They make room for happiness.

The best way to begin working on frustration tolerance with your child is to build an anger toolbox. Remember, some tools will feel miraculous to some kids and like a complete waste of time to others. Helping your child develop coping skills involves trial and error, and it's important to listen to your child's individual anger cues to build a toolbox that works for your child. If you believe that you have a high-intensity child on your hands, please refer to "Tips for Helping High-Intensity Kids" on page 261 and begin there.

Tips for Teaching Frustration Tolerance

Create a "Mad" List

Kids need to get their feelings out. And throwing an enormous temper tantrum is actually one way to do that. But it's not the most adaptive coping strategy out there. Often they feel exhausted and remorseful following a huge meltdown. They might even be more prone to illness if the meltdowns are frequent (it takes a lot out of them physically). They need to learn to express their emotions in a calm and more adaptive way.

Have your child write a list of the things that make him feel really, really frustrated. (Do the writing for your child if he doesn't write—just be sure to let him come up with the answers.) Join him in the process by making your own list. When we work through difficult emotions with our children, they feel less alone. When the list is complete, read it out loud in a dramatic fashion. (A few well-timed "Oh, that makes ME mad, too!" comments go a long way toward conveying empathy.)

And then it's time to start tearing. Hand the mad list back to your child and ask him to tear it up into as many pieces as possible and crumple those pieces into tiny little balls. My son is fond of exclaiming, "See you later, mad stuff!" while tearing and crumpling. The act of tearing and crumpling provides a physical release of the pent-up emotions. Take those feelings out to the trash and get rid of them.

This is a fun and engaging frustration-tolerance exercise that actually relieves the frustration and makes kids smile during the process.

The Paper Towel Game

You know what feels good when you're mad? Throwing stuff. Kids do it all the time (and some adults do it, as well). On the one hand, at least they're not hitting. So that's a good thing. On the other hand, they might break a favorite toy or something else in the house, and they might put siblings in danger.

Feeling frustrated isn't just an emotional state; it has a physical component, as well. Kids often report feeling hot, a racing heart, and like their arm and leg muscles are cramped or tight when they are frustrated. This is a very normal reaction to anger, and some physical relief is necessary.

The paper towel game can help. Soak a bunch of paper towels in a bowl of cold water and bring the bowl outside (or someplace where messiness is okay—your call). Pick up one paper towel at a time and squeeze out the excess water. Hand it to your child and ask her to throw it against the wall while yelling out what makes her mad. Repeat until the bowl is empty.

The act of throwing the wet paper towels provides the physical relief of symptoms. Yelling out the triggers provides emotional release. And the funny sound that results from the paper towels hitting the wall often brings laughter.

When kids internalize their negative emotions, they get stuck. They develop negative core beliefs and begin to think in negative phrases such as: "I can't, I won't, and/or I'm bad." These emotions build up over time, leaving them feeling angry and depressed. When kids get their feelings out on a regular basis, happiness can be restored.

Break It Down

You know what's frustrating beyond belief? IKEA instruction manuals. Page after page of drawings of furniture parts and the necessary hardware to somehow piece the furniture together line the pages of an instruction manual intended to guide you through the construction of something as small as a child's desk. You know that feeling that erupts in the very pit of your stomach when you open the box and see the parts, hardware, and instructions? That's *exactly* how many kids feel when something they really, really want feels just out of reach. Puzzles, building blocks, lack of communication skills, friends who just don't understand what you're saying, and teachers who tell you to do it over and over again when you have no idea what the teacher even wants you to do—these are all examples of kid-sized IKEA manual frustration.

Adults know that they need to break down overwhelming tasks into manageable parts (and possibly top it off with a latte or a glass of wine, depending on the time of day) in order to solve difficult problems, but kids don't. A three-hundred-piece puzzle looks a lot less fun when you dump the pieces out of the box and they completely cover the floor in the process. Learning to attack frustrating tasks one step at a time is an important life skill for little ones, and it helps decrease frustration in the process.

Little kids love to sort and organize, and that's a great first step toward breaking down overwhelming tasks later on. Although sorting and organizing peaks in the preschool years and slowly fades away as older children learn new skills, it's important to keep those skills fresh. Help your child learn to sort and organize before reacting to an overwhelming situation so that your child can learn to tackle obstacles one step at a time. For toddlers and preschoolers, sorting and organizing blocks by size, shape, and color helps them learn to create a plan before building the tower. Puzzles are great for older children because they can sort and organize by end piece versus middle piece and where the pieces fit in relation to the whole. Other ideas: Encourage collections, crafting without specific instructions, laundry (hooray for extra help!), cooking together, and organizing the toys.

Board Games

Believe it or not, playing fifty-seven rounds of Chutes and Ladders (or any other board game that probably drives you bananas) actually helps your child build frustration tolerance. Board games involve turn taking, waiting, a little bit of luck (which can induce frustration when you're feeling unlucky), flexibility (sometimes you have to develop a new strategy due to that unforeseen bad luck), winning, and losing. It's hard to lose when you're little. Who doesn't want to be the first one to the Candy Castle in Candyland? Who doesn't want to draw the special ice-cream sea card? Sadly, you can't win them all.

Sometimes parents cheat to lose when playing board games with young children. I can understand that. That coveted one-on-one time is supposed to be fun and engaging. Who on earth wants to spend that time consoling a five-year-old who falls down every chute along the way? Not me. And there's a place for amending rules and working together to complete a game. But if you let your child win every single time, you're missing an important opportunity (and you're not doing your child any favors).

The frustration that can crop up during board games provides a springboard for building coping skills. When frustration occurs in the safety of the home with a calm and loving parent present, kids can learn to work through their emotions and develop problem-solving skills. Sure, they might cry for a period of time, but once the emotions are on the table you can work together on problem-solving skills. You can help your child reframe the situation so that he wants to try again.

Take Relaxation Breaks

Time-out is often a first line of defense for tired parents when kids have lengthy meltdowns for unknown reasons. On some level, it makes sense. Separate the child from the trigger until the child calms down. Sean and I never had the strength for time-out, if I'm being honest. It takes some serious parental will to leave a screaming child alone in a room, and we just can't do it. Beyond that, it seems counterintuitive.

When a child is in the midst of a tantrum, that child often feels scared and overwhelmed. The loss of control that occurs during tantrums and meltdowns might be frustrating for parents, but it's downright terrifying for the child who can't regain control. Have you ever noticed that your child appears lethargic or worn-out following a meltdown? That's because an emotional release of that magnitude is physically exhausting.

Instead of leaving an emotional child alone with her feelings, try a relaxation break instead. We've always made certain that the kids have a space of their own to calm down and relax. While my daughter might be found drawing on her bed when she needs a break, my son is likely to fill his with cars and books. They do this now because we took relaxation breaks with them when they were little.

The important thing to remember about meltdowns is that they will come to an end. They are time-limited. They might feel like forever in the moment, but eventually the screams become whimpers and the whimpers become sighs and then you're left with a tired child. Relaxing music, rocking, and holding them close always helped mine calm down in the moment, but your children have their own needs. Create a calming space for each child and spend time there both when your child is calm and when your child is upset. When you see those red flags emerging, suggest a relaxation break together to help your child manage her emotions before they become overwhelming.

Empathize

I know empathy is a running theme throughout this book, but for good reason. Never underestimate the power of empathy. Children confront difficult emotions every day. Sometimes they navigate their feelings with ease, and other times they blow. It's confusing and scary for young children. Knowing that you've been there before helps.

Calming phrases to convey your understanding of the situation (e.g.: "Your brother broke your favorite car and that's frustrating. You feel angry. I know what that feels like.") help center your child during a meltdown and communicate your understanding of the event. You might even find that your child snaps out of the tantrum to ask follow-up questions about your experiences with anger or asks those questions while sobbing in your arms. Kids want to feel heard and understood. (Don't we all?) Empathizing with them normalizes those enormous emotions.

Trigger Tracker

Certain kids have certain triggers, and those triggers can change as kids grow. Sharing seems an impossible task for many toddlers, for example, but by the time they hit kindergarten kids are more likely to be set off by things involving perceived injustice ("That's NOT fair!"). As previously mentioned, many kids struggle with a few common triggers, including transitions, feeling misunderstood, surprises, etc. Tracking triggers, and helping your child learn to track triggers, is a great way to establish patterns so that you can troubleshoot with your child.

Observe your child carefully during tantrums. What was happening prior to the tantrum? What time of day is it? When did your child last eat? What are your child's sleep habits? Keep a log of details that might help you understand potential triggers of tantrums for your child. Once you've established a pattern, talk to your child about it. So often we try to fix things for kids without actually telling them what we're doing. Using age-appropriate language to discuss these topics with your child will help increase your child's understanding of her feelings. That will help her learn to manage her feelings more effectively in the future.

Begin the conversation (during a calm moment) with something like: "I noticed that you get pretty frustrated in the afternoons lately. I wonder if you're feeling hungry or tired during that time." True story: Growth spurts always set Liam off. I have to stay on top of snacks and rest periods when he's growing. Have your child help you create a trigger tracker sheet so that she can take an active role in investigating the causes of her meltdowns. She can write or draw or check off a column after she experiences frustration and you can work together to think about possible solutions.

Calming Sensory Activities

It feels good to release the physical tension in your body. I don't know about you, but a good run always helps me view a situation through a different lens. When I've released the tension trapped in my body, I'm better able to take a calm approach to the problem and rely on adaptive coping strategies. Kids reap the same benefits from calming sensory activities.

Daily physical activity is always necessary for healthy and happy children, but you can't send a child out for a run when he's upset. You can, however, have your own toolbox of calming sensory activities to help relieve the physical stress.

- Paper tearing or crumpling
- Finger painting
- A mini–sand tray (think a large Tupperware container with soft play sand, smooth stones, and a few toys)
- Water play (you don't need anything fancy for this—just a kitchen sink and some plastic cups and bowls!)

- Make your own play dough (add a few drops of vanilla for a calming scent)
- Clay
- Get outside and make mud pies

Be Forgiving

I know this sounds like a given, but if you have a child who endures frequent tantrums, you know how frustrating it can be for the parent. It's overwhelming, tiring, and feels never-ending. Be forgiving.

Many kids carry around feelings of guilt and shame following a tantrum. They didn't mean to lose control. They didn't mean to upset the balance of the family or disappoint their parents in some way. Even though you might carry on as if nothing happened, your child is likely to carry around feelings related to the event (even if those feelings seem irrational). Kids need to be forgiven . . . out loud. They need to hear you say that you're not upset, you're not mad, and you have forgiven them. Unconditional love makes for happy kids, and being forgiving plays an important role in expressing unconditional love for your child.

Tips for Helping High-Intensity Kids

Tone Things Down

Among other things, high-intensity kids tend to react to sensory information. They get overstimulated quickly, and can have a negative response to everything from fabrics to lights to the people around them. It's important to watch for environmental triggers and try to make adjustments whenever possible.

- Try low lighting or soft lighting to soothe.
- Music is great, but resist the urge to turn it up for a dance party. Low music is preferable at first—gradual increases can get it to your (or your child's) preferred level.
- Choose soft fabrics without tags.

High-intensity kids need a soothing environment to help them calm down when they become upset or overstimulated. Take a look at your child's bedroom and see where adjustments can be made. Even something as simple as a soothing color (think muted colors like tans, creams, blues, and greens that are rich in color but not bright and overstimulating) for wall paint can make a big difference.

Offer Physical Comfort

Believe me, I know, when your child is in midtantrum and probably throwing things around the room, the last thing you want to do is pick her up and cuddle her. But that's exactly what she needs during those moments. High-intensity kids lose control quickly, and that is a very scary feeling. They don't know what to do or how to calm themselves again.

You can provide physical comfort by:

- Holding your child close to slow down the physical response. Touch can decrease the heart rate and alleviate the rapid breathing that often accompanies such events.

- Gently massaging her back or legs for stress relief.
- Wrapping a favorite soft blanket around her and snuggling her close.

Providing physical comfort can help slow down the acute stress reaction so that your child can begin to work through her feelings. Resist the urge to problem-solve right away. Often, high-intensity kids need time to recover and work through their emotions.

Acknowledge Temperament

Have you ever caught yourself making a comment about your child's temperament under your breath to another parent? Or perhaps you've called it out as an explanation for something. Parents do this frequently because we like to make sense of things. If there is an explanation for something, we provide it. But we don't always provide an explanation for our children.

Talk to your child about his temperament in a way that makes sense to him. Acknowledging that your child gets upset quickly and experiences emotions passionately will help your child learn to understand his own reactions. When a child can understand that he always gets more excited than other kids, for example, he can learn to use self-talk to tone down his reactions at school or during team sports so that he doesn't lose control. Understanding what makes us tick helps us learn to manage our emotions and make choices to increase our overall happiness.

Channel Energy

High-intensity kids need to learn to channel their energy to positive outlets. Yes, team sports are the obvious first choice because they are generally easy to access at any age. But not every kid enjoys team sports, and sometimes the competition underlying team sports can heighten intensity. It's not just about releasing physical energy by running around and kicking a ball. It's about channeling that added physical and emotional energy to a safe place.

Solo sports actually tend to work well for high-intensity kids because they are focused on their own goals. Karate and gymnastics can be great outlets. But many high-intensity kids enjoy channeling their energy to building projects, art, or even science. Find an outlet that appeals to and excites your child for the best results.

Avoid Power Struggles

You have to choose your battles when it comes to high-intensity kids. They will dig in their heels and fight you just for the sake of fighting, so be certain that the battles you choose are the battles worth winning. I can't tell you how many parents of high-intensity children have expressed some version of the same complaint: "It doesn't matter what I ask her to do—she just wants to do it differently."

High-intensity kids don't dig in their heels on seemingly meaningless issues just to annoy you, they just experience big emotional shifts and sometimes it feels good to say no first and think about it later. This is easily mediated by offering choices (two choices, not ten) and providing plenty of warning about changes to the status quo.

Kids engage in power struggles when they feel a loss of control. What begins as a yes-or-no argument can escalate to a full-blown meltdown as tempers flare (for both children and parents). Giving your child two choices that you can live with (e.g.: we can leave now or we can leave in three minutes) and factoring in extra time for transitions will help your high-intensity child remain calm instead of overreacting to every request.

Parent Breaks

Having a high-intensity child means that parents are always "on." This can be exhausting. Parents need breaks. Keeping your cool during your child's intense emotional reactions is an essential component of helping your child learn to tone down her reactions, but it isn't always easy to do.

It's important to avoid walking away in frustration during these moments. If you feel yourself hitting your own limit, set an egg timer for three minutes and gently explain to your child that you need three minutes to cool off in another room so that you can regroup. Try to create a relaxing atmosphere for your child before you leave the room with self-soothing activities on hand (e.g.: stress balls, relaxing music, clay or Play-Doh on the table, etc.).

Three minutes might not sound like much right now, but it will give you enough time to do some relaxation breathing and collect your thoughts so that you can help your child. *Note: If your child is in the middle of a major tantrum and might not be able to keep herself safe, it is always better to calm your child first and give yourself a break after.*

Teach Appropriate Expression of Emotions

News flash: High-intensity kids don't actually understand that running around screaming at the slightest hint of excitement isn't really appropriate. They do what feels right in the moment, and often that seems like overreacting to other people. They need to learn appropriate expression of emotions.

Role-play is a great way to help high-intensity kids learn to express their feelings in an appropriate manner. Make a list of common triggers (positive and negative) that your child might encounter during the day. Examples might include: the teacher gives you extra recess time (excitement), a friend leaves you out (sadness), or Mom doesn't let you go on a playdate (anger). Try to use examples that you know will trigger your child. Take turns acting out emotional responses to the triggers. Stop your child when she overreacts and talk about how she's feeling in the moment and where she can channel those feelings. Use video to record your role-plays so that you can revisit them another time.

Feelings Report

High-intensity kids struggle to understand their emotions. A feelings report can help. A feelings report is a little bit like a book report, except your child won't be graded on it. When your child has an intense emotional reaction, either positive or negative, have your child write or draw a report detailing the reaction so that you can work together to help your child tone down a similar reaction in the future.

It's often easier for kids to draw their feelings than write them.

Writing can be time-consuming and sometimes feels like home-work (who needs more of that?). Create a form with a few boxes that include specific prompts. The first box might say: "The feeling I experienced was . . ." A second, larger box might say: "Something that happened right before I felt that way was . . ." The third box should cue your child to describe (or draw) exactly how he reacted. The last box should ask your child to describe how he felt following the event. In processing emotional reactions after the fact, kids can learn to assess how they reacted in proportion to the event. They can also begin to consider how they might handle that particular feeling in the future.

Anger Thermometer

The anger thermometer is a great tool to help high-intensity kids gauge their reactions to frustrating situations. As the temperature rises, the reaction becomes stronger. When kids use the anger thermometer daily, even when they're calm, they learn to predict how they might react to triggers. They also learn to spot their trouble zones so that they can seek help before they explode.

You can download a template of a thermometer online or draw one. The point of the thermometer is to help kids understand how they feel when they're cool, how they feel when they're somewhere in the middle, and how they feel when they're hot. Cue your child to fill in the thermometer at various points throughout the day. They should use a red marker to fill in the thermometer to indicate the "heat" of their emotions and talk about why they feel that way. Help your child identify his hot spots and talk about strategies he can utilize when feeling hot.

Teach the Stoplight

The stoplight is a great metaphor for teaching kids how to react to events that trigger various emotions. It works just as well for excitement and overstimulation as it does for anger and frustration. It's a simple concept, but the visualization of the stoplight changing colors will stay with your child for years to come.

Draw, paint, or print a picture of a stoplight and place it in the most used room of your house. You might even want to create mini versions of the same stoplight for bedrooms, backpacks, and desks. Explain to your child that the colors of the stoplight represent different actions your child should do to confront emotional situations.

- **Red: STOP**—Stop what you're doing, take three deep breaths, and think about the situation.

- **Yellow: THINK**—Think about your options. Who can help? Should you walk away? What is the best way to react?

- **Green: ACT**—Choose the best strategy to fit the situation and proceed.

Practice the stoplight as a family to show your child that everyone can benefit from taking some time to stop and assess before reacting to emotionally charged triggers.

Factor in Downtime

I know that your high-intensity child might seem like she wants to go, go, go! But she also needs plenty of downtime to decompress.

Make downtime a priority, particularly on weekends. Factor in at least forty-five minutes of quiet, soothing activities per day, longer on the weekend if you can. Over time, your child will learn to self-soothe and choose calming activities to keep herself on an even keel.

Different activities will work for different kids, so try to find soothing activities that fit your child's personality. Examples include:

- Yoga
- Knitting or sewing
- Baking
- Painting
- Crafting
- Reading in a rocking chair or hammock for the calming swinging motion
- Nature walks
- Water play

12

Happy Parents Raise Happy Kids

When my kids become wild and unruly, I use a nice safe playpen.
When they're finished, I climb out.

—ERMA BOMBECK

JESSICA APPEARED completely exhausted when she first approached me. Apologizing over and over for what she seemed to think would be an imposition (she had tracked me down without an appointment), she appeared near tears and her eyes were rimmed with dark circles. The kind you get when you just can't get a break.

She started the conversation by describing the behavior of her older daughter. She was defiant, refused to follow directions, and aggressive toward her younger sister on a regular basis. She taunted her brother constantly and talked back whenever her mother tried to redirect her. And the little sister seemed to be picking up on the behavior. Both girls were struggling in school. The behavioral reports coming home left her feeling helpless. She was sure that therapy wouldn't work. They didn't need to talk; they needed to behave. She wanted a quick fix. After spilling her problems and venting her frustration with her children, she stared at me, wide-eyed and hopeful.

I let the information hang in the air for a few minutes as I considered what might be helpful for her. Referrals? Books? In the end, I chose empathy. I told her that it sounded like things were hard for her. It sounded like she had a lot on her plate. It seemed like a recipe for exhaustion and stress. With that, the tears began to flow. She told me that she and her husband were at odds. That they didn't know how to help the kids. That she was constantly worrying and running around and felt like the kids just didn't listen. She admitted that she yelled at them frequently. Daily. That she just couldn't stop herself from getting angry over small things, like messy rooms and homework battles. Jessica was under stress, and that stress was trickling down to her children.

Stress, and negative responses to stress, can have a lasting impact on children. A study reported in *Child Development* (2013) revealed that when parents are significantly stressed during their child's first few years of life, some of the child's genes can be altered and show effects years later, even into adolescence.[11] There's no denying that stress affects the way we parent our children. When the stars are aligned and everything is good, we are present and less reactive to the small moments of parenting frustration. When something shakes things up and our stress levels increase in response, we are short-tempered, tired, less present, and more reactive to small moments of parenting frustration. And that pressure to be perfect that many parents feel at various stages of parenting? That can add another layer of stress. In fact, according to a study published in 2011 in *Personality and Individual Differences*, new parents who believe society expects perfection from them experience increased stress and are less confident in their parenting skills.[12]

Stress has a tendency to accumulate over time, particularly when it's not dealt with along the way. People, and moms in particular, often tell me that they thrive under stress. Pressure, they say, makes them more productive. I believe that feels accurate in the moment. I write fairly quickly when the ticking of the clock grows louder with each passing second. But that feeling, and that productive state, is short-lived. If you don't get to the heart of the matter and address the actual stressor (as in time management, for example), the stress begins to build. Eventually, something breaks. Stress can lead to sleeplessness, weight gain, weight loss (not the good kind), high blood pressure, heart problems, anxiety, and depression. Stress can affect your mood, your productivity, your relationships, and your ability to parent your child. It can also have a profound effect on your children.

Believe it or not, children actually do pick up on just about everything. You might think your child is playing quietly with his trucks while you scream at the cable guy for missing yet another appointment that caused you to stay home all day long, but chances are he's taking in the stress response unfolding before his eyes while he zooms those trucks around. Children might not understand the triggers of stress, but they certainly pick up on the stress level in the home, in school, and just about everywhere else they go. Even infants are known to cry more often and have difficulty eating and sleeping when Mom is under stress.

High levels of stress hormones can suppress the body's immune response, leading to more frequent illness and even chronic illness. In some cases, prolonged exposure to high-level stress can even damage portions of the growing brain that affect memory and learning. Children exposed to frequent environmental stress are known to have frequent colds, show poor school performance, have difficulty sustaining social relationships, and become overreactive to adverse events. What does this mean? It means they're not happy, and they're not enjoying childhood, that's for sure.

Why are parents so stressed out right now? There isn't a simple explanation for that one. Kids bring incredible happiness, unconditional love, and many gifts into our lives, but they also bring some added stress. Parenting is demanding. It's a full-time job from which there is no vacation. Ever. And while many parents will say that the joys outweigh the demands most of the time, those demanding moments can be very, very stressful. Although all families are different and each parent experiences unique stressors, there are some stressors that seem to be fairly common among parents:

- **Self-doubt:** I don't care how high your self-esteem is going into this parenting gig, kids will make you doubt yourself over and over again. The commitment to nurture a child from birth to adulthood is huge and full of mysteries, crises, and unexpected turns. Am I a good enough mom? Did I handle that well? Is it my fault my child refuses to leave her bedroom? It's easy to say that all parents make mistakes and you have to keep moving forward, but that doubt that plagues parents can trigger significant emotional stress.

- **Time demands:** People love to joke about the lack of sleep that new parents face when an infant wakes every two hours around the clock. What they don't tell you is that you never get your time back. Caring for and nurturing kids of all ages requires a lot of time, whether or not you work, have a spouse or partner, or have help of some kind. Parenting is a 24/7 job with a lifetime commitment (just ask my mom, she's been trying to retire for at least fifteen years). On top of the demands of being a parent, there are also things like laundry, grocery shopping, and countless other tasks that add up quickly. Many parents feel that there simply aren't enough hours in the day, and that is stressful.

- **Insufficient "me" time:** All people need time alone to engage in calming activities. I like to run. I also like to read, and I always enjoy a steaming cup of Irish tea. Believe it or not, I can't fit in all those things every day of the week (unless I want to be up all night reading after drinking my tea once the kids go to bed). But I always make sure to carve out some little something for me each day. Whether it's shuttling older kids to school and activities or caring for newborns and toddlers, many parents feel they don't have time for themselves.

- **Relationships suffer:** Friendships and marriages tend to take a backseat when kids enter the equation. Many parents struggle with balancing meeting the needs of their kids and having the energy to keep their adult relationships thriving. In addition to the stress of trying to balance everyone's needs, this can be very isolating for parents.

- **The urge to protect:** People are always telling parents to stop trying to protect their kids from the darkness of the world (sink-or-swim parenting is big), but those natural mama/papa bear instincts are strong. From safety concerns to behavioral issues to academic stress to social development, parents always have a worry list a mile long. (Don't worry, that's natural.) Even when parents learn to step back and let kids fail, they don't stop worrying about them, and that triggers the stress response.

- **Finances:** Spoiler alert: Kids are expensive. It starts with diapers, but it doesn't end when potty training is complete. Clothing, child care, food, schooling, enrichment activities, and countless other things can place a significant strain on a family's finances.

Daniel began therapy because he had trouble relating to others. Truth be told, he was a bit of a loner. Contrary to popular belief, he didn't really mind being alone. He had a rich internal world and he enjoyed karate classes after school twice a week. But he did show symptoms of depression. His mother preferred to blame his depression on his school. They weren't meeting his unique academic needs, she told me over and over again during brief cell phone calls on her way to work multiple times each week. He deserved better. He did. I agreed with her on that. But it wasn't the school that was to blame. It was family stress.

Daniel's parents divorced when he was young, and his father moved a few hours away shortly after the split. Daniel's brother attended a different school and didn't particularly like Daniel. He ignored him as much as possible. His mother had a high-stress job with a long commute and long hours. She was always on the go and rarely took time off. The financial stress of the divorce had left her no choice. What she didn't realize, however, was that her high stress level was affecting the boys. She was quick to yell and prone to screaming at teachers, and often me, on her way from here to there. She was short on patience and carried with her significant unresolved anger. Daniel suffered because of it.

When I finally convinced her to give family therapy a try, the result was eye-opening. She had no idea how much she yelled. She didn't know that her tendency to rush everywhere triggered stress for Daniel. And she didn't see the negative interactions between the siblings. She was so busy trying to be everything for everyone and make ends meet that she couldn't process the stress level in her own home.

Stress can be sneaky. It starts out small and feels manageable on some level, until one day it permeates everything and completely alters family functioning. Happiness might come from within, but it also comes from the top. Raising happy kids isn't simply about taking care of their needs and making sure that they are emotionally stable. Raising happy kids is about creating a stable, happy, and loving home environment, and that begins with parents. No matter your family situation, your own happiness is important. Your emotional well-being matters.

Tips for Decreasing Parental Stress

Know the Signs

You can't beat stress if you don't even realize that it's happening. While symptoms of stress will vary from person to person, there are some telltale signs that are difficult to ignore.

Cognitive Symptoms

- Memory problems
- Inability to concentrate (or poor concentration)
- Racing thoughts
- Constant worry

Physical Symptoms

- Headaches, backaches, and other pains
- Stomach irritability
- Dizziness
- Chest pain and/or rapid heartbeat
- Frequent illness
- Low (or no) sex drive

Emotional Symptoms

- Irritability
- Feeling overwhelmed
- Feeling isolated
- Agitation—difficulty relaxing
- General unhappiness

Behavioral Symptoms

- Sleep disturbance
- Eating more, or eating less
- Isolating
- Procrastinating

Know Your Limits

One thing I've learned over and over again along this parenting journey is that too many commitments means increased stress for the
family. My husband travels a lot, which means that I have to be
everything a lot of the time. Making choices and paring down

commitments helps me keep my own stress in check, which in turn helps my kids stay calm during his absences.

Remember that trigger tracker I suggested in Chapter 11? You might want to create your own version to track your stress. Knowing the specific causes of your stress will help you determine what changes can be made to decrease your overall stress level. Parents have a tendency to push their own limits to meet the needs of their children. While this is sometimes necessary, it shouldn't become the norm. Constantly pushing your own limits puts you at risk for symptoms of stress, which can have lasting effects on your physical health.

Raise the White Flag

No mom (or dad) is an island. I'm not sure when the trend in parenting shifted from "It takes a village" to "Don't worry, I got this," but we are long overdue for a shift back to the village mentality. Parenting isn't about doing everything independently while baking the best cookies on the block. There is no room for competition in this gig. Parenting requires balance and harmony, and asking for help is a great first step toward finding your own parenting happy place.

Your people can't help you if they don't know that you're struggling. You don't have to tell the whole world, which really just means Facebook, but you can choose to confide in a family member or a close friend who might be able to help you out. Perhaps one of your mom friends knows of a great "mother's helper" in the neighborhood who won't break the budget. Or maybe you have family in the area that can come help with laundry, dishes, or entertaining wiggly toddlers so that you can get some sleep. The truth is that people usually love to help other people, but they can only offer so many times. Make that first brave phone call. You deserve it.

Hone Your Time Management Skills

If you spend your days running around chasing your tail, you're probably not getting much done. Time management is a critical part of parenting. It begins with feedings and sleep schedules and moves into school, classes, sports, and homework. There is always something that needs to get done and somewhere that you need to be.

Focus on time management.

A great place to start is by setting some limits. You simply can't make it to every birthday party *and* every sporting event. Plan ahead. Don't overextend yourself. Make choices. Teach your children the value of establishing priorities. When you teach your kids how to set limits and avoid stretching themselves too thin, you teach them how to avoid stress overload.

There are endless options when it comes to apps and digital calendars to keep your to-do list in order, but sometimes a good old-fashioned wall calendar and handwritten to-do list are the best ways to stay on track. Find a system that works for you and implement it. Check it first thing in the morning (before the kids start jumping all over you) and revise it after the kids are down for the night. Take charge of your to-do list; don't let it take charge of you.

Increase Your Support Network

Find your tribe.

From the moment you see those coveted two blue lines on the stick, you start hearing about the importance of mom friends. Mom friends get it. They know about things like peeing *while* nursing an infant and scraping vomit off the side of a crib at 3 AM. They know when to laugh, when to hug, and when to cry out in disgust. Mom friends (and dad friends) are superimportant. You need them. Trust me on this one.

Even if you are constantly busy and struggle to find time for friendships, you need at least one mom on the other end of the text exchange who always knows what to say. Having a strong support network will give you an outlet when the days are hard. It will keep you centered. It will help you feel less alone when the days are short and the nights are long.

Not every mom friendship works—that's okay. We all bring different personalities to the table and some friendships take off while others fade away. Find a few mom (or dad) friends with whom you can weather the storms and enjoy the highs. You are likely to find that the more support you have, the better able you are to cope with parental stress.

Prioritize Sleep

Many parents will boast that they have the nighttime routine down to a science. (I will, anyway.) Creating the perfect bedtime routine to ensure that your kids get enough sleep is important, and also feels like an Olympic sport at times. We keep on trying until we find what works because we want well-rested, healthy, and happy children. Then we stay up way too late watching Love It or List It in bed because oh my God we need to decompress. (Okay, maybe that's just me.)

While parents take bedtime for kids seriously, they have a tendency to forget about their own sleep requirements. Getting adequate sleep is crucial for parents. Yes, infants will wake you up. But there's no rule stating that you have to mop the floors the moment your infant naps. Take a nap instead. And yes, many parents use the quiet nighttime hours to catch up on work, e-mail, or various other commitments. But you have to know when to turn it off.

Create your own bedtime routine and set timers to keep yourself on track. You need seven or eight hours of sleep a night, and it's up to you to get them. If you happen to have a day job plus an infant plus a teething toddler on your hands? Refer back to asking for help, and train yourself to fall asleep early. You need it, and you also deserve it!

Set Realistic Expectations

You can't meet every need at every possible moment and take care of yourself at the same time. There is no such thing as parenting perfection, despite what you might find on the Internet. It's up to you to create realistic expectations for yourself and your family, and to set reasonable limits to help you meet those expectations.

Some parents genuinely enjoy volunteering for the PTA and helping out in the classroom. Others prefer to coach a team or help out with scouts. Some don't have the time to volunteer, but are happy to send snacks for parties or games. And some do none of the above. You have to learn to do what works for your family. When you take on too much and feel overwhelmed, you can't be the parent that you want to be. If you want the health and happiness of your family to come first, you have to begin by setting realistic expectations and sticking to them.

Prioritize Your Partnership

The best parenting advice my mother has given me to date came thirty seconds before I walked down the aisle to marry my husband. At the time, I was heavily focused on *not* falling down the rickety wooden stairs and thought she might be losing her mind just a little.

I mean, who dishes out parenting advice before the bride even says "I do"? Nonetheless, this little gem has stayed with me through the years: "Love him more. You will have kids and you will love them more than you can even imagine, but you have to love him more. When things are good and when things aren't so good, he will never stop needing you to love him." Moms know stuff.

It's nearly impossible to quantify love, and the heart-stopping love that I have for Sean is different from the indescribable love that I have for my kids. But I love him just the same.

Parenthood has ups and downs and can place a significant strain on a marriage or partnership at times. It's essential to prioritize that relationship. Adult relationships need nurturing just as children do. Left unattended, relationships can dwindle. Nagging takes center stage and pent-up emotions come out in bits and pieces. It takes a couple to be a couple. You have to find the time for your loved one so that you can set the stage for a happy and harmonious family.

Work Together

Whether you are married, divorced, or single-parenting for one reason or another, presenting a calm and united front helps families thrive. Being on the same page and working together toward agreed-upon parenting goals helps kids feel calm, self-confident, and happy, even when parents live in separate homes.

Increase Me Time

Parents need time to decompress and reenergize. While it would be great if we could all run off to the spa once a week, that's not possible for most parents. Some parents give up on the idea of "me time" because they feel like it needs to be an event. Pedicures are nice and I hear going to the movies alone is a great way to catch up on sleep, but you don't need a babysitter and three hours to fit in some me time.

There are ways to fit in exercise at home. Getting lost in a great book can completely change your outlook on life. A bubble bath with a glass of wine while the little ones sleep can feel like that much-dreamed-about spa day for a little while. And although reality television isn't my favorite thing, sometimes checking out so that you rejuvenate your soul to check back in really helps. Find little things that you can do just for you so that you can relax and get back to being the parent that you want to be. Note: *Would you please put down that mop, already? You'll catch up on cleaning when they're older!*

Trade Favors

A great way to factor in me time and, okay, mop the floors if you must, is to trade favors with your mom friends. I have a theory that chaos is chaos, so adding a couple of extra kids to the mix for an hour or two won't actually be as stressful as it might seem. More often than not, this theory works.

Find the other moms in your area who are willing to trade child care once a week. I've done this with my own friends, and it can be a huge relief. (I mean, have you been to Target without kids? Heaven on earth!) Set up a rotating schedule so that you can all help each other out. This will decrease the stress level for all and show your little ones the importance of friendship.

Take a Digital Vacation

If I'm being completely honest, I have a love/hate relationship with technology. I love that FaceTime keeps my kids connected to Sean when he's on the road. He recently attended our son's preschool open house from Australia via FaceTime. You can't put a price on that. But I hate the constant white noise of social media. Don't get me wrong, Facebook put me in touch with old friends and, as it turns out, I have some very funny friends. But sometimes it feels as if the world is just a little too connected. There is a dependence on and expectation of immediate interaction that can cause burnout. And then there's the whole Pinterest perfect-parenting thing . . . Let's not get started on that.

Give yourself a break from digital overload. When you're constantly connected to your phone or your laptop, you're actually disconnected from a real live human being in your presence. And that human being might be small and cute and wanting to play or get a hug. Human connection is important. Technology has its place in this world, but nothing is more real or more intimate than face-to-face interactions, hugs, and holding hands with those we love. Give yourself the gift of freedom by setting limits on your digital consumption. Take it from me, it will work wonders for your family.

At the end of the day, happiness is a choice we make. Life will present obstacles, and things won't always go as planned, but we always have the choice to find a happier way. When we raise kids to choose happiness, to understand that darkness happens but light follows, we give them the power to choose positive emotions. When we allow them to be themselves and follow their dreams and teach them to cope with bumps in the road, we set them up for a lifetime of hope, resilience, and happiness.

They say that the years are short but the days are long when you're lost in the world of parenting. I say savor the small moments, screenshot the happiness, and play as if no one is watching. You won't regret it. That much, I can promise.

ACKNOWLEDGMENTS

I'VE BEEN A DREAMER since I can remember. At ten years old, I sat on my bed in my pink-and-green room on a cold winter day and wrote my first story on my own. There was no assignment from a teacher, no deadline to meet, and no one to grade me on the final product. That first act of independent creativity sparked a lifetime of writing. From that day forward, I dreamed of writing a book that would somehow help someone else the way that countless books helped me along the way.

The Happy Kid Handbook came to me one foggy morning while jogging with my kids in my happy place: a little beach town on the Connecticut coast. As I watched my kids ride ahead of me with the wind in their hair and smiles on their faces, hearing only snippets of their conversation, it hit me: Childhood should be full of bike rides, laughter, love, and silliness. It should be full of wonder, curiosity, courage, and support. Childhood should be happy. Every child has the right to be a child, and every child has the right to play. These days childhood seems to slip through the cracks for some. The race to the finish can overshadow the moments of messy play and boundless curiosity that *should* define childhood. I finished that run, e-mailed my agent, and began writing this book that very night.

Of course, turning an idea into a book is no easy task, and it requires a team of supportive and enthusiastic people. I am truly grateful to every single member of my amazing team.

To Lauren Galit, my literary agent, for your unwavering support, for pushing when I needed a push and cheering when I needed a cheer, for believing in me, for guiding me through absolutely everything, and for your friendship. I am forever in your debt. We did this together.

To Sara Carder, my inspiring editor, who earns the adjective "enthusiastic" ten thousand times over, for your support, for your love of *Happy Kid*, for the edits that made it better, and for turning this particular dream into a reality. Thank you to everyone at Tarcher/ Penguin, from the brilliant minds in the art department (have I mentioned how much I love the cover?) to the copy editors to the publicity team—you are a joy to work with. Special thanks to Erica Rose for the beautiful copyedits, Joanna Ng for absolutely everything, and Keely Platte—a great publicist is a game changer. I am one lucky writer.

To Ryan D'Agostino, an old friend and great writer who popped up at exactly the right moment and, in a single sentence, convinced me that I could do this. I owe you one.

To the friends and writers who eagerly agreed to read the manuscript and cheer me on, I can't thank you enough. Special thanks to Idina Menzel, Peter Gray (who continues to inspire my work both in my office and on the page), Rick Ackerly, Jill Smokler, Rachel Stafford, Amy McCready, Heather Turgeon, and my friend Soleil Moon Frye (who brings a smile to my face each and every time I see her).

A few years ago, thanks to the Internet, I met a fellow writer who would change my life for the better. One million thanks to my other half, Jenny Feldon. You've been there start to finish, and your friendship means the world to me.

If it takes a village to raise a child, it takes an army of writers to launch a writing career. Thank you to everyone who helped me along the way, with special thanks to Jody Arsenault, Nichole Beaudry, Galit Breen, Dawn Dais, Elizabeth Flora Ross, Nicole Hempeck, Liz Jostes, Sherri Kuhn, Jessica Lahey, Marilyn Price-Mitchell, Andrea Nair, Shell Roush, Laura Willard, and Maureen Wallace to name just a few. Truly, there are so many of you out there, and I appreciate each and every one of you.

Thank you to my editors at the Huffington Post, EverydayFamily, mom .me, and Momtastic for taking me on and publishing my words.

I found my path at Boston College. At the University of Pennsylvania School of Social Policy and Practice, I honed my skills and learned how to put my dream of helping kids and families into action. But I learned the art of writing at the Kingswood-Oxford School in West Hartford, Connecticut. To all of my teachers during those six years, thank you for helping me become me.

To everyone at the Help Group in Los Angeles, with special thanks to Susan Berman and Pat Sandler, my work there shaped my career, and I am proud to have worked among so many inspiring educators and clinicians.

To the children and families who shared their lives with me along the way—although the details were changed, your kind hearts inspired this book. I learned as much from you as I hope you learned from me.

To my very dear friend and mom-away-from-mom, Nancy Rosenfelt, for the big shoulders and even bigger heart.

I am lucky in friendship and grateful beyond words for the friends who love me for me.

To Sarah Walker Tonetti, best friend of (gulp) forty years, thank you, thank you, thank you for every kind word, every hug (real and through the phone), every ounce of support, and every container of rainbow chip. I wouldn't be me without you.

To Stacey Bogue Foster, your friendship, love, and support are everything. I am grateful for you every single day.

To Emily Dolan, the friendships that last a lifetime are the best kind of friendships.

To Sondra Abrams, my partner in crime. Thank you for every text, every joke, every word of support, and every cup of coffee (I mean glass of wine). I am lucky to have you in my life.

Friendship plays a leading role in happiness. Extra special thanks to Caroline and Jon Dawes, Cheryl Eskin, Brian Federman, Carly Friedberg, Nicole Greenblatt, Amy Hoffman, Jen and Marc Kalan, Stacey and Brian Kelly, Dave Lavine, Claire Kelly Maxwell, Yvonne Portillo, Courtney Ronald Platt, Matt Scannell (love you, mean it), and Tracy and Jeremy Stahl.

To Brian Madden, for taking such great care of my babies and for answering every e-mail (even in the middle of the night).

Every mom needs a tribe and I am truly grateful to my mom tribes, in California and Connecticut (you know who you are), for your willingness to jump in at the sound of a text tone and for the constant reminders that we are all in this together.

To the best babysitter ever, Barbie Thierjung, for loving my babies as much as I do and for showing up day or night . . . even at 2:00 AM. The words wouldn't have made it to the page without you and I am forever grateful for you.

I've always been a believer in the power of family. A family provides unconditional love and support, and a family always makes you feel at home. Love and thanks to the great big Hurley-Godbout-O'Keefe-Corwin family who always welcomes me home.

Special thanks to my brother, John Godbout, for laughing at my jokes and cheering me on since 1974. They say that you can choose your friends, but you can't choose your family, but I would choose you every time.

To my sister, Kara Corwin, head cheerleader and endless source of support. I'm happy that you're my sister, but I'm grateful that you're my friend.

To my mom, Kathy Godbout DiFrancesca, for supporting me every step of the way and for answering every single call. Your love and friendship mean the world to me. Extra special thanks to Don DiFrancesca for giving my mom the happy ending she so deserves.

To my uncle, Sean O'Keefe, who was given the title "Godfather" but happily stepped in to play "Dad" more times than I can count.

To Riley Ann and Liam James, my happy little miracles, you are my everything. It is my privilege to watch you grow, and I love you to the moon and back one million gazillion times . . . and then some.

To my husband, Sean Hurley, dream catcher of the Universe. For fifteen years (and counting) of love, support, adventure, and happily ever after. You are the smile on my face, the light in my eyes, and the love in my heart. Love you all the way.

RESOURCES

Rick Ackerly, *The Genius in Every Child: Encouraging Character, Curiosity, and Creativity in Children* (Guilford, CT: Lyons Press, 2012).

Jeffrey S. Allen, M.Ed., and Roger J. Klein, Psy.D., *Ready . . . Set . . . R.E.L.A.X.: A Research-Based Program of Relaxation, Learning, and Self-Esteem for Children* (Watertown, WI: Inner Coaching, 1996).

Alliance for Childhood "Promotes policies and practices that support children's healthy development, love of learning, and joy in living"; allianceforchildhood.org.

Johann Christoph Arnold, *Their Name Is Today: Reclaiming Childhood in a Hostile World* (New York: Plough Publishing House, 2014).

Children & Nature Network supports people and organizations working to reconnect children with nature; childrenandnature.org.

DEY (Defending the Early Years), "Working to support and nurture the rights and needs of young children," endorses appropriate practices in early childhood classrooms; deyproject.org.

Peter Gray, *Free to Learn: Why Unleashing the Instinct to Play Will Make Our Children Happier, More Self-Reliant, and Better Students for Life* (New York: Basic Books, 2013).

Making Caring Common Project (MCC): Harvard Graduate School of Education. MCC helps educators, parents, and communities raise children who are caring, respectful, and responsible toward others and their communities; http://sites.gse.harvard.edu/making-caring -common/about.

Roots of Empathy: an evidenced-based classroom program focusing on increasing empathy and reducing aggression among school children; rootsofempathy.org.

Rachel Macy Stafford, *Hands Free Mama: A Guide to Putting Down the Phone, Burning the To-Do List, and Letting Go of Perfection to Grasp What Really Matters!* (Grand Rapids, MI: Zondervan, 2013).

Susan Stiffelman, MFT, *Parenting with Presence: Practices for Raising Conscious, Confident, Caring Kids* (Novato, CA: New World Library, 2015).

NOTES

1 Shawn Achor, *The Happiness Advantage: The Seven Principles of Positive Psychology That Fuel Success and Performance at Work* (New York: Crown Business, 2014).

2 ———, *Before Happiness: The 5 Hidden Keys to Achieving Success, Spreading Happiness, and Sustaining Positive Change* (New York: Crown Business, 2013).

3 J. S. Allen, M.Ed., and R. J. Klein, Psy.D., *Ready . . . Set . . . R.E.L.A.X.: A Research-Based Program of Relaxation, Learning, and Self-Esteem for Children* (Watertown, WI: Inner Coaching, 1996).

4 Peter Gray, "Play as a Foundation for Hunter-Gatherer Social Existence," *American Journal of Play* (Spring 2009): 476–522.

5 J. Almon and E. Miller, "The Crisis in Early Education: A Research-Based Case for More Play and Less Pressure," Alliance for Childhood (November 2011).

6 C. Van Oyen Witvliet, T. Ludwig, and K. Vander Laan, "Granting Forgiveness or Harboring Grudges: Implications for Emotions, Physiology, and Health," *Psychological Science*, volume 12, number 2 (March 2001): 117–123.

7 Emory University Health Sciences Center, "Emory Brain Imaging Studies Reveal Biological Basis for Human Cooperation," *ScienceDaily* (July 18, 2002). Retrieved June 4, 2014 from www.sciencedaily.com /releases/2002/07/020718075131.htm

8 T. D. Bonner and D. N. Aspy, "A Study of the Relationship Between Student Empathy and GPA," *Humanistic Education and Development*, volume 22, issue 4 (1984): 149–154.

9 Peter Gray, *Free to Learn: Why Unleashing the Instinct to Play Will Make Our Children Happier, More Self-Reliant, and Better Students for Life* (New York: Basic Books, 2013): 100.

10 J. S. Middlebrooks and N. C. Audage, "The Effects of Childhood Stress on Health Across the Lifespan" (Atlanta, GA: Centers for Disease Control and Prevention, National Center for Injury Prevention and Control, 2008).

11 M. J. Essex, W. T. Boyce, C. Hertzman, L. L. Lam, J. M. Armstrong, S. M. Neumann, and M. S. Kobor, "Epigenetic Vestiges of Early Developmental Adversity: Childhood Stress Exposure and DNA Methylation in Adolescence," *Child Development*, volume 84, issue 1 (January/February 2013): 58–75.

12 M. A. Lee, S. J. Shoppe-Sullivan, and C. M. Kamp Dush, "Parenting Perfectionism and Parental Adjustment," *Personality and Individual Differences*, volume 52, issue 3 (2011): 454–457.

INDEX

ALSO FROM TARCHER

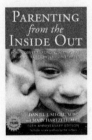

"Dan Siegel and Mary Hartzell have quite deftly managed to translate highly complex neuroscientific and psychological matters into lay strategies for effective parenting."
—MARILYN B. BENOIT, MD, FORMER PRESIDENT, AMERICAN ACADEMY OF CHILD AND ADOLESCENT PSYCHIATRY

978-0-39916-510-8 • $16.95

"If there's one thing parents need to teach their kids—well beyond getting into college or finding a job—it's how to be humble, contributing citizens of the world. If you're a weary parent trying to do just that, you'll find encouragement and practical know-how in the clear and enjoyable pages of this book."
—DANIEL H. PINK, NEW YORK TIMES BESTSELLING AUTHOR OF DRIVE: THE SURPRISING TRUTH ABOUT WHAT MOTIVATES US

978-0-399916-997-7 • $26.95

"A must read! *If I Have to Tell You One More Time* delivers practical, step-by-step tools for well-behaved kids and happy families."
—DR. MICHELE BORBA, AUTHOR OF THE BIG BOOK OF PARENTING SOLUTIONS, AND TODAY SHOW CONTRIBUTOR

978-0-39916-059-2 • $15.95